C

307

THE NEW ENGLAND PURITANS

THE INTERPRETATIONS OF AMERICAN HISTORY

★ ★ ★ JOHN HIGHAM AND BRADFORD PERKINS, EDITORS

THE NEW ENGLAND PURITANS

EDITED BY

Sydney V. James

University of Iowa

HARPER & ROW, PUBLISHERS
NEW YORK, EVANSTON, AND LONDON

Library of Congress Catalog Card Number: 69-11114

CONTENTS

EDITORS' INTRODUCTION

This volume—and companions in the series, "Interpretations of American History"—makes a special effort to cope with one of the basic dilemmas confronting every student of history. On the one hand, historical knowledge shares a characteristic common to all appraisals of human affairs. It is partial and selective. It picks out some features and facts of a situation while ignoring others that may be equally pertinent. The more selective an interpretation is, the more memorable and widely applicable it can be. On the other hand, history has to provide what nothing else does: a total estimate, a multifaceted synthesis, of man's experience in particular times and places. To study history, therefore, is to strive simultaneously for a clear, selective focus and for an integrated, over-all view.

In that spirit, each book of the series aims to resolve the varied literature on a major topic or event into a meaningful whole. One interpretation, we believe, does not deserve as much of a student's attention as another simply because they are in conflict. Instead of contriving a balance between opposing views, or choosing polemical material simply to create an appearance of controversy, Professor James has exercised his own judgment on the relative importance of different aspects or interpretations of a problem. We have asked him to select some of what he considers the best, most persuasive writings bearing on the New England Puritans, indicating in the introductory essay and headnotes his reasons for considering these accounts convincing or significant. When appropriate, he has also brought out the relation between older and more recent approaches to the subject. The editor's own competence and experience in the field enable him to provide a sense of order and to indicate the evolution and complexity of interpretations. He is, then, like other editors in this series, an informed participant rather than a mere observer, a student sharing with other students the results of his own investigations of the literature on a crucial phase of American development.

John Higham
Bradford Perkins

INTRODUCTION

No part of American history has been studied longer than the Puritan era in New England; no part is more generally conceded to have significance for the understanding of the whole; no part has inspired wider disagreement over its significance. While some interpretations have been discredited and will live on only as objects of study in the field of intellectual history, a spirited controversy is in progress between proponents of points of view advanced within the last forty years.

The Puritans themselves offered the first explanation of their historical role. They pondered this subject on their way to the New World, and after their arrival a few men immediately began recording events to show how the settlers were carrying out their purposes. Naturally, the earliest writers could not relate their narratives to an American national experience, but this did not matter to them. Puritans from William Bradford in the seventeenth century to Thomas Prince in the eighteenth agreed on a conception of Christian history which gave meaning to the founding of New England. The devout men who led the Puritan Great Migration had understood the hints of God's will to require them to flee the corruption in England and Holland and go to America, where they should establish a godly society and complete the reformation of Christ's church begun by

Wycliffe and Luther. Accordingly, these early historians dwelt on ecclesiastical history, where the holy purpose was best shown—Bradford in *Of Plimmoth Plantation* as much as he could, Edward Johnson in *The Wonderworking Providence of Sions Saviour in New England,* William Hubbard in *A General History of New-England,* and Cotton Mather in *Magnalia Christi Americana,* to mention outstanding examples. By contrast, the connection between divine purposes and civil history was often vague, even though God's hand was to be seen in everything that happened. External threats from Indians or London officials could be related to the divinely given mission, but the formation of governments and towns, election of officials, and economic developments, while worth noting, tended to appear as a series of nearly unrelated facts. During the seventeenth century no other ideas about historical perspective inspired efforts to put these items into a meaningful pattern.

In the eighteenth century, however, the proposition began to gain favor even among the clergy that New England could take pride in carrying out a mission to establish civil and religious liberty. For almost two hundred years this view dominated historical thinking in one form or another. At first historians argued that the colonists had successfully used their charter privileges for two interlocking purposes: preserving their rights as Englishmen, and protecting their churches from the wicked control of an episcopal hierarchy. But by the nineteenth century, when the old Puritan states finally cut their churches off from public support, expounders of the liberty theme likewise began to separate the two aspects that this theme had originally united. Most historians played down the ecclesiastical side, as the evidence convinced them that Puritans advanced the cause of freedom much more in their political than in their religious institutions. Church history became a separate field, slowly turning into Congregationalist or Unitarian denominational history.

In secular history the Protestant reformation and Puritanism figured only as stages of progress toward a secular conception of human freedom, not as the achievement of ultimate goals. The historian had to select for praise the tendencies of Puritanism to foster civil and religious freedom and condemn or find excuses for holdovers from the benighted past, such as intolerance and persecution of dissidents. Men who followed this program took what has been called the filiopietist approach on account of their solicitude for the reputation of their forbears. John Gorham Palfrey, a painstaking scholar, represents this category well. His aptly named *Compendious History of New England* (1858–1890), which contains a great deal of solid information and sound judgment, is best remembered for a few passages such as the one on Roger Williams, in which Palfrey seems willing to go to any lengths to whitewash the Puritans.

With a highly Puritanical zeal to face up to the world's ugliness, a group of New Englanders made a bad name out of Palfrey and earned from historians the label "antifiliopietist." Their sneers at ancestor-worship enliven the *Proceedings* of the Massachusetts Historical Society in the late nineteenth century. Convinced that the honor of the present generation did not depend on the virtue of the past, they were determined to analyze impartially and distribute blame, where due, unflinchingly. On balance they found Puritanism a hindrance to the progress of freedom. Among the antifiliopietists the best known are Charles Francis Adams, Jr., and his brother Brooks. (Curiously, they found nothing in their own family tree that did not deserve veneration and nothing in their home town to criticize). Charles Francis Adams, Jr., dealt with the earliest days in *Three Episodes of Massachusetts History* (1892), significantly devoting a third of the space to the Antinomian controversy, in which he made Anne Hutchinson a heroine and her opponents illiberal bigots. In *The Emancipation of Massachusetts* (1887) Brooks Adams surveyed the rest of colonial history to show how secular-minded men, especially lawyers, freed the province from the tyranny, superstition, and obscurantism imposed by the Puritan clergy. He wanted to show how Massachusetts fitted into a grand pattern of human progress, not merely to assemble antiquarian lore, and in later writings sought basic causes in world history that could provide a scientific basis for predicting the future.

The antifiliopietists quite logically joined forces with the men who were introducing graduate training in historical research into the universities. The standards set by those who "professionalized" history in this way were partly the same as those of the best nonacademic writers—devotion to primary sources and exactitude in detail, a critical view of evidence, and constant struggle for objectivity. The professors agreed with the antifiliopietists in denouncing homage to the past and in striving for a scientific method to find meaning in the record of events.

But where antifiliopietists tried to be scientific by using all-embracing theories, professional historians after toying with such ideas boiled scientific method down to inductive reasoning from evidence. The professors also insisted on thinking about early New England as part of the nation's history, not the region's—or, rather, on thinking about early New England as only part of the nation's origins, not the fountain of American religion and culture which regional patriots took it to be.

It was not easy to see at first that the academic historians were adopting a new point of view. At the end of the nineteenth century they were much preoccupied with the evolution of institutions. Some of their first efforts were devoted to the New England town, an institution much admired even by antifiliopietists, and of course by local antiquarians. Many people who feared the advance of bigness and corruption in America looked back fondly to the New England town as humanity's best device to reconcile democracy, freedom, and community solidarity. Widespread interest followed efforts to discover how this exemplary social unit had come into existence. Debate raged over the priority to be given to Teutonic, English, Puritan, or strictly local, origins, but the results were inconclusive. The professionals went on to larger subjects, such as colony governments or the structure of the British empire. Most of the discussion of institutions focused on the transfer of British forms and laws, thus subduing interest in Puritanism. Herbert Levi Osgood did write a noteworthy article, "The Political Ideas of the Puritans," *Political Science Quarterly,* Vol. VI (1891), pp. 1–28, 201–231, tracing democracy from them, but more commonly a legalistic view prevailed on the transformation of the rights and institutions of Englishmen into American democracy.

Even this rather antiseptic approach seemed like filiopietism to a few influential writers who flourished in the 1920s. In the estimation of James Truslow Adams (no relation to Charles and Brooks) and Vernon L. Parrington, American freedom, far from being an outgrowth of Puritanism or even colonial governments, was won by overcoming these things. Puritanism meant intolerance, snooping, repression, and authoritarianism instigated by the ministers and enforced by the magistrates. The true origins of American ideals must be found elsewhere—in frontier individualism, in liberating ideas imported from Europe, in innate aspirations for freedom felt by the common man everywhere. Adams triumphantly concluded that the New England colonies had not really been founded for religious purposes, but for economic ends. He even persuaded himself that the bulk of the population was anti-Puritan from the start. Parrington was willing to see a subcurrent of liberalism in Puritan ideas which survived even the persecutions in Massachusetts to support new forms of liberalism when a better day dawned.

To both these men the heart of the evil in American Puritanism was the use of governmental power to assert the will of the clergy, a practice which they called theocracy. Many people saw the same evil in the contemporary policy of prohibition, and a hue and cry was raised against the influence of Puritanism on America. Prohibition was denounced as a Puritan tyranny—though in the colonial period only Anglicans in Georgia had tried to use government to prohibit drinking—and prudery was thrown in for good measure, even though it was obviously of Victorian origin. The public swilled down a succession of shoddy books "debunking" early New England.

All this was outrageous enough to elicit a counterattack to publicize accurate information, but amazingly it did more: it kindled a zeal for the study of Puritanism in America that has produced work to rank with the best historical writing and has left all previous scholarship on the topic inadequate by comparison. Respectable as the works of Parrington, Osgood, Brooks Adams, or John G. Palfrey may have been in their times, they have been superseded. Until recently the best of James T. Adams remained worth quarreling with, but new studies of demography, church membership, commercial life and the merchants make his work look sadly superficial. All the valid controversies over the interpretation of Puritanism are those between practitioners of the new scholarship.

The modern study of Puritanism falls roughly into two parts, of which the first may be called the Harvard school, and the more recent (for lack of a better name) the new look. The Harvard school made its first appearance in print with Kenneth B. Murdock's *Increase Mather* (1925), but truly got under way with the work of Samuel Eliot Morison as teacher and writer. Morison, a Bostonian of distinguished ancestry who taught history at Harvard, investigated Puritan thought and behavior in a great variety of fields while writing *Builders of the Bay Colony* (1930). This book may be regarded as the manifesto of the school. Morison made it clear that he was not performing an act of ancestor worship or denominational defense; he took an interest in New England Puritans because he admired their characters and their dedication to ideals, a dedication that he respected although he shared few of the ideals themselves. *"The ways of the puritans are not my ways,"* he wrote, *"and their faith is not my faith; nevertheless they appear to me a courageous, humane, brave, and significant people."* His research convinced him that Puritan character and ethics dominated early Massachusetts; Puritan parsons guided church and state and even economic enterprise according to their principles—all with the support of the populace at large. Morison went on to make a specialty of Puritanism and learning, but after 1936 left heavy labor in this field to fellow workers.

He remained combative in writing about Puritans. He championed them against undeserved slurs and misunderstanding; writing with his opponents in mind, he sometimes overstated his case. He tended to make his defense a regional one, showing that the laudable qualities of the Puritans reappeared in their New England descendants. In this respect he did not completely maintain the detached position announced in *Builders of the Bay Colony*. Still, he steadfastly studied the Puritans in the light of their thought and aspirations—taking what they wrote seriously—and regarded early Massachusetts as a colony shaped by devotion and ideas rather than by economic determinism or greed.

Many of Morison's students lent a hand to the task of applying sound scholarship to the Puritans, but few stayed with the subject long. Morison's most important associate, though not one of his students, was Perry Miller. A Chicagoan, Miller had no local pride to justify by explaining early New England; moreover, as an outspoken atheist, he was just as detached from Puritan belief as Morison. After graduate study at the University of Chicago, where new interest in Puritan thought was springing up, Miller joined the Harvard English department. Far more than Morison, he delighted in constructing huge webs of explanation in which each strand was necessary to hold every other strand in place. Where Morison wrote a series of biographies, using personal careers to explain various facets of Puritanism, Miller wrote about a structure of ideas and how it was used. Even more deeply committed than Morison to the proposition that intellect can direct history, he believed that early New England offered a splendid proof.

During the 1930s Miller produced a series of articles and books expounding the view that the Massachusetts Bay leaders brought to America a special form of Puritanism, the "covenant theology" or "federal theology." This work culminated in *The New England Mind; the Seventeenth Century* (1939). To some of his admirers his best book, it showed as a systematic whole the elements of Puritan thought that remained constant during the years from 1630 to about 1720, explaining only the changes that Puritans made as a result of wrestling with problems of internal consistency or strictly intellectual challenges from outside the system. A book of exceptional simplicity of organization, it presented ideas of exceptional subtlety—some believe that Miller found in Puritan writing a more complex and ramified and consistent structure of ideas than was there. It was a dazzling performance, but at first few were dazzled. Even Morison once claimed to find it too hard to understand, a modesty as uncharacteristic as it was unwarranted.

When World War II imposed a vacation on it, the Harvard school had accomplished a great deal, yet it had made little impression on historians at large. For example, Thomas J. Wertenbaker's *The Puritan Oligarchy* (1947) showed only superficial effects of the new research. Suspicion still prevailed that admiration for Puritans was merely New England ancestor-worship not to be taken seriously elsewhere, and that seeing more in Puritan writing than crude theological logic-chopping was a mental disease fortunately confined to Harvard Yard. The new work on Puritanism had been almost entirely a Harvard enterprise so far; moreover, Morison had gravitated to the study of *alma mater*. Miller and Murdock, who went on investigating all aspects of Puritanism, taught in the English department and stimulated a modest interest in Puritan literature, considerably advanced by a model anthology, *The Puritans* (1938), edited by Perry Miller and Thomas H. Johnson. So the historical profession at large ignored new studies of Puritanism as parochial or the province of literature professors. Ignoring them was all the easier because interest in colonial history was at an all-time low in the New Deal years, when the times seemed to call for breaking with the past to cure the ills of an industrial society.

The Harvard school encountered other, even more serious, obstacles among historians, obstacles posed by views of causation popular in the 1930s and 1940s. During the depression years economic interests seemed the most potent causes of historical developments, and ideas at best were fig leaves for them. (The chief alternative to economic explanations was a mindless eclecticism that took pride in piling up causal "factors," regardless of their compatibility.) The Second World War inspired increased willingness to see political ideals and power politics, along with economic interests as driving forces in history, but religious doctrine still did not seem important. A change began after 1945, when postwar concern with ideological conflict (real or fancied) set off renewed interest in a national heritage and elevated ideas and religious beliefs to a high prestige.

The Harvard school finally received due notice in the 1950s. Miller's *The New England Mind; from Colony to Province* (1953) demonstrated the immense possibilities for understanding history through Puritan writing. Though based almost exclusively on "what was said and done publicly" without resort to private papers, this book presented the development of Puritan ideas in the context of an elaborate general history of politics, economics, and social change from 1650 to about 1725. Miller had to improvise much of the general history, but until other work revealed its shortcomings his improvisation seemed to have been done in masterly fashion. Furthermore, when he published a collection of shorter pieces in *Errand into the Wilderness* (1956) he finally got attention to what he had been saying all along less bluntly: that he had set out to explain "the movement of European culture into the vacant wilderness of America," and that the story commenced "with the Puritan migration." Regardless of the greater antiquity of Virginia, the coherent development of the American mind, he believed, began with the New Englanders.

This assertion, so far from general opinion in the 1920s or 1930s, met no resistance in the 1950s. A nationwide resurgence of scholarship on colonial history was in progress, with the participants taking it for granted in a vague way that the "roots" or "foundations" of American history lay in pre-Revolutionary times. With Puritan writing vastly exceeding all the rest in the seventeenth century, and so full of abstruse thought, it could hardly seem controversial to claim that it represented the beginning of the nation's cultural history. The Harvard school won adherents across the land, and its books were reprinted to become daily fare for graduate students. Acquiescence in Miller's assertion was all the more remarkable because he offered no explanation of how the New England mind influenced modern America and did not live to complete an analysis that would show a coherent pattern of intellectual development from 1630 to the twentieth century .

Similarly, Miller's new admirers were not greatly troubled by his belief in the dominance of intellectual development in the national experience as a whole, a belief for which he did not offer a full defense. For all his zeal to show that ideas control history, Miller could not show that they always did. *The New England Mind; from Colony to Province* is a narrative of ideas losing mastery as they interacted with a changing world. As systematic thought lost dominance, Miller's sense of causality lost coherence; he relied on economic interests, chance, and other "factors" suggested by topics at hand. Much of Miller's intellectual uncertainty went unnoticed, but at least one man saw it at once. In his review in *The New England Quarterly,* Vol. XXVII (1954), pp. 112–118, Bernard Bailyn pointed out that Miller had needed a more "detailed, sophisticated history of colonial society" than any yet written, and had attempted to deduce one from "literary and theological sources," an effort bound to fail. Different kinds of evidence had to be examined to get precise information on what merchants and men of business were doing or to make a political analysis that could account for the appearance of imperial-minded colonials at the end of the seventeenth century.

The Harvard school goes on—for example, in the work of Alan Heimert, or more broadly speaking in the continued pursuit of literary and intellectual history—but dissatisfaction with its commitment to the dominance of ideas in human affairs has led a number of scholars to seek new ways to assess the role of Puritanism. Among the first to do so was Bernard Bailyn, whose study of *The New England Merchants in the Seventeenth Century* (1955) supplied some of the information that Miller had lacked. Bailyn found that Puritan ideals were far from a sufficient explanation of the economic lives of early New Englanders. He put their behavior in a context that scaled down the importance of ethical precepts and then showed how the precepts were quickly overborne by mundane considerations. Puritanism, though its economic implications were never more sharply defined, became in his hands merely one influence on New England; a web of quite different sorts of causality had to be woven to explain events about which Miller had written.

Like Bailyn, others have insisted that Puritanism needs to be re-examined in the light of much more accurate and comprehensive knowledge of what happened in early New England. They outdo the Harvard school in thoroughness and precision, much as it outdid previous scholarship, but they can make this advance only because the Harvard school has gone before them. Although as yet there is little coherence to the conclusions of these partisans of rigor, they share enough in purposes and standards to warrant grouping them and provisionally naming their work the new look.

To begin with, they take a Missourian stance on the dominance of Puritan ideas over actions: they will believe it only to the extent that it can be shown decisively. In this respect their basic impulse is markedly different from Morison's or Miller's. They have a willingness to try a variety of alternative explanations. Bailyn, with a technique that appears to owe much to the structural-functional type of sociological theory, weaves an all-encompassing fabric of explanation out of diverse materials. Emery Battis, in *Saints and Sectaries; Anne Hutchinson and the Antinomian Controversy in the Massachusetts Bay Colony* (1962), put together but did not fully integrate a fairly conventional historical narrative, medical and psychiatric expertise, and a sociological analysis of the behaviorist variety. Less flamboyantly, George L. Haskins, in *Law and Authority in Early Massachusetts* (1960), described how Puritan ideas and ideals shaped law and government in a fashion that would do credit to the Harvard school, but just as ably showed the effects of non-Puritan English law and traditions.

In the second place, the new look has involved a search for alternatives to doctrine as a framework of continuity. Richard S. Dunn, in *Puritans and Yankees; The Winthrop Dynasty of New England* (1962), used a family as the register of changes which Miller had viewed from the standpoint of Puritan thought. Somewhat farther afield, Anthony Garvan, in *Architecture and Town Planning in Colonial Connecticut* (1951), used the changing spatial relationships of New England towns as a guide to town development. He cavalierly ignored Puritanism, apparently because he found no need of it to explain his data. Interest is growing in church institutions as a central subject matter, with the hope that the study of ecclesiastical organization in conjunction with religious doctrine and town life will improve the understanding of all three topics.

The search for alternative frameworks has so frequently led to the study of individual communities as to make this an important trait of the new look. Only when examining a small arena can there be any hope of taking all the evidence into account and arriving at a comprehensive analysis. Best known is Sumner C. Powell's *Puritan Village* (1963), an account of Sudbury, Massachusetts, and the English communities that supplied its leaders and provided models for some of its ways. The book demolishes all simple formulas about the relation between English experience and the New England town, though Powell cautiously concludes that Sudbury was unique. Religion and the church figure slightly, partly because of the absence of church records for the town and the fact that its minister wrote little that survives, but partly because Powell was content with secular explanations for the town's development. He hinted broadly that the parson's influence rarely radiated beyond the religious sphere.

Darrett B. Rutman has treated Boston with even greater detail in *Winthrop's Boston* (1965), but in quite a different way. Not as concerned as Powell with distinguishing imported ways from those assumed in New England, Rutman in effect used Boston as a test for the propositions of the Harvard school on the purposes of the Massachusetts Bay founders, the extent of Puritanism's domination of institutional and social life, the nature of the community. The Harvard school kept failing. The Great Migration, Rutman finds, was not extensively planned; there was no clear connection at the outset between it and any particular stripe of Puritanism; the religion of the settlers did not foster compact settlements in a cluster of church-centered communities. Quite the contrary: the first years of the colony were characterized by lay leadership and improvisation; multinuclear settlement came about because the leaders quarreled over how to implement their plan of a single community; a rough unity of religious views and church practice appeared among church members only after the Antinomian nightmare—and when this happened an exclusive policy on membership resulted in the church dividing rather than uniting the community.

Elsewhere Rutman has bluntly argued that the concept of "Puritanism" is a misleading creation of historians and one that "as any intimate view of a 'Puritan' community will show, has little to do with reality in New England."* He will admit the importance of religious beliefs, once accurately identified in an actual historical setting, and sees even more importance in ecclesiastical regulations, but insists that such things explain only part of what happened. In his opinion, the Harvard school was devoted to intellectual history while mistakenly believing that its investigations yielded a comprehensive understanding of Puritan life; Rutman agrees that generalizations should be made about early New England, but cautions that all kinds of evidence must be examined first.

Studies of other towns now under way—of Dedham by Kenneth A. Lockridge and Andover by Philip Greven, for example—may yield results just as corrosive of the Harvard school as the conclusions of Powell or Rutman. There is even reason to hope that the findings on the various towns will agree sufficiently to allow generalizations about New England as a whole. It is likely that these generalizations will reduce once again the importance assigned to Puritanism—deprive it of the role of presiding

* Darrett B. Rutman, "The Mirror of Puritan Authority," in George A. Billias (ed.), *Law and Authority in Colonial America* (1965), p. 149.

intellectual system, deprive it of credit for fostering compact towns, emphasize its lack of homogeneity in New England, and shift the emphasis in religious influences from doctrine or theology to ecclesiastical institutions. If such is the case, new ideas will have to be found to relate Puritan New England to the whole of American history; incomplete as the work of the Harvard school has been on this problem, the new look critics have yet to tackle it.

The Marrow of Puritan Divinity

PERRY MILLER

Beyond any doubt there was such a thing as Puritanism, yet describing it clearly and accurately has proved to be hard. One source of difficulty is the fact that in most respects Puritans were like their non-Puritan neighbors. Puritans did insist upon a few telltale points of personal conduct and church practice. They also endorsed distinctive theological justifications of religious doctrine, but did not entirely agree among themselves—a further source of trouble in defining Puritanism. Subdivisions proliferated among English Puritans, especially after 1630, but earlier ones created the varieties that appeared in America. The Harvard school fostered by Samuel Eliot Morison and Perry Miller found in New England Puritanism an integrated system of religious feeling and theology with corollaries to regulate ecclesiastical organization and all aspects of personal and civil life—indeed, the only such system in American history.

Critics of the Harvard school have questioned the existence of such a comprehensive structure. They have leveled two charges particularly at Perry Miller, who went further than anyone else in delineating a rationally coherent system. First, the critics have accused Miller of disregarding the central core of piety. Second, they say he neglected to distinguish parts of the system that were simply the views of Englishmen in general during the early seventeenth century. The second of these accusations has some truth, and its significance is being investigated. The first of the accusations, however, is based on little except a superficial observation that Miller wrote much more on the system of ideas than on the central religious feelings. In the first chapters of *The New England Mind; the Seventeenth Century* (1939), Miller in fact argued that "Puritan theology was an effort to externalize and systematize" a mood or sensibility which he called "the Augustinian strain of piety." He described this piety as a yearning for communion with divine perfection, a yearning felt by men convinced that the world had been created perfect, that man's sin had corrupted it, that man cannot know God except in fleeting glimpses afforded by divine grace.

Still, Miller's interest centered on the expression of ideas, on theology and its interaction with experience in New England. He delighted in vigorous phrases, in vast concatenations of ideas, in the discovery of meanings hidden behind seemingly straightforward statements. He found in American Puritan writing a unity of thought derived from a particular subvariety of English

Perry Miller, "The Marrow of Puritan Divinity," *Publications of the Colonial Society of Massachusetts,* XXXII (1937), pp. 247–300; also in P. Miller, *Errand into the Wilderness* (1956), pp. 50–98. The article is reprinted here without footnotes and with deletions where indicated.

Puritanism: the covenant theology. Having explained how this special form of Puritanism came to New England in *Orthodoxy in Massachusetts, 1630–1650* (1933), he went on to expound its contents in "The Marrow of Puritan Divinity" and later more fully in *The New England Mind; the Seventeenth Century.* Miller's proposition that the covenant theology predominated in Massachusetts and Connecticut, and so made New England Puritan culture unique, put the study of early New England on a new foundation. The proposition showed up previous formulations as too ill-informed to be taken seriously or too vague to be verified and, by contrast, stimulated precise research and thinking, whether by supporters or critics of Miller's interpretation.

WE INVARIABLY THINK OF THE ORIGINAL SETTLERS OF NEW ENGland as "Calvinists." So indeed they were, if we mean that in general terms they conceived of man and the universe much as did John Calvin. But when we call them Calvinists, we are apt to imply that they were so close in time and temperament to the author of the *Institutes* that they carried to America his thought and system inviolate, and to suppose that their intellectual life consisted only in reiterating this volume. Yet students of technical theology have long since realized that Calvinism was in the process of modification by the year 1630. There had come to be numerous departures from or developments within the pristine creed, and "Calvinism" in the seventeenth century covered almost as many shades of opinion as does "socialism" in the twentieth. The New England leaders did not stem directly from Calvin; they learned the Calvinist theology only after it had been improved, embellished, and in many respects transformed by a host of hard-thinking expounders and critics. The system had been thoroughly gone over by Dutchmen and Scotchmen, and nothing ever left the hands of these shrewd peoples precisely as it came to them; furthermore, for seventy years or more English theologians had been mulling it over, tinkering and remodelling, rearranging emphases, and, in the course of adapting it to Anglo-Saxon requirements, generally blurring its Gallic clarity and incisiveness.

Much of this adaptation was necessitated because, to a later and more critical generation, there were many conundrums which Calvin, and all the first Reformers for that matter, had not answered in sufficient detail. He had left too many loopholes, too many openings for Papist disputants to thrust in embarrassing questions. His object had been to compose a sublime synthesis of theology; he sketched out the main design, the architectural framework, in broad and free strokes. He did not fill in details, he did not pretend to solve the metaphysical riddles inherent in the doctrine.

He wrote in the heyday of Protestant faith and crusading zeal, and it is not too much to say that he was so carried along by the ecstasy of belief that an assertion of the true doctrine was for him sufficient in and for itself. There was no need then for elaborate props and buttresses, for cautious logic and fine-spun argumentation.

Hence the history of Reformed thought in the late sixteenth and early seventeenth centuries reveals the poignant inability of Calvin's disciples to bear up under the exaction he had laid upon them. He demanded that they contemplate, with steady, unblinking resolution, the absolute, incomprehensible, and transcendent sovereignty of God; he required men to stare fixedly and without relief into the very center of the blazing sun of glory. God is not to be understood but to be adored. This supreme and awful essence can never be delineated in such a way that He seems even momentarily to take on any shape, contour, or feature recognizable in the terms of human discourse, nor may His activities be subjected to the laws of human reason or natural plausibility. He is simply the sum of all perfections, that being who is at one and the same time the embodiment of perfect goodness and justice, perfect power and mercy, absolute righteousness and knowledge. Of course, man will never understand how these qualities in unmitigated fullness exist side by side in one being without conflict or inconsistency; though man were to speculate and argue to the end of time, he can never conceivably reconcile plenary forgiveness with implacable righteousness. . . .

It is of the essence of this theology that God, the force, the power, the life of the universe, remains to men hidden, unknowable, unpredictable. . . . The English Puritans may be called Calvinists primarily because they held this central conception, though the thought is older in Christian history than Calvin, and they did not necessarily come to it only under Calvin's own tuition. "Now, sayth the Lord, my thoughts go beyond your thought as much as the distance is betweene heaven and earth." William Ames, whose *Medulla Sacrae Theologiae* was the standard text-book of theology in New England, lays it down at the very beginning that "what God is, none can perfectly define, but that hath the Logicke of God himselfe," and argues that therefore our observance of His will can never be based upon God's "secret will," but only upon His explicitly revealed command. William Perkins, from whom Ames and English Puritans in general drew a great share of their inspiration, asserted squarely once and for all that even the virtues of reasonableness or justice, as human beings conceive them, could not be predicated of God, for God's will "it selfe is an absolute rule both of iustice and reason"; and that nothing could therefore be reasonable and just intrinsically, "but it is first of all willed by God, and thereupon becomes reasonable and iust." . . .

This system of thought rests, in the final analysis, upon something that cannot really be systematized at all, upon an unchained force, an incalculable essence. For the period of Protestant beginnings, for the years of pure faith and battle with Babylon, this doctrine, as Calvin expressed it, was entirely adequate. . . . But by the beginning of the seventeenth century Protestant schools and lectureships had been established; the warfare with Rome had become a matter of debate as well as of arms, and logic had become as important a weapon as the sword. Calvinism could no longer remain the relatively simple dogmatism of its founder. It needed amplification, it required concise explication, syllogistic proof, intellectual as well as spiritual focus. It needed, in short, the one thing which, at bottom, it could not admit—a rationale. . . . Even if the specific doctrines of Calvinism were unchanged at the time of the migration to New England, they were already removed from pure Calvinism by the difference of tone and of method. It was no longer a question of blocking in the outlines; it was a question of filling in chinks and gaps, of intellectualizing the faith, of exonerating it from the charge of despotic dogmatism, of adding demonstration to assertion—of making it capable of being "understood, known, and committed to memory."

The history of theology in this period indicates that the process of development was accomplished in many guises. Learned doctors wrote gigantic tomes on the Trinity or the Incarnation, and soon were creating for Protestantism a literature of apologetics that rivalled the Scholastic, not only in bulk, but in subtlety, ingenuity, and logic-chopping. For our purposes it is possible to distinguish three important issues which particularly occupied the attention of Dutch and English Calvinists. These are not the only points of controversy or development, but they may be said to be the major preoccupations in the theology of early New England. Calvinism had already by 1630 been subjected to attack for what seemed to Catholic, Lutheran, and Anglican critics its tendency toward self-righteousness at the expense of morality; in spite of Calvin's insistence that the elect person[1] must strive to subject himself to the moral law—"Away, then," he cried, "with such corrupt and sacrilegious perversions of the whole order of election"—there was always the danger that the doctrine of predestination would lead in practice to the attitude: "If I am elected, I am elected, there is nothing I can do about it." If man must wait upon God for grace, and grace is irrespective of works, simple folk might very

[1] EDITOR'S NOTE: Calvin (and Calvinists after him) believed that God has made an irrevocable decision to confer the divine grace which brings saving faith—and, ultimately, heavenly bliss—on certain persons, the predestined elect, and to leave the others just as inevitably to obey their sinful natures and reap their just reward of eternal damnation.

well ask, why worry about works at all? Calvinist preachers were often able to answer this question only with a mere assertion. Calvin simply brushed aside all objection and roundly declared: "Man, being taught that he has nothing good left in his possession, and being surrounded on every side with the most miserable necessity, should, nevertheless, be instructed to aspire to the good of which he is destitute." . . . Ames restated this doctrine; yet at whatever cost to consistency, he had to assert that though without faith man can do nothing acceptable to God, he still has to perform certain duties because the duties "are in themselves good." The divines were acutely conscious that this was demanding what their own theory had made impossible, and they were struggling to find some possible grounds for proving the necessity of "works" without curtailing the absolute freedom of God to choose and reject regardless of man's achievement.

Along with this problem came another which Calvin had not completely resolved, that of individual assurance, of when and how a man might reach some working conviction that he was of the regenerate. . . . The curve of religious intensity was beginning to droop [by 1600], and preachers knew that a more precise form of stimulation had to be invoked to arrest the decline; men wished to know what there was in it for them, they could not forever be incited to faith or persuaded to obey if some tangible reward could not be placed before them. Yet to say roundly that all the elect would be immediately satisfied by God of their promotion was to say that God was bound to satisfy human curiosity. The theologians could only rest in another inconsistency that was becoming exceedingly glaring in the light of a more minute analysis. Assurance is sealed to all believers, said Ames, yet the perceiving of it "is not always present to all"; this uncertainty, he was forced to admit, is a detriment to "that consolation and peace which Christ hath left to believers."

In both these discussions the attempt to arrive at bases for certainty led directly to the fundamental problem: no grounds for moral obligation or individual assurance could be devised as long as God was held to act in ways that utterly disregarded human necessities or human logic. In order to know that God will unquestionably save him under such and such circumstances, man must know that God is in reality the sort of being who would, or even who will have to, abide by these conditions, and none other. He must ascertain the whys and wherefores of the divine activity. In some fashion the transcendent God had to be chained, made less inscrutable, less mysterious, less unpredictable—He had to be made, again, understandable in human terms. If the sway of the moral law over men were to be maintained, men must know what part it played in their gaining assurance of salvation; if men were to know the conditions upon which they could found an assurance, they must be convinced that God would be bound by those conditions, that He would not at any moment ride roughshod over them, act suddenly from an abrupt whimsy or from caprice, that salvation was not the irrational bestowal of favor according to the passing mood of a lawless tyrant.

The endeavor to give laws for God's behavior was attended with apparently insuperable obstacles, for it was clear that such principles as men might formulate would be derived from reason or from nature, and Calvin had made short work of all rational and natural knowledge in the opening chapters of the *Institutes*. Not only does God transcend reason and nature, but the corruption of the universe which followed the sin of Adam has vitiated whatever of value once existed in them. Reason was originally endowed with an inherent knowledge of God, which is now hopelessly extinguished by ignorance and wickedness; the knowledge of God may be conspicuous in the formation of the world, but we cannot see it or profit by it. We may still have the light of nature and the light of reason, but we have them in vain. "Some sparks, indeed, are kindled, but smothered before they have emitted any great degree of light." Ames went as far as he dared toward bringing order into God's character by saying that since God is obviously perfect, He must be perfectly rational; that in His mind must preëxist a plan of the world as the plan of a house preëxists in the mind of an architect; that God does not work rashly, "but with greatest perfection of reason." But we can never in our discourse attain to that reason. The principles of other arts may be polished and perfected "by sense, observation, experience, and induction," but the principles of theology must be revealed to us, and "how ever they may be brought to perfection by study and industry, yet they are not in us from Nature." Divinity may utilize "Intelligence, Science, Sapience, Art or Prudence," but it cannot be the product of these natural faculties, but only of "divine revelation and institution." Knowledge and rational conviction may be prized by the theologian, and may be preached by him as much as doctrine, but in the final analysis he must declare that reason is not faith, that it is not necessary to justification, and that in itself it cannot produce the effects of grace. He may also study nature and natural philosophy, but his knowledge will always be vain and useless; his faculties are too corrupted to observe correctly; nature is under God's providence, and God's ways are past finding out; and, finally, the works of nature "are all subject to corruption."

Here, then, was the task which seventeenth-century Calvinists faced: the task of bringing God to time and to reason, of justifying His ways to man in conceptions meaningful to the intellect, of caging and confining the transcendent Force, the inexpressible and unfathomable Being, by the laws of ethics, and of doing this somehow without losing the sense of the hidden God, without reducing the Divinity to a mechanism, without depriving Him of unpredictability, absolute power, fearfulness, and mystery. In the final analysis this task came down to ascertaining the reliability of human reason and the trustworthiness of human experience as measurements of the divine character—in short, to the problem of human comprehension of this mysterious thing which we today call the universe.

The Arminian movement in Holland (and the "Arminian" theology in the Church of England) represented one Calvinist attempt to supply a reasonable explanation of the relation of God to man. . . .[2]

The Arminians yielded too far to the pressure for construing theology in a more rational fashion and so succumbed to the temptation of smuggling too much human freedom into the ethics of predestination. A more promising, if less spectacular, mode of satisfying these importunities without falling into heresy was suggested in the work of the great Cambridge theologian, William Perkins, fellow of Christ College, who died in 1602. Anyone who reads much in the writings of early New Englanders learns that Perkins was a towering figure in Puritan eyes. . . . I cannot find that in making wholesome meat out of controversy Perkins added any new doctrines to theology; he is in every respect a meticulously sound and orthodox Calvinist. What he did contribute was an energetic evangelical emphasis; he set out to arouse and inflame his hearers. Consequently, one of his constant refrains was that the minutest, most microscopic element of faith in the soul is sufficient to be accounted the work of God's spirit. Man can start the labor of regeneration as soon as he begins to feel the merest desire to be saved. Instead of conceiving of grace as some cataclysmic, soul-transforming experience, he whittles it down almost, but not quite, to the vanishing point; he says that it is a tiny seed planted in the soul, that it is up to the soul to water and cultivate it, to nourish it into growth.

This idea was palliative; it lessened the area of human inability and gave the preacher a prod for use on those already, though not too obviously, regenerate. In Perkins's works appear also the rudiments of another idea, which he did not stress particularly, but which in the hands of his students was to be enormously extended. He occasionally speaks of the relationship between God and man as resting on "the Covenant of Grace," and defines this as God's "contract with man, concerning the obtaining of life eternall, upon a certaine condition." He uses the covenant to reinforce

[2] EDITOR'S NOTE: The Arminians were followers of Jacobus Arminius (1560–1609), a Dutch Protestant who in 1604, when he was professor of theology at the University of Leyden, denounced the doctrine of predestination and proceeded to argue that good works can earn salvation. Protestants who hold these views have been called Arminians ever since, even when they do not agree with Arminius in all respects.

his doctrine of the duty that man owes to God of cultivating the slightest seed of grace that he may receive.

The most eminent of Perkins's many disciples was Dr. William Ames, who in 1610 was so prominent a Puritan that he found it advisable to flee to Holland, where he became professor of theology at the University of Franeker. He was the friend and often the master of many of the New England divines, and I have elsewhere claimed for him that he, more than any other one individual, is the father of the New England church polity. Like Perkins, Ames was an orthodox Calvinist. His was a more logical and disciplined mind than that of his teacher, and his great works, the *Medulla Sacrae Theologiae* (1623) and *De Conscientia* (1630), became important text-books on the Continent, in England, and in New England because of their compact systematization of theology. There is very little difference between his thought and Perkins's, except that he accords much more space to the covenant. He sets forth its nature more elaborately, sharply distinguishes the Covenants of Works and of Grace, and provides an outline of the history of the Covenant of Grace from the time, not of Christ, but of Abraham.

In 1622, John Preston became Master of Emmanuel College, Cambridge. . . . In the elaborate exegesis which Preston devoted to unfolding and expounding the philosophy of the covenant, which he held to be "one of the main points in Divinitie," he contrived the seeming solution of the problems which then beset his colleagues. His greatest work on this subject (though all his many books deal with it to some extent) was entitled *The New Covenant, or The Saints Portion* (London, 1629). This work is prerequisite to an understanding of thought and theology in seventeenth-century New England.

Another [leading exponent of the covenant concept] . . . was Richard Sibbes, preacher at Gray's Inn from 1617 until his death in 1635, and Master of St. Catherine's Hall, Cambridge, from 1626. . . .

In the work of all these authors the covenant plays a conspicuous part. Furthermore, this group seems to coincide frequently with the coherent group who formulated the peculiar philosophy of Non-Separating Congregationalism. They were students or friends of Ames, whose works they quote frequently. Sibbes owed his conversion to a sermon of Paul Baynes, and he edited Baynes's *Exposition of Ephesians*. There are many ascertainable relations of almost all the school with one or more of the New England divines; their works were read in New England, and Perkins, Ames, Preston, and Sibbes are clearly the most quoted, most respected, and most influential of contemporary authors in the writings and sermons of early Massachusetts. Sibbes revealed his awareness of the great migration in the year 1630 when he said in *The Bruised Reed:* "The gospel's course hath hitherto been as that of the sun, from east to west, and so in God's time may proceed yet further west." Both in the works of all these men, including Cotton, Hooker, Shepard, and Bulkley, and in their lives there is evidence for asserting that they constituted a particular school, that they worked out a special and peculiar version of theology which has a marked individuality and which differentiates them considerably from the followers of unadulterated Calvinism. And the central conception in their thought is the elaborated doctrine of the covenant.

The word "covenant" as it appears in the Bible presents for the modern scholar a variety of meanings. Possibly suspecting or intuitively sensing these confusions, Luther and Calvin made hardly any mention of the covenant, and the great confessions of sixteenth-century Protestantism avoided it entirely. But with Preston and his friends the word seemed to suggest one simple connotation: a bargain, a contract, a mutual agreement, a document binding upon both signatories, drawn up in the presence of witnesses and sealed by a notary public. Taking "covenant" to mean only this sort of commitment under oath, Preston proceeded, with an audacity which must have caused John Calvin to turn in his grave, to make it the foundation for the whole history and structure of Christian theology. . . .

The theology of the Covenant of Grace, invested with such importance by these authors, proceeds upon a theory of history. It holds that man has not only been in relation to God as creature to creator, subject to lord, but more definitely through a succession of explicit agreements or contracts, as between two partners in a business enterprise. God entered into such a bond with man as soon as He created him. He stipulated that if Adam performed certain things He would pledge Himself to reward Adam and Adam's posterity with eternal life. In order that man might know what was required of him, Adam was given specific injunctions in the form of the moral law. In addition, the law was implanted in his heart, built into his very being, so that he might perform his duties naturally and instinctively. The original Covenant of Works, therefore, is the Law of Nature, that which uncorrupted man would naturally know and by which he would naturally regulate his life. Of course, Adam failed to keep his covenant, and by breaking the bond incurred the just penalties. But God did not rest there. Beginning with Abraham, He made a new covenant, and the seventeenth chapter of Genesis, which describes the new bargain, becomes thereby the basic text for the school. The new covenant is just as much an agreement as its predecessor, stipulating terms on both sides to which the contracting parties are bound.

. . . these words containe the *Covenant* on both sides, sayth the *Lord,* this is the *Covenant* that I will make on my part, *I will be thy God* . . . you shall haue all things in me that your hearts can desire: The *Covenant* againe, that I require on your part, is, that you be *perfect with me,* that you be *upright,* that you be without *hypocrisie*. . . .

The idea of a mutual obligation, of both sides bound and committed by the terms of the document, is fundamental to the whole thought. . . . In the Covenant of Grace, God, observing the form, contracts with man as with a peer. But since the Fall man is actually unable to fulfil the law or to *do* anything on his own initiative. Therefore God demands of him now not a deed but a belief, a simple faith in Christ the mediator. And on His own side, God voluntarily undertakes, not only to save those who believe, but to supply the power of belief, to provide the grace that will make possible man's fulfilling the terms of this new and easier covenant. "In the Covenant of works a man is left to himselfe, to stand by his own strength; But in the Covenant of grace, God undertakes for us, to keep us through faith." Man has only to pledge that, when it is given him, he will avail himself of the assistance which makes belief possible. If he can believe, he has fulfilled the compact; God then must redeem him and glorify him.

The covenant which God made with Abraham is the Covenant of Grace, the same in which we are now bound. The only difference is that Abraham was required to believe that Christ would come to be mediator for the covenant and compensate God for the failure of Adam; since Christ we have merely to believe that He has come and that He is the "surety" for the new covenant. . . .

This legalized version of Biblical history may at first sight seem to offer nothing toward a solution of the problems of Calvinism. It may even appear an unnecessarily complicated posing of the same issues, for the grace which gives salvation even in the covenant comes only from God and is at His disposing. But in the hands of these expert dialecticians the account leads to gratifying conclusions. In their view it succeeded in reconciling all contradictions, smoothing out all inconsistencies, securing a basis for moral obligation and for assurance of salvation while yet not subtracting from God's absolute power or imposing upon Him any limitations prescribed by merely human requirements.

Because a definition of the divine nature must be preliminary to deductions concerning assurance and morality, the problems enumerated may be considered in reverse order. The first effect of the doctrine was to remove the practical difficulty of conceiving of the Deity as a definite character. He might still remain in essence anything or everything, incomprehensible and transcendent. That no longer need concern mankind, for in His contacts with man He has, voluntarily, of His own sovereign will and choice, consented to be bound and delimited by a specific programme. He has promised to abide by certain procedures comprehensible to the human intellect. He has not, it is true, sacrificed His sovereignty by so doing; He has not been compelled by any force of reason or necessity. He has merely consented willingly to conform in certain respects to stated methods. For all ordinary purposes He has transformed Himself in the covenant into a God vastly different from the inscrutable Divinity of pure Calvinism. . . .

As soon as the theologians of this school had explained what a covenant involved, they realized that they had come upon an invaluable opportunity to present the hitherto stern Deity in a new light. The very fact that God allows Himself to become committed to His creature must be in itself some indication of His essential disposition. Hence, if God condescends to treat with fallen man as with an equal, God must be a kindly and solicitous being:

. . . how great a mercie it is, that the glorious God of Heauen and Earth should be willing to enter into *Couenant,* that he should be willing to indent with vs, as it were, that he should be willing to make himselfe a debtor to vs. If we consider it, it is an exceeding great mercie, when wee thinke thus with our selues, he is in heauen, and wee are on earth; hee the glorious God, we dust and ashes; he the Creator, and we but creatures; and yet he is willing to enter into Couenant, which implyes a kinde of equality betweene vs. . . .

We need no longer torture ourselves trying to imagine a being made up at once of both justice and mercy, because in stooping to the covenant the Lord has shown that His mercy takes command of His justice. He is bearing in mind the frailties and desires of man, He is endeavoring to bind His will and His requirements to suit man's abilities. . . .

Some of the deductions which followed these premises carry us still further from the conventional notion of the Puritan Jehovah. For one thing, the terms of the contract are decidedly reasonable. God has not only limited Himself to specific propositions, but to propositions that approve themselves to the intellect. . . . Though by virtue of His absolute sovereignty God might have promulgated any laws He chose, those which He has voluntarily invested with moral significance are exactly the same laws which reason finds ethical, precisely as the terms to which He has voluntarily consented in the covenant are humanly understandable ones. "It is his will and good pleasure to make all laws that are moral to be first good in themselves for all men, before he will impose them upon all men." Goodness is consequently discoverable by right reason; the goodness of a moral law "is nothing else but that comely suitableness and meetness in the thing commanded unto human nature as rational, or unto man as rational, and consequently unto every man." Theoretically God is above and beyond all morality as we formulate it; yet by committing Himself to the covenant God has sanctioned as His law not just any absurdity, but things which are in their own nature suitable, good, and fitting. The difficulty of reconciling God's will with reason vanishes in this interpretation; reasonable justice and His sovereign power of enactment "may kiss each other, and are not to be opposed one to another."

A God who conforms thus cheerfully to reasonable terms must obviously be all-excellent, "and therefore reasonable, he must have the most excellent faculties," and would therefore be such a one as would endeavor also to abide by reason in the ordering and governing of nature. Probably no other tenet reveals so clearly how earnestly these writers were striving to bring Calvinism into harmony with the temper of the seventeenth century. They made their gesture of obedience to the unconfined Deity of Calvinism. They prefaced their remarks with the statement that He always *could* interrupt the normal course of nature if He wished to, but they said that a God who voluntarily consented to a covenant would generally, as a matter of choice, prefer to work through the prevailing rules. The realm of natural law, the field of scientific study, and the conception of mathematical principle presented few terrors to this variety of Calvinist. . . . He may come to the aid of His people by direct interposition in moments of crisis, as in the passing of the Red Sea; more often He will contrive that assistance come by guiding the natural causes, and when He has arranged "a course of means, we must not expect that God should alter his ordinary course of providence for us." . . .

The historical theory of the Covenant of Grace, its progressive unfolding from Abraham to the Christian era, permitted these theologians to add the final touches to their portrait of the divine character. God did not simply present the covenant point-blank to fallen man, but introduced it by degrees, unfolding it gradually as men could be educated up to it. . . . He first administered it through conscience, then through the prophets and ceremonies, now through Christ, preaching of the Word, and the sacraments. . . . The effect of this theory was to introduce an element of historical relativity into the absolute dogmatism of original Calvinism. God is seen deliberately refraining from putting His decisions fully into effect until man can cope with them and profit by them. He is not so much a mail-clad seigneur as a skillful teacher, and He contrives on every hand that men may be brought to truth, not by compulsion, but by conviction. For these reasons theologians of this complexion were eagerly disposed to prize knowledge, logic, metaphysics, and history. They were prepared to go as far as their age could go in the study of Biblical history and commentary, for truth to them resided in the history as well as in the doctrine. Preston confesses that intellectual persuasion and historical research are not in themselves sufficient for absolute faith in the Scriptures unless God also "infuseth an inward light by his Spirit to worke this faith." Yet even so he holds that sufficient testimonies exist in the Scriptures "to give evidence of themselves." Knowledge is not to be despised because faith also is necessary: "Wisedome is the best of all vaine things under the Sunne." Knowledge and faith must go hand in hand:

I deny not but a man may haue much knowledge, and want Grace; but, on the other side, looke how much Grace a man hath, so much knowledge he must haue of necessity. . . . You cannot haue more Grace than you haue knowledge. . . .

It is a significant indication of the bent of his mind that Preston argues for the reliability of Scripture because heathen histories corroborate Old Testament chronology.

To describe this theology as "rationalism" would be very much to overstate the case; before the triumph of Newtonian science reason did not have the rigid connotation it was later to carry. Preston drew back from out-and-out mechanism, and he never doubted that even where God was steering events by the rudder of causation, He was charting the course according to His own pleasure. But in this way of thought appears an entering wedge of what must be called, if not rationalism, then reasonableness. It is a philosophy that put a high valuation upon intellect. Its tendency is invariably in the direction of harmonizing theology with natural, comprehensible processes. The authors were prepared to welcome the scientific advance of the century with open arms, until some of their successors in the next century were to realize too late that they had let the wooden horse of rationalism into the Trojan citadel of theology. But thus early there were few misgivings; the Puritans were so secure in their faith that they could with perfect serenity make it as understandable as possible. If we today insist upon supposing that their philosophy was an absolute authoritarianism, we ought to be very much disconcerted by their continual appeals to experience and reason, appeals which, from our point of view, imply assumptions altogether at variance with those of the creed. John Winthrop, in his manuscript debate with Vane[3] in 1637, took it as axiomatic that man is a reasonable creature, and his statement of political theory in these papers owes more to logic than to the Word of God. Thomas Hooker constantly reinforced a dogma by such statements as that it "hath reason and common sense to put it beyond gainsaying," or that to deny it "is to go against the experience of all ages, the common sense of all men"; and Samuel Stone eulogized his colleague because "He made

[3] EDITOR'S NOTE: Sir Henry Vane (1613–1662) went to Massachusetts in 1635, was elected governor the following year, but left the colony after he was defeated for re-election in 1637 as a result of his siding with Anne Hutchinson.

truth appear by light of reason."[4] Professor Morison has found that Elnathan Chauncy, while an undergraduate at Harvard in the 1660's, copied into his commonplace book the remark, "Truth and the rational soule are twins." According to the conventional notions of New England Calvinism this would seem to be somewhat startling. In view, however, of the disposition of the covenant theology, this truism was as appropriate to young Chauncy's background as some admonition concerning the integration of complexes might be to the undergraduate of today. Such passages make it increasingly clear that our notions of the Puritan philosophy, derived in the main from a casual acquaintance with "Calvinism," are in need of drastic reconsideration.

Setting forth from the nature of God as defined by the covenant, these theologians enjoyed clear sailing to the haven of assurance. The Covenant of Grace defines the conditions by which heaven is obtained, and he who fulfils the conditions has an incontestable title to glorification, exactly as he who pays the advertised price owns his freehold. . . . The contract between God and man, once entered into, signed by both parties and sealed, as it were, in the presence of witnesses, is ever afterwards binding. This exceedingly legal basis furnishes the guarantee, not only for the assurance of the saints, but even for their perseverance. In the covenant, says Hooker, the soul "is inseparably knit to Christ"; though you falter in action and fall short of holiness, if you have once become a member of the covenant, the covenant "doth remain sure and firm," said John Cotton. "If we be hemm'd in within this Covenant, we cannot break out."

Thus bound by His own commitment, God must live up to His word. If you do your part, He must, willy-nilly, do His. As Bulkley says, "He hath passed over those things by covenant, and he cannot be a covenant breaker"; hence, "we might have the more strong consolation, assuring ourselves of the fulfilling of his gracious promise towards us." Pursuing this logic, these men broached one of their most daring ideas: if a man can prove that he has faith, he has then done his part and can hold God to account, hale Him into court and force Him to give what has become the man's just and legal due: "You may sue him of his own bond written and sealed, and he cannot deny it." . . .

The covenant theory admitted into the official theology many ideas that bade fair to undermine it entirely, and this idea, that man can by fulfilling terms extort salvation from God, might well seem the most incongruous. . . . Stating the theory of predestination within this frame shifts the point of view from that maintained by Calvin. We no longer contem-

[4] EDITOR'S NOTE: Thomas Hooker (1586?–1647) went to Massachusetts in 1633 and three years later became the founder and first minister of Hartford, Connecticut. Samuel Stone (1602–1663) was Hooker's colleague in the ministry at Hartford.

plate the decrees in the abstract, as though they were relentlessly grinding cosmic forces, crushing or exalting souls without regard for virtue or excellence; instead we are free to concentrate our attention upon what immediately concerns us. We do not have to ask whether God be ours; we need ask only whether we be God's. Sibbes presented this reversal in emphasis most clearly, though it can be found consciously recognized in the works of all the covenant theologians. A man has no grounds, he says, to trouble himself about God's election as it exists in God's own mind. "It is not my duty to look to God's secret counsel, but to his open offer, invitation, and command, and thereupon to adventure my soul." . . . In fact, Sibbes carried this argument so far that he can actually tell men to reach out for the covenant, to promise to abide by it, to take it upon themselves, before they have had any recognizable experience of regeneration. If they can succeed, they can very probably secure faith, not only by prayer and fasting, but by demanding that God reward them according to His bond.

. . . The subtle casuistry of this dialectic is altogether obvious. Yet the spectacle of these men struggling in the coils of their doctrine, desperately striving on the one hand to maintain the subordination of humanity to God without unduly abasing human values, and on the other hand to vaunt the powers of the human intellect without losing the sense of divine transcendence, vividly recreates what might be called the central problem of the seventeenth century as it was confronted by the Puritan mind.

These considerations as to the grounds of assurance paved the way for the supreme triumph of the school—the establishment of a code of ethics and of moral obligation. In two respects they could achieve this end: first, by partial rehabilitation of natural man, and second, by incorporating moral effort into the terms of the covenant. For in this theory man as well as God is no longer left in precisely the state decreed by original Calvinism. God is seen condescending to behave by reason because in man there exists at least a potential rationality. Calvin himself had admitted that in depraved man lingered some remnants of the divine image in which Adam had been created, but, as we have seen, he held them too feeble to be of any use. The Federal theologians also held that these remains, in the form of natural reason or "the light of nature," were exceedingly unreliable, but they rescued them from the rubbish heap where Calvin had cast them. . . . Preston's sermons frequently remind his hearers that the soul, though fallen, "is the Image of the Essence of God," that it possesses both understanding (which in these discussions is used synonymously with "reason") and will, so that man "understands all things, and wils whatsoever he pleaseth." The speculative faculty he defines as "that by which we know and judge aright concerning God and morall vertues," and its decisions are corroborated by the natural conscience and an innate inclination in the will:

There is in naturall men not onely a light to know that this is good, or not good, and a Conscience to dictate; this you must doe, or not doe, but there is even an Inclination in the will and affections, whereby men are provoked to doe good, and to oppose the Evill. And therefore the proposition is true, that naturall men have some truths, because they have this Inclination remaining, even in the worst of them. . . .

Even when he insists that something more is necessary to man than the deductions of natural wit, Preston does not view them as antagonistic to faith. Imperfect as they are, they do not run contrary to supernatural illumination. Within the sphere of demonstration, for instance, the evidence of the senses is sound, Calvin to the contrary notwithstanding:

Of all demonstrations of reason that we have to prove things, nothing is so firme as that which is taken from sense: to prove the fire is hot, we feele it hot, or honey to be sweet, when we taste it to be sweet: There is no reason in the world makes it so firme as sense: As it is true in these cases, so it is an undoubted truth in Divinity, that in all matters of sense, sense is a competent judge.

Faith may be above reason but since reason comes as directly from God as does revelation, there can be no conflict between them:

But, you will say, faith is beyond sense and reason, it is true, it is beyond both, but it is not contrary to both; faith teacheth nothing contrary to reason, for sense and reason are Gods workes as well as grace, now one worke of God doth not destroy another.

Seen in this light, the imperfections of the human mind are not so much a vitiation resulting from sin, as simply the limitations under which a finite being inevitably labors. Confined in time and space, we cannot conceivably "see all the wheeles, that are in every businesse" or if we do see them, we are "not able to turne euery wheele." In these purely physical terms Preston occasionally interprets original sin, and ideas of this sort can be matched in all the writings upon the covenant. . . .

If traces of the image of God are still to be found in the soul, they should even more clearly be manifested in the material universe, where all can decipher them if they will. "The heavens are the worke of his hands, and they declare it, and every man understands their language." "When a man lookes on the great volume of the world, there those things which God will have known, are written in capital letters." Quite apart from faith, therefore, there are two important sources of truth to which man has immediate access: himself and his experience of the world. Hence, secular knowledge—science, history, eloquence, wisdom (purely natural wisdom) is doubly important for these Puritans; for knowledge is not only useful, it is a part of theology. Of course, the writers are always careful to stipulate, we must have Scripture to supplement the discovery of God in nature and providence, but having made that concession, they go on valiantly to exonerate the study of nature from the charge of obscuring the religious goal, and confidently press it into the service of theology. They insist that we can reach God through science as well as through revelation:

For, though I said before, that Divinity was revealed by the *Holy Ghost,* yet there is this difference in the points of *Theologie:* Some truths are wholly revealed, and have no foot-steps in the creatures, no prints in the creation, or in the works of *God,* to discerne them by, and such are all the mysteries of the *Gospell,* and of the *Trinitie:* other truths there are, that have some *vestigia,* some characters stamped upon the creature, whereby wee may discerne them, and such is this which we now have in hand, that, *There is a God.* [Preston]

"The workes of Nature are not in vaine," and it behooves us to study them with as much care and precision as the Bible:

Can we, when we behold the stately theater of heaven and earth, conclude other but that the finger, arms, and wisdom of God hath been here, although we see him not that is invisible, and although we know not the time when he began to build? Every creature in heaven and earth is a loud preacher of this truth. Who set those candles, those torches of heaven, on the table? Who hung out those lanterns in heaven to enlighten a dark world? . . . Who taught the birds to build their nests, and the bees to set up and order their commonwealth?

Shepard[5] pronounced a flat condemnation upon those who would cast the Law of Nature from the domain of theology merely because it is not so perfect today as at the Creation; these, he said, "do unwarily pull down one of the strongest bulwarks."

The theologians were treading on dangerous ground at this point; they were perilously close to talking Arminianism. But in their own opinion they were still safe. They were carrying the frontiers of reason to the very boundaries of faith, yet they were not allowing them to encroach. They were careful to point out that regeneration cannot come by the intellect without the inspiration of grace, at the same time adding that the road to grace is also the highway of knowledge. They denied that faith imparts any new doctrines or enlarges the scope of the understanding; the doc-

[5] EDITOR'S NOTE: Thomas Shepard (1605–1649) went to New England in 1635 and served as minister in Cambridge, Mass.

trine, as such, can be grasped by anyone. "They may be enlightened to understand all the truths of God; there is no Truth we deliver to you, but an unregenerate man may understand it wholly, and distinctly, and may come to some measure of approbation." Consequently, though by understanding alone no man may achieve salvation, any man does by nature learn so much of God's law that he cannot plead ignorance as an excuse for not obeying it. Here was indeed a triumph in the justifying of God's ways to man! Natural knowledge, such as all men can attain, cannot make a man holy, but it can at least render him inexcusable, and God is exculpated from the charge of injustice in His condemnations. An individual may not be able to deliver himself from the bondage of sin, but in the meantime he can be held personally responsible for doing what the light of nature teaches him is wrong. . . .

In accordance with their disposition to enlarge the sphere and opportunities of natural reason, the authors redefined, or rather redescribed the nature of grace itself. They did not forget that grace is an influx from the supernatural, but they preferred to concentrate upon its practical operations in the individual, and to conceive of it, not as a flash of supernal light that blinded the recipient, but as a reinvigoration of slumbering capacities already existing in the unregenerate soul. As in the ruins of a palace, so runs one of their favorite metaphors, the materials still exist, but the "order" is taken away, grace reëstablishes the order by rebuilding with the same materials. Or as another image has it, natural promptings, passions, and desires are like the wind; holiness is the rudder. "So Nature, the strength of nature, affections, or whatsoever they be, are like the wind to drive the ship, thou mayst retaine them, only godliness must sit at the Sterne." Grace, once infused into the soul, becomes itself "natural," just as when a man has learned to play a lute, the instrument becomes second nature to him; "so is this, it is planted in the heart, as the senses are, it is infused into the Soule, and then we exercise the operations of it; so that it is another Nature, it is just as the thing that is naturall." Hence the faith preached in early New England was not the violent convulsion of the camp-meeting, but the exercise, under divine guidance, of reason and virtue. Thomas Hooker conceived that "the main principall cause of faith is rather an assisting power working upon, than any inward principall put into the soule to worke of its self." In this description, faith emerges, not as prostration on the road to Damascus, but as reason elevated. It enables us to see existing truths exactly as a telescope reveals new stars:

. . . and therefore they are said to be *revealed,* not because they were not before, as if the revealing of them gave a being unto them; but, even as a new light in the night discovers to us that which we did not see before, and as a prospective glasse reveales to the eye, that which we could not see before, and by its own power, the eye could not reach unto. . . .

Faith does not require acquiescence in irrationalities, but empowers us to believe thoroughly in that which we can also accept intellectually. Faith is not intoxication, it is education. . . . Preston appears the most audacious of the school in this intellectualizing of grace, but his friends in New England were not far behind him. Shepard, for example, declared that God does not work upon believers as upon blocks, propelling them by an "immediate" act, because believers are rational creatures and therefore capable of acting as rational creatures. Grace is the renewal of God's image in them, "like to the same image which they had in the first creation, which gave man some liberty and power to act according to the will of Him that created him." Hooker said that after grace has done its work and removed the obstructions of sin, "now Conscience is in commission and hath his scope, & the coast is now clear that reason may be heard." According to this theology, the regenerate life is the life of reason.

This line of argument indicates a predisposition in the minds of early New England theologians to minimize the power of original sin, so that by pointing out the advantages which all men inherently possess, they could at least hold the unregenerate responsible for their own damnation. As far as we have followed them at this point, their conclusions concerning what remains of God's image in man since the Fall resulted simply from their strong bent toward making the most of what reasonable elements they could find in the original doctrine of Calvin, and thus far did not necessarily involve the covenant theory. But from the theory they were able to derive an ingenious support for their contentions, to construct a theoretical basis for maintaining that the image of God in man was not so hopelessly debauched as Calvin had imagined. For by conceiving the relationship between man and God as a contract, the sin of Adam appeared in a new light. Adam in his disobedience had broken a bond, had violated a lease. The punishment which he received as a consequence was not deterioration so much as it was the infliction of a judicial sentence; it was expulsion for non-payment, it was not inherent pollution. . . . Adam had stood as the agent, the representative of all men, the "federal" head of the race. When he, as the spokesman for man in the covenant, broke it and incurred the penalty for disobedience, it was imputed to his constituents as a legal responsibility, not as an inherent disease. These writers did not openly deny that all men were by birth partners in Adam's guilt, as Augustine had said and Calvin had repeated after him, but they were very much inclined to give lip-service to this historic theory of transmission and then concentrate upon their own version of legal imputation. Both theories at once are outlined by Ames, and amplified by Preston, who argues that men are corrupted first because they come from Adam's loins, but secondly and more importantly because they, as the heirs of Adam, have imputed to them the blame for breach of covenant. . . . Shepard taught that this was justice itself, "it being just, that as if he standing, all had stood, by imputation of his righteousness, so he falling, all should fall, by the imputation of his sin." . . . Man is born owing God a debt; his creditor compounds with him, making a new agreement out of consideration for his bankrupt state. When man fulfils the new and easier terms, the debt is cancelled. Though the debt is a serious hindrance to man's freedom of action, it is not an utterly crushing burden, and it does not entirely obliterate the qualities of reason and intelligence he possessed before he acquired it. So something of these qualities remains in him, enough to make him inexcusable for a neglect of God's law, enough to leave him no defence if he fails in moral effort, particularly since God in the covenant has condescended to deal with him by appealing to precisely these qualities and ordering the scheme of salvation in just such a fashion as he can understand by virtue of them.

Thus the Federal theory, freeing man from the absolute moral impotence of the strict doctrine, first made possible an enlargement of his innate capacities. Secondly, it provided a logical device for immediately enlisting these capacities in the service of morality, even before they had been further invigorated by divine grace. It had been with these considerations in mind that God framed the covenant precisely as He did, and thereby demonstrated His cleverness by devising a scheme to insure the continuation of moral obligation even in a covenant of forgiveness. He did not discard the Covenant of Works after Adam's fall; He included it within the Covenant of Grace. "For the Morall Law, the Law of the ten Commandments, we are dead also to the covenant of that law, though not to the command of it." But in this arrangement it exists no longer as a command, the literal fulfilment of which is required of man, but as a description of the goal of conduct toward which the saint incessantly strives. The Law, which no man can perfectly fulfil any more, exists as a "schoole-master"; it teaches us what we should do, whether we can or no, and as soon as we realize that we cannot, we flee to Christ for the assistance of grace. And since Christ has satisfied God by fulfilling the Law, there is no necessity that we do it also. It is only necessary that we attempt it. . . . The demand made upon benighted human nature in the Covenant of Grace is not exorbitant, and demonstrates again how solicitous God appears as He is pictured by this school. It is indeed a little surprising to the modern student to find how large a part of Puritan sermons was devoted to proving to people that they need not be weighed down with too great a sense of sin. The ministers seem to have been fully aware that the stark predestination of early Calvinism was too often driving sincere Christians to distraction, and that it needed to be softened, humanized. Hence they said again and again that there need be very little difference between the performances of a saint and the acts of a sinner; the difference will be in the aims and aspirations of the saint and in the sincerity of his effort. The proof of election will be in the trying, not the achieving. "God accepts at our hands a willing minde, and of childe-like indeavours; if we come with childe-like service, God will spare us; a father will accept the poor indeavours of his childe for the thing it selfe."

Yet while our endeavors will be satisfactory though poor, they must still be real endeavors. Since the conception of grace in this theory is not so much that of rapture as of the reawakening of dormant powers, grace is by definition the beginning of a moral life. It is a strengthening of the remains of the Law that still exist in the natural heart, in unregenerate reason, and in conscience. Saints are not able to do all they should, "yet this they doe . . . they carry a constant purpose of heart to doe it. . . . They never come to give over striving to doe it." . . . Conversely, it follows as night the day that sanctification is a very handy evidence of justification, and that we may even receive grace first in the form of a moral ability before we have any inward experience of regeneration. God's predestination is of course absolute, He picks and chooses without regard to merit. But in the covenant He has consented to bestow His favor upon those who fulfil the conditions, and to guarantee to those who do so the assurance of their salvation. . . . "Though God's grace do all," said Sibbes, "yet we must give our consent," and Thomas Shepard wrote:

> God hath so linked together the blessing of the Covenant (which is his to give) with the duty and way of it (which is ours to walk in) that we cannot with comfort expect the one, but it will work in us a carefull endeavour of the other.

Peter Bulkley[6] reveals what the New England divines thought this version had gained over that of primitive Calvinism when he explains that if God simply predestined without imposing conditions, morality would fall to the ground, nothing would be required of men one way or another; but in the covenant our endeavors are made, not the cause, but the *sine qua non* of a heavenly future: "But hereby he would teach us, that when he makes with us a Covenant of Grace and mercy, he doth not then leave us at liberty to live as we list; but he binds us by Covenant to himself. . . ." . . .

[6] EDITOR'S NOTE: Peter Bulkley (1583–1659) went to Massachusetts in 1635 and became the first minister at Concord.

Armed by this logic at every point, the theologians were prepared to concentrate their attack upon the question of passivity. They were equipped to counteract the danger of lassitude which threatened to result from the fatalistic doctrine of predestination. They could show that men are responsible for a great deal, even though God alone bestows grace, and in more ways than one they could prove that a sinner brings reprobation upon himself. All those who live within the hearing of Christian doctrine —particularly of covenant doctrine—are offered the opportunity of taking up the covenant, because to them its terms are made clear. An offer of the covenant from God includes also an offer of enabling grace, because God is under obligation to supply grace when He presents the contract to men. Therefore, when the convenant is presented, through the sermon of a minister, to a particular individual, and the individual does not then and there embrace it, or attempt to embrace it, then he must be resisting it. Though faith comes from God, yet because it is not forced upon any, but is presented through reasonable inducements, and is conveyed by "means," by sermons, and by sacraments, men have of themselves the power to turn their backs upon it, to refuse to be convinced by the most unanaswerable demonstrations, to sneer at the minister, and to pay no attention to the sermon. Thereafter the onus is entirely on their own shoulders:

> Take heede of refusing the acceptable time . . . Beloued, there is a certaine acceptable time, when God offers Grace, and after that hee offers it no more . . . there are certaine secret times, that *God* reserues to himselfe, that none knowes but himselfe, and when that time is past ouer, he offers it no more.

Consequently, men must be constantly in readiness to take up the covenant, so that they will not fail to respond when the acceptable time comes to them individually.

The covenant theory, then, was an extremely strategic device for the arousing of human activity: it permitted divine grace to be conceived as an opportunity to strike a bargain, a chance to make an important move, an occasion that comes at a specific moment in time through the agency of the ministry. If an individual does not close the deal when he has the chance, he certainly cannot blame God because it gets away from him. "The Lord is a suitor to a many a man," said Shepard, "that never gives himself to him." . . . Hooker says that if persons have lived under a "powerful ministry" a half-dozen years or so and have not profited therefrom, "It is no absolute conclusion, but . . . it is a shrewd suspicion, I say, that God will send them downe to hell." Consequently, it behooves us all not to lie back until the Lord comes to us, but to exert ourselves at once in accordance with the instructions of our pastor.

On these grounds the school carried on Perkins's tendency to reduce the actual intrusion of grace to a very minute point. They not only insisted that the tiniest particle is sufficient to start a man on the road to salvation, they even argued that before any faith is generated, a man can at least "prepare" himself for it. He can put himself in an attitude of receptivity, can resolve with himself not to turn down the covenant when it seems to be offered to him. God may decree, but a man must find out whether the decree applies to himself; "the kingdom of heaven is taken with violence." "You must not thinke to goe to heaven on a feather-bed; if you will be Christs disciples, you must take up his crosse, and it will make you sweat." If any man excuse himself by the sophistry that Christ must work for him and that he cannot under his own power "bring forth fruit to him," that man despises Christ's honor, and in that act rejects the Covenant of Grace.

In this respect, as in others, the covenant doctrine did not intend to depart from essential Calvinism; it did not openly inculcate free-will. But by conceiving of grace as the readiness of God to join in covenant with any man who does not actively refuse Him, this theory declared in effect that God has taken the initiative, that man can have only himself to blame if he does not accede to the divine proposal. This was indeed a marvellous stratagem for getting around a thorny difficulty in theology, a hazard which Calvin had simply taken in stride by asserting roundly that though God elects or rejects according to His pleasure, the responsibility for damnation is man's own. The generation of Peter Bulkley could no longer accept so brusque or unsophisticated an account as this. They were under greater compulsion to clear God of the charge of arbitrary condemnation and to place the responsibility for success or failure squarely on human shoulders. The result was the conception, not of conditional election, but of conditional covenant, according to which the absolute decree of God is defended, and yet the necessity of activity by man is asserted:

The Lord doth not absolutely promise life unto any; he doth not say to any soule, I will save you and bring you to life, though you continue impenitent & unbelieving; but commands and works us to repent and believe, and then promises that in the way of faith and repentance, he will save us. He prescribes a way of life for us to walk in, that so wee may obtaine the salvation which he hath promised. . . .

. . . The final outcome of the intricate system was a shamelessly pragmatic injunction. It permitted the minister to inform his congregation that if any man can fulfil the covenant, he is elected. The way for him to find out is to try and see: "Therefore goe on boldly, God hath promised to heare you, hee cannot deny you." Whatever the differences among the various writers, there is a marvellous unanimity among them on the ultimate moral: "The way to grow in any grace is the exercise of that grace," said Preston. "It is not so much the having of grace, as grace in exercise, that preserves the soul," said Sibbes. And John Cotton[7] said in Boston: "If thou hast but a thirsty soule, and longest for grace under sense of thine owne droughtinesse, then God will not deny the holy Ghost to them that aske him."

The conclusion toward which the doctrine of the covenant shapes is always the practical one that activity is the essence of a Christian life, that deeds are not merely the concomitants of faith, but can even be in themselves the beginning of faith. Some kind of revision of Calvinism seemed absolutely inevitable if the doctrine of justification by faith were not to eventuate in a complete disregard of moral performance. The covenant theology was the form that that revision took among this particular group of thinkers. It was the preliminary to their proving that faith without performance is an impossibility, a contradiction in terms, and that that which must be performed is the moral law, the law which reason and common sense know to be good in itself. In dogmatic Calvinism morality could exist only as a series of divine commands. It had no other basis, and to Calvin it needed no other. The covenant theology is a recognition on the part of a subsequent generation that this basis was inadequate, that it reduced morality to an arbitrary fiat, that it presented no inducement to men other than the whip and lash of an angry God. Consequently, in New England morality was first of all the specific terms of a compact between God and man, and rested, therefore, not upon mere injunction but upon a mutual covenant in which man plays the positive rôle of a coöperator with the Lord. In the second place morality was also that which can be considered good and just.

This conception was of tremendous value to the leaders of Massachusetts, not only in the realm of faith and personal conduct, but just as much in the realm of politics and society. The sphere of moral conduct includes more than such matters as individual honesty or chastity; it includes participation in the corporate organization and the regulation of men in the body politic. The covenant theology becomes, therefore, the theoretical foundation both for metaphysics and for the State and the Church in New England. An exhaustive study of the social theory would lead too far afield for the purposes of this paper, but a brief indication of the connection between it and the theology will demonstrate that without understanding this background we shall misread even such a familiar classic as

[7] EDITOR'S NOTE: John Cotton (1584–1652) went to Massachusetts in 1633 and was chosen teacher (i.e., second minister) of the church in Boston.

Winthrop's speech of 1645 on liberty. That address is not what it is most often described as being—an expression of pure Calvinism. All that strictly Calvinistic political theory needs to contain is in the fourth book of the *Institutes*. It amounts in effect to the mandate that men must submit to magistrates because God orders them to submit, to the assertion that the power of the governor is of God, never of the people. But Winthrop outlines a much more subtle conception in his account, and by invoking the covenant theory secures the sway of morality in the State in precisely the same fashion in which the theologians secured it in the religious life. He distinguishes between the liberty all men have in the state of nature, the liberty to do anything they wish, which generally means something bad, and the liberty men exercise in society:

The other kind of liberty I call civil or federal, it may also be termed moral, in reference to the covenant between God and man, in the moral law, and the politic covenants and constitutions, amongst men themselves. This liberty is the proper end and object of authority, and cannot subsist without it; and it is a liberty to that only which is good, just, and honest.

I do not believe that the real connotation of Winthrop's words has been altogether recognized in modern accounts. He is saying that just as the covenant between God and man is a coming to terms, and as the validity of that which is by its nature good, just, and honest rests not upon its intrinsic quality but upon its being agreed to by the contractors, so also in the State, the rule of law rests upon a similar agreement among the participants. The covenant theory cannot claim for that which is inherently good the force of a cosmic law, because the universe and man are corrupted; it cannot identify the good completely with the thought of God, because God transcends all systematic formulations. But being arrived at by compact, the good then acquires the power to compel obedience from those who have covenanted to observe it, be they gods or men. . . . The mutual consenting involved in a covenant, says Hooker, is the "sement" which solders together all societies, political or ecclesiastical; "for there is no man constrained to enter into such a condition, unlesse he will: and he that will enter, must also willingly binde and ingage himself to each member of that society to promote the good of the whole, or else a member actually he is not." The implanting of grace, being by definition an acceptance of the covenant, produces by the same token a people prepared and ready to be disciplined in a holy society. "The same Spirit quickneth us unto holy duties; so that . . . the Spirit sanctifying draweth us into an holy Confederacy to serve God in family, Church, & Common-wealth." . . .

The covenant upon which a Congregational church was founded was viewed by the theologians in the same light as the political compact. It was held to be a miniature edition of the divine covenant. The saints come together and formally agree to carry out in ecclesiastical life the obligations to which they stand individually bound by their covenant with God. The duties and requirements are those determined in the Covenant of Grace. The church compact is the agreement of the people in a body to constitute an institution which will facilitate the achievement of these ends. "The rule bindes such to the duties of their places and relations, yet it is certain, it requires that they should *first freely ingage* themselves in such covenants, and *then* be carefull to fulfill such duties." The creation of a church by the saints is necessary, furthermore, because the church makes possible the machinery of "means." The argument from the covenant, therefore, clinched the theoretical justification for the existence of a formal ecclesiastical order, for the dispensing of sacraments, and for the application of such regulatory measures as censure and excommunication, while at the same time protecting the liberty of God to enter into covenant with anyone He chose, inside or outside the church. Yet as long as it seemed that God would normally work through the regular means, He would therefore generally dispense grace through the ordinances of the church. Consequently the children of the saints should be baptized as a means toward their conversion, and should be taken into the church covenant:

> *The Covenant of Grace* is to be considered, either according to the *benefits* of saving grace *given* in it, or according to the *means* of grace *offered*. . . . [The church covenant] is not the Covenant of the Gospel in the first sense; but it is within the verge, and contained within the compasse of the Covenant in the second sense.

In this distinction between the covenant as faith and the covenant as the provision of means for the engendering of faith were contained the seeds of the difficulties which later produced the Half-Way Covenant. But in the first decades of New England history no difficulties were anticipated because the theologians were so supremely confident that grace would almost inevitably accompany the means. "God delights in us, when we are in his Covenant, his Covenant reacheth to his Church, and wee being members of that Church: Hence it comes to passe, that we partake of all the pleasant springs of Gods love."

Thus the sign of true faith is not only a desire on the part of the regenerate individual to fulfil the moral law, but it is also a determination to join in the setting up of the one and only polity which Christ has outlined in Scripture. For this reason New England was settled: "When faith is stirring, it longs and desires much after the strongest, purest, and liveliest Ministry, and every Ordinance in the greatest purity."

I have not attempted in this account of the covenant theology to give more than a rapid survey; the summary of each point could easily be amplified and revealing quotations multiplied indefinitely. But in even as compressed a treatment as this, the bent of the thought becomes clear. In every position there is a remarkable consistency of tone, a resolute determination to solve the riddles of Calvinist theology, as far as may be possible by the ingenuity of man or the subterfuges of metaphysics, in a reasonable, comprehensible fashion, and yet at the same time to preserve, in form at least, the essential structure of Calvinism. To understand why these men should have been driven by this urgency, it is necessary to remember what was taking place in the intellectual life of Europe at the time, in science, in politics, in the work of Bacon, of Descartes, and of Hobbes. Within the limits of their particular theology, within the framework of their creed, these Puritans were responding to the same impulses as their philosophical contemporaries. They were seeking to understand, to draw up explicable laws, to form clear and distinct ideas, to bring order and logic into the universe. They could not interpret it as extension and movement as did Descartes. They could not reduce it to atoms as did Hobbes. They could not deify its natural construction as did the Newtonians. But oddly enough they could take many steps in the same direction once they had seized upon their fundamental discovery that God has voluntarily engaged Himself to regular, ascertainable procedures. The rest followed surely and easily from this premise: the validity of reason in man, the regularity of secondary causes in nature, the harmony of knowledge and faith, the coincidence of the arbitrary with inherent goodness, the intimate connection between grace and the incitements that generate grace, the necessity for moral responsibility and activity. Everywhere along the line the method of the divine dispensation, while authorized only by God and remaining under His constant control, is actually synchronized with a completely scientific account. God works grace in the soul, not by compulsion, but by persuasion and reasonable inducements, by the sermon of the minister which penetrates the sinner's mind. Was the real cause God working through the sermon, or was it the sermon itself? The authors had no hesitancy in saying that the sermon was simply the efficient cause and that God was the final cause, but they were delighted to find that God's activity could take the form of a natural stimulus. This seemed to make religion doubly secure and to enhance it by the addition of comprehensibility.

Yet there is a caution to be observed before we rest in this conclusion. By marshalling from the works of Cotton and Hooker passages which deal only with the covenant and its implications, an impression could easily be created that New England thought had ceased to have any affinities with Calvinism, that there was really no difference between the Puritans of the covenant school and the rational theologians of the century who, like John Smith listening to the Arminians at Dort, had bidden Calvin good-night. . . .

The achievement of this theology was that it did everything that could be done to confine the unconfinable God in human terms. It transformed the revealed Word from an exaction arbitrarily imposed by a conqueror into a treaty of mutual obligation. But it never forgot that at the long last God is not to be fathomed, understood, or described with absolute certainty. Such certainty as we do have is temporary, the result of an agreement, of God's having consented to be bound in the main by such and such conditions, of His condescending for the moment to speak the language of men. There is no absolute guarantee that *all* His manifestations will appear within the scope of the covenant. The essence of Calvinism and the essence of Puritanism is the hidden God, the unknowable, the unpredictable. In this sense the Puritans were indeed Calvinists. They hedged the undiscoverable Essence about with a much more elaborate frame than did Calvin. They muffled it and cloaked it (to borrow Cotton's phrase), they cabined it and circumscribed it up to a point; and though the point was far beyond anything Calvin would have allowed, there was still a limit beyond which even the Federal theologians could not go. They could not say that natural law was immutable and eternal, though they might say it was generally reliable. They might say that God's justice was for all intents and purposes the same as human justice, but they could not say that it was invariably the same. Always they had to leave a loophole, they had to be wary and circumspect; for behind the panorama of the world, behind the covenant and behind the Scriptures there loomed an inconceivable being about whom no man could confidently predict anything, who might day in and day out deal with man in stated forms and then suddenly strike without warning and scatter the world into bits. There was no telling with unqualified certitude what He might do; there was only the rule of thumb, the working agreement that by and large He would save and reject according to reason and justice as we understand the words. For ordinary purposes this was enough; we could feel fairly secure, we need not be too distraught. But the Puritan, as long as he remained a Puritan, could never banish entirely from his mind the sense of something mysterious and terrible, of something that leaped when least expected, something that upset all regularizations and defied all logic, something behind appearances that could not be tamed and brought to heel by men. The covenant thought kept this divine liberty at several removes, placed it on a theoretical plane, robbed it of much of its terror, but it could not do away with it entirely.

The respects in which these men, for all their efforts at intellectualization, remained essentially Puritans may perhaps appear if we briefly compare the Puritan reasonableness of John Preston with the Anglican reasonableness of Jeremy Taylor. In the *Ductor Dubitantium* Taylor's exposition of the Law of Nature and his determination of the segment of it that is also moral law are so very close to the pronouncements of Preston and Thomas Shepard that at first sight there seems to be no philosophical conflict between them. But for Taylor the conclusions reached by right reason, the dictates of justice, and the ideals of goodness cannot be invested with divine sanction merely because God, out of sovereign pleasure, elected to give them a binding force when He might just as well have enacted rules contrary to all human expectations. Taylor denies that it is even remotely possible that there remain a hidden God, outside and above reason. God *is* reason. There cannot be one justice on earth and another in heaven. . . . God cannot have a secret will distinct from his revealed one. He does not commit Himself to any rules simply through choice; the rules in themselves must be good, and God must inevitably, inescapably, instinctively follow them and no others. There can be no such thing as an offer of the covenant, an invitation to all men, and yet a secret withholding of grace without which man cannot respond. . . .

For Preston and the Puritan theologians of the covenant it was enough that God had consented to reason and had made an effort to fit His will to the requirements of abstract justice. They would not dogmatize further about His essence, and they felt that no man had a right to. They would expound the laws of reason and the laws of nature step by step with Taylor, they would extol justice and virtue as much as he, but they would not affirm that these human constructions, these intellectual values, were necessarily part and parcel of the cosmos. God's will coincides roughly with such conceptions, but not always exactly. The universe is almost always regular and orderly, but there is the one chance in a million, the one inexplicable accident, the one fact that will not fit into any scheme. There is every so often the apparently good man who cannot be saved or the hopeless wretch who is lifted from the gutter to glory in spite of all that we think appropriate. "If he take pleasure to breathe in a man, there is nothing can hinder him, it will blow upon the most noysome dunghill in any place, and be never a whit the more defiled." In a Christian community the machinery of conversion is set up, the covenant proposed, the terms made explicit, the means set in order, and yet in spite of all the best intentions this or that individual may never be able to join the covenant. And there is no explaining why, except that it is God's pleasure to withhold the ability from that particular man. Even the godly, after they have become partakers of the covenant, will not dwell in happiness and comfort. . . .

We should doe thus, stand upon the shore, (as it were) and behold his infinite Essence . . . and goe no further; as a man that stands upon the sea-shore, and sees the vastnesse of the sea, but dares goe no further, for if he goes into the deepe, he is drowned: You may looke into *Gods* Essence, and see and admire it; but to thinke that thou couldest comprehend *God* is as if a man should think to hold the whole sea in the hollow of his hand. . . .

The Puritan wished to bring his theology into harmony with science and reason wherever they might be made to coincide, but he could never lose his hunger for the inward exultation that came from a union with God which, though it might be brought about by natural causes, was yet something supernatural, something different from the causes, something which was bestowed only at the pleasure of God. Faith adds no new doctrine, teaches us no new facts, is not an addition to the contents of the mind. It is a glow of inspiration that quickens knowledge, and for that reason is all the more valuable and indispensable:

There is indeed a common faith, which the others may have, and thou mayest have, but the strong faith ariseth from the Spirit, *God* dispenseth it where he pleaseth; this infused faith is not gotten by strength of argument, or perspicuitie of the understanding; it is not brought in by custome, but *God* doth worke it; it is not all the antecedent preparation that will doe it, but *God* must first worke it, and then you are able to beleeve these principles of faith, and able to beleeve them to the purpose.

Morality and God's decree may, as we have seen Shepard saying, kiss each other and agree, but the Puritan could never forget that the agreement comes of God's own choice, and Shepard must add that the agreement is not always perfect, that the will of God remains superior to the demands of human equity. "When they [moral precepts] are called perpetual and unchangeable, we must understand them in respect of God's ordinary dispensation; for he who is the great Lawgiver may, and doth sometimes extraordinarily dispense with moral laws." The Puritan temperament is nowhere so well illustrated as in the contrast between the tenor of these passages and the tendency of the Puritan metaphysic. As far as possible Puritans would explain, draw diagrams, plot the course of God's will, and generalize upon His character. But it would be the end of Puritanism if they ever succeeded completely in penetrating the ultimate secret, if they could reach the point of saying that thus and so is not simply the way God does behave, but the way in which He must behave for these and those reasons. If the covenant theology is, as I think it is, a characteristic product of the Puritan mind, then we are perhaps justified in describing Puritanism as a willingness to follow nature and reason as far as possible, but not completely; for though Puritanism will use reason and enjoy nature, it can never overcome a fundamental distrust. . . .

To be wise unto sobriety was the purpose of this theology, to elucidate the laws of God's universe, but to keep a wary eye upon the unpredictability, the mystery of God. The evidence of subsequent history, both in England and in New England, would seem to be that it failed. Eventually the ideas which it introduced into the creed, reinforced by the triumph of Newtonian physics, displaced the theology in the estimation of such men as Charles Chauncy.[8] The moral of this episode in the story is, I think, that the Calvinism to which the Puritans were ostensibly dedicated was already in the process of far-reaching modification at the hands of English theologians before it was transported to Massachusetts. The men who directed the intellectual life of seventeenth-century New England left Cambridge and London when their tradition was in the first flush of transformation. They did not depart until into that tradition, under the guise of a doctrine of covenants made by God with man, there had been injected many ideas which derived, not from theology and revelation, but from law, from the study of nature, from the principles of reason and common sense. As time went on, the incompatibility of these ideas with the official confession was bound to become more apparent. Seen in this light, the development of rationalism in eighteenth-century New England is not a phenomenon produced entirely by the stimulation of imported ideas. The intellectual life of American Puritans in the seventeenth century was by no means so sparse and monotonous as it has sometimes been accused of being. The pristine doctrine was not rigorous, iron-clad, and inflexible; it had in it the elements of complexity, the seeds of future growth, making for diversity and contradiction. That period which is sometimes spoken of as the "glacial age" was not an era of intellectual dearth and philosophical sterility, but one of slow progression toward the ultimate separation of the diverse attitudes which had somehow been awkwardly and unwittingly put together in the covenant theology of Ames, Preston, and Sibbes. . . .

[8] EDITOR'S NOTE: Charles Chauncy (1705–1787) was a Boston minister who opposed revivalist preaching, favored rationality in religion, and pioneered in Unitarianism.

"The Heart of New England Rent": The Mystical Element in Early Puritan History

JAMES FULTON MACLEAR

James Fulton Maclear, a historian who did graduate work at the University of Chicago and teaches at the University of Minnesota at Duluth, should be classified as a critic of the Harvard school. Like Alan Simpson (see p. 159), Maclear differed with Miller by viewing Puritanism as a whole (on both sides of the Atlantic) rather than seeking to define a special subvariety that was carried to Massachusetts Bay. Accordingly, Maclear used definitions that were more inclusive than Miller's. But Maclear, like other critics, also implied that Miller had regarded Puritan piety in New England as more uniform and internally consistent from the outset than it actually was. By focusing on the mystical element in transatlantic Puritanism, Maclear produced a new interpretation of the Antinomian crisis and showed that the rational-minded approach to religion, which Miller had thought dominant from the founding of Massachusetts, was only part of the original mixture and did not prevail until after 1637. At first glance a return to the interpretation of Charles Francis Adams, Maclear's analysis is really more subtle and provides explanations for such previously puzzling phenomena as the emphasis that anti-Antinomians put on preparation for grace and the endemic susceptibility to Quakerism in New England, a susceptibility that enables us to understand the panicky persecution of Quaker missionaries by Puritan magistrates.

THOUGH RECENT YEARS HAVE SEEN MEANINGFUL REINTERPRETATIONS of New England Puritanism and of certain key figures within it, one important strain has been almost entirely neglected. This is the mystical element in Puritan thought and piety. . . .

. . . The neglect of this theme has resulted in a seriously distorted

James Fulton Maclear, " 'The Heart of New England Rent': The Mystical Element in Early Puritan History," *Mississippi Valley Historical Review,* XLII (1955–56), pp. 621–652. Reprinted without footnotes and with minor deletions where indicated, by permission of the author and the Managing Editor of the *Journal of American History*.

picture of New England Puritanism. It has prevented a true appreciation of the real warmth and vitality of much of early New England piety. It has made the "antinomian controversy" not only an enigma but an alien intrusion into the historical development of the Puritan mind. It has resulted in a tendency to view Quakerism as something to be dealt with only in terms of the external relations of Puritanism, neglecting the very real inner connections which existed. It has fostered the temptation to regard the Puritan mind as static rather than dynamic, as an entity installed in the New England landscape in 1630 rather than a development which within the first decade of settlement underwent ferment, revolution, decision, selection, and purgation. And lastly, it has created the greatest confusion with regard to the relation of American to English Puritanism. Massachusetts, it is said, constituted a refuge of the older and orthodox English Puritanism of the 1630's, free from the spiritual upheaval and fragmentation which dominated England after 1640; but in actuality the seeds of upheaval and fragmentation had arrived with Winthrop's company in the *Arbella,* and the comparative quiet of the New England scene in the 1640's can have been due only to the fact that the inevitable theological explosion had taken place in New England before that time.

These confusions can be eliminated only by recourse to a radically different approach. Such an approach begins with a full recognition of the emotional, the experiential, and ultimately the mystical element in the synthesis which stood at the center of Puritan evangelical religion. It takes seriously the effect on this synthesis of the new American situation and regards the establishment of "New England Puritanism" as coming only in crisis and agonizing decision. It appreciates that in the early 1640's English and American Puritanism were indeed dwelling in different stages of the religious development of the Puritan movement, but that New England stood in the post- rather than the pre-disintegration stage. And finally, it views the spiritual Puritanism of New England as unfolding in precisely the same pattern as that of Old England, even to the culmination in the Quaker harvest of the 1650's and 1660's.

A first step in such a portrayal is to summarize briefly the character of Puritan piety in England, with particular attention to the mystical strain. From that background the New England story evolves.

The Puritanism which reached Massachusetts with the first planters in 1630 formed a complex pattern, a piety which contained within it diverse elements maintained in rather precarious balance. There was, for one thing, its notorious Biblicism, the simplest identifying feature of the movement both then and now. At best expressing itself as a resolve to subject all life to the will of God as disclosed in Scripture, at worst degenerating into a narrow bibliolatry and legalism, it was responsible for the prominence in Puritan thought of such themes as authority, law, and moral reform at both the personal and institutional levels. As the spur to a search for an ecclesiastical polity prescribed by the Word, this Biblicism was also the source of the most dramatic chapter in the history of the Puritan movement, its fragmentation and resultant sectarianism, particularly after 1640. But in addition to its Biblicism, the Puritan complex held other elements—elements which when emancipated in the upheaval of the Puritan Revolution were to produce an intellectual fragmentation paralleling external schism. One of these elements was the "hidden rationalism" in Puritanism which has interested Perry Miller. Rooted deeply in the Puritan fascination for natural law, in the universally accepted "covenant theology," and even in the formal theological discipline imposed by the searching out of God's purposes in Scripture, traces of rationalism were present in all Puritan thinkers, though rarely dominant even after the beginning of the Revolution. And lastly, there was the element with which this essay is most concerned—the deep emotional longings for personal encounter and direct communion with God, in independence and contempt of all mediatory principles. In the form of the conversion experience, this experiential note stood, in fact, at the very heart of Puritan faith, as every Puritan biography testifies.

The strain produced within the Puritan synthesis by the tensions between these diverse parts was often very great, and balance was upheld only with increasing difficulty. That it was upheld at all was due in part to the curbs on religious innovation provided by Archbishop Laud's machinery of repression,[1] and more importantly, by the isolation from power which freed Puritans from the necessity of effectuating a constructive program of their own. But even so, occasional heterodoxy appeared, and when restraining factors were removed with the launching of the Revolution in 1640, the whole Puritan community was to be cast into a religious ferment in which the various components of Puritan piety often found pure expression. On the one hand, the obsession with polity was to lead many men to a preoccupation with externals. Others, relatively unconcerned with law or institutions, developed patterns of genuine mystical piety. Still others, though few in number, disgusted with the religious strife and stressing the tradition of natural law in the Puritan heritage, turned in the direction of rationalistic modes of thought. By 1644 this dissolution, centering chiefly in Independency, was well advanced, and an alarmed Scottish observer could describe precisely this threefold disin-

[1] EDITOR'S NOTE: William Laud (1573–1645) as Archbishop of Canterbury favored a form of Arminianism and directed the repression of Puritanism in England during the reign of Charles I.

tegration, though in the language of seventeeth-century polemic: "The most of their partie are fallen off to Anabaptisme, Antinomianisme, and Socinianisme; the rest are cutted among themselves."

It was out of this religious environment, then, though before the stage of actual dissolution had been reached, that the Puritanism of the Bay Colony was drawn. To discern more clearly the mystical element in New England Puritanism we must examine more closely the state of spiritual Puritanism in England in the decade of the great migration to the New World.

From its earliest beginnings, Puritanism had exhibited a drive toward immediacy in religious experience. It was this which stood at the root of its utter rejection of all sacerdotalism, whether Roman or Anglican. Here was a thirst for "experimental" knowledge of God, a craving for the most intimate relating of the soul to the divine "in independence of all outward and creaturely aids." Getting Christ in one's soul was perhaps the goal most emphasized in Puritan homiletics, just as deadness of heart appeared as the most heavy and burdensome affliction. The conventionalized Puritan hagiography customarily reached its crisis in the dramatic moment when, in the words of Thomas Goodwin, "God took me aside and as it were privately said unto me, do you now turn to me, and I will pardon all your sins." The popularity of prophesyings and testimonies, the emphasis on private extempore prayer, the introspection and self-analysis of the Puritan diary, were all variations on the same theme.

In early years this piety did not assume unconventional forms, but beginning in the 1620's and 1630's a new note was struck. There was, for one thing, the tremendous popularity of Lewis Bayly's *Practise of Piety*. Here was a spiritual guide which provided a most detailed and precise program of exercises—prayer, contemplation, and holy duties—by which the earnest seeker might come to enjoy a real possession of God, and "he that hath not by experience tasted his goodness, knows not how good he is." This work was thoroughly to penetrate the English Puritan community. By 1633 it was in its thirty-first edition; a Welsh version had been published, and John Eliot[2] was soon to translate it into Algonquin for the use of his Indian charges.

But even more revealing as a symptom of this mounting absorption with religious experience were certain changing emphases in Puritan

[2] EDITOR'S NOTE: John Eliot (1604–1690) went to Massachusetts in 1631 and served as minister at Roxbury. One of the few Puritans to devote much attention to the Indians, Eliot began to preach to those near his town in about 1644, went on to organize and supervise communities of converted natives, and translated the Bible and other books into their language.

theology and preaching, particularly the growing preoccupation with the doctrine of the Holy Spirit and resulting changes in the way in which the religious life was conceived. Geoffrey F. Nuttall has called attention to the great interest that Puritanism developed in this doctrine after a neglect which extended back to the church of antiquity. While this interest was to reach its climax in the radical mystical Puritanism of the Commonwealth and Interregnum, there was much preparation earlier. In pre-Revolutionary Puritanism there was evident an increasing emphasis on the concept of the indwelling Spirit as a means by which the closest possible communion with God might be achieved. Rebirth in the Spirit, the dwelling of the Spirit in the saint, and the continuing guidance of the Spirit were themes dwelt upon by every reputable divine, while hortatory literature stressed the necessity of striving for the Spirit. "If we would have the Spirit of God," declared Richard Sibbes, the most influential Puritan theologian of the 1630's, "let us attend upon the sweet promises of salvation, upon the doctrine of Christ; for together with the knowledge of these things, the Holy Ghost slides and insinuates and infuseth himself into our souls."

Indeed it was Sibbes who more than any other was responsible for this direction to Puritan piety in the second quarter of the century. Quoted repeatedly, sought out for spiritual advice, his works perhaps the most widely read of any writer on theology of the 1630's, Sibbes was the premier theological scholar of Puritanism until his death in 1635—even Laud grudgingly acknowledging the veneration which was accorded him. Nor was his influence confined to Old England. Almost every known library in early Massachusetts contained his works, while in John Cotton he had a devoted convert and disciple. And in scores of sermons and treatises Sibbes sounded the call to a spiritual religion, even to the warning, "Shut out of your hearts too much relying on any outward thing." Sibbes, to be sure, was orthodox. Judgment and redemption in history were never overlooked; no emphasis ever supplanted an evangelical faith and trust as the central element in his piety; the witness of the Spirit was always carefully joined to the hearing of the Word. But there was occasionally a flavor of mysticism too:

> Desire Christ by his Spirit to blow upon us. . . . Desire him to plant those blessed spices of grace in our hearts, and that he would blow upon them by his Spirit, that they may prosper and thrive, that so he may come into his garden and solace himself. Let us desire further and further communion with him; never be content. . . . He hath been familiar, but I desire more still. . . . "Thy love is sweeter than wine" and therefore "let him kiss me with the kisses of his mouth."

It was no accident that Sibbes preached twenty sermons on Canticles, the favorite book of all Christian mystics, making use of the bridal symbol to describe the soul's passionate longing for Christ.

In the limits within which Sibbes and other divines cautiously placed them, these doctrines were not immediately disruptive. But they were potentially so. Cautions against "grieving the Spirit," against abridging the freedom of the Spirit to blow where it listeth, not only militated against prepared prayers and sermons but also provided additional stimulus to the lay movement, already appearing in Puritanism. In particular, the encouragement given the old practice of lay prophesying—soon to be justified in some circles as "the opening and interpreting the word of God by a proper gift of the Spirit for the work"—was to make inevitable the great flowering of lay preaching after 1640. Moreover, an invincible assurance of union with God through his Holy Spirit could result only in a devitalization of all Puritan ecclesiasticism and externals. "Trust not in sacraments above their place," Sibbes had warned, and the teaching that sacraments, however beneficial, were not of the essence of the church nor absolutely necessary to the life of a Christian was accepted as reputable. . . .

This change in Puritan piety was still within the pale of religious respectability, but in certain isolated individuals and conventicles, particularly in the separatist underworld of Puritanism, much more sweeping inferences were being explored. Here the mode of the possession of the Spirit was in the more radical form of a personal indwelling. The role of the Spirit was the subject of excited discussion, whether viewed intellectually, in terms of special revelations, or morally, in terms of preservation from sin. Insistence on preaching and praying by movement of the Spirit was betraying a nascent but fierce iconoclasm toward traditional concepts of ministry and church order and a gravitation toward that spiritualized church where, according to a later description, "Christ and the Spirit are the onely Officers and men onely, so far as Christ and the Spirit dwel and manifest themselves in them." Changing attitudes toward sacraments—progressing from indifference to disuse, and finally to overt and unrestrained enmity—eventuated in their proscription as things external and carnal, not fit for men who had been baptized in the Spirit and who had fed on Christ spiritually. Even the Bible, though deeply precious as the testimony of the Spirit, could command no unique reverence from those in whom the same Spirit had become articulate.

These were yet gropings, but ultimately they were to coalesce into a genuine Spirit-mysticism in which the substantial and abiding presence of the Holy Spirit in the hearts of men freed them from reliance on any of the marks of institutional Christianity. This Spiritism differed from traditional conceptions of Christian mysticism (which also existed, but less significantly, in the period) not only in its different conception of the union as the inbeing of the Spirit rather than the more classic bridal relationship with Christ the heavenly spouse, but also in its consequences. With Spiritism, the central point was not an experience of transitory bliss but a rebirth and a subsequent life permanently transfigured, resulting in the consistent iconoclasm which the man who had entered the kingdom of the Spirit, unlike the conventional mystic, necessarily displayed. The flowering of Spirit-mysticism was to attain its full promise in the 1640's and 1650's when, as a serious contender for the domination of a shattered Puritanism, it was to find expression in such diverse figures as John Saltmarsh, William Dell, Gerrard Winstanley, Sir Harry Vane, George Fox, and even, to some degree, Oliver Cromwell.

Where did such advanced Spiritism exist in the 1630's? This is not an easy question to answer satisfactorily, though the mounting concern of the government and church authorities over the increase of "familism," the usual epithet for such ideas, is transparent. Probably, for many men the journey to these discoveries was a lonely one. In revolt against a rampant ecclesiasticism or in despair of reconstituting the church of the apostles, they turned to an anxious waiting for the new age of the Spirit and to seeking the signs of its coming within themselves. Foreshadowings of some such pattern as this can be seen perhaps as early as 1612 when the pioneer sectarian, John Smyth, drew up his final statement of belief. Within a few decades there were to be hundreds of such confessions, all claiming lonely and unassisted pilgrimages to their spiritual discoveries, of which those of Anne Hutchinson and George Fox are perhaps the most familiar.

But there were also more organized cultures of this Spiritism. London, where every radical religious current found a welcome, was certainly one. Here preparation for a Puritan mystical flowering had been made by the celebrated minister, John Everard, preacher at St. Martin's-in-the-Fields after 1618, whose large congregations included both gentlemen and "mechanicks." By the 1630's "mysticall Wolves," as a preacher at Paul's Cross in 1627 termed partisans of extravagant emphasis on the Spirit, were actively involved in the subterranean religious ferment of the capital, as increasing cries of familism and antinomianism attest. And the North was perhaps even more important than London as a center of this ferment. At Grindleton in Yorkshire, beginning about 1618, Roger Brierly (or Brerely) had started a movement of great notoriety, teaching

> Its not brain knowledge that doth make men free,
> But where God's Sp'rit is, there is liberty.

Brierly's views certainly tended toward antinomianism, and though he occasionally erected cautionary safeguards, his followers could be excused for concluding such things as "the Scripture is but for novices"; "wee must not now goe by motives but by motions [of the Spirit]"; and "when God comes to dwell in a man, he so fills the soule that there is no more lusting." Grindletonianism soon became the best-known as well as the most abhorred of contemporary heresies, and its spread throughout the North may have helped prepare the way for the rise of Quakerism in that area three decades later.

Were there other centers as well? This is impossible to answer with certitude. But the rapid flowering of mysticism in the Civil War period argues considerable preparation. In particular, the early history of Quakerism, the Buckinghamshire Levellers, and the Digger movement in Surrey all offer significant clues. Only of one area can we speak with greater assurance: in Ely, where there was apparently a small Spiritist conventicle which, by its own claim, had been meeting since 1631.

But to alarmed conservatives, caught in the religious anarchy of the Civil Wars and looking back in an effort to discern the origins of their troubles in the 1630's, there was still another nursery of this Spiritism. Ephraim Pagitt, Robert Baillie, Samuel Rutherford—all turned to Massachusetts as the locus of the most prominent outburst of pre-Revolutionary "familism." Thus Rutherford could identify Saltmarsh and Dell, the leading Spiritist preachers of his own day, with the doctrines condemned at the Cambridge Synod of 1637. So, too, Baxter could provide the Quakers with a pedigree which included not only "those in Yorkshire called Grundletonians [*sic*]" but also "in New England Mrs. Hutchinson and Mr. Wheeler [Wheelwright]." In so doing, these writers in the 1640's were groping toward some true vision of the way in which the mystical element had contributed to the fragmentation process which had now overtaken Puritanism. One of their own contemporaries could have given them the key. Viewing the spiritual road which he himself had traveled, William Erbury observed in 1652 that truth had advanced by several stages, the legalism of Elizabethan Puritanism giving way to the free grace of Sibbes, and the movement culminating in the knowledge of Christ in the Spirit as manifested in such Spirit-mystics as William Sedgwick, the "apostle of Ely," and Joshua Sprigg, the chief disciple of Sir Harry Vane. In England propulsion toward the final stage was to be provided by the events of 1640, but in New England freedom and the necessity of construction had come earlier, and so too had the dissolution of the Puritan synthesis. The horror with which Massachusetts viewed the English religious scene of the 1640's and 1650's was genuine, but by no means novel. For the "heart of New England" had been "rent," not, as John Norton thought, in the relatively minor Quaker annoyances of the late 1650's, but in the much more fundamental and decisive eruption which had taken place two decades earlier.

There is no reason to suppose that the polarities which existed in English Puritanism were not faithfully reproduced on the New England scene. True, some selective process was at work in the recruitment for the new colony, but this does not seem to have produced distortion. The majority of the settlers came from London, Essex, East Anglia, and Lincolnshire, but these were the areas of greatest Puritan density at home. Other "selective" factors in the migration did not disturb the pattern of piety so much as intensify already existing tensions within it. It is likely, for instance, that the colonization project primarily attracted only those for whom religious purity was the dominant concern, rather than those so-called "political Puritans" to whom the real issue was the outcome of the constitutional struggle in England. Thus religious issues were likely to assume greater importance and religious disagreements to generate greater heat than in the more complex quarrels in England. The predominantly Congregational auspices of the colonization had similar consequences. On the one hand, by dwelling on the issues of polity, the correctness of ecclesiastical externals was made central from the very beginning, but at the same time the limitation of church membership to a religious elite whose members could openly confess their spiritual experience laid an antithetical stress on the experimental qualities of Puritan spirituality. The consequence was the heightened tension which always characterized the "gathered" church and which was to make Independency the locus of Puritan fragmentation in both Old and New England.

There can be no doubt, in any case, that the piety transplanted to the new home harbored a drive toward experimental knowledge of God as potent as that in the parent Puritanism of the mother country. The sermons, spiritual guides, private correspondence, and personal diaries of New England bear witness to this. The popularity of Bayly in the devotional life of the colonists and the universality of Sibbes' works in colonial libraries have already been noted. Writing years later, Roger Clap tried to recapture the spiritual atmosphere of those early days:

> The Discourse not only of the Aged, but of the Youth also, was not, How shall we go to England? . . . but How shall we go to heaven? Have I true Grace wrought in my Heart? Have I Christ or no? O how did Men and Women, young and old, Pray for Grace, beg for Christ in those Days.

There may have been in this a touch of the nostalgia of old age, but it was not wholly so. In 1672 William Coddington, formerly treasurer of Massachusetts but at that time a Rhode Island Quaker, pronounced impassioned judgment on the revolution which he discerned as having taken place in the religion of the Bay Colony. His words to William Hawthorn were typical of his remembrance of the spirit of the entire colony in the days when he had been one of its leading magistrates:

I know thou wast tender, serious and retired . . . (for I had Speech with thee many times) and both then and afterward barest thy Testimony against Persecution, and stinting or limiting the Spirit of Prophecy in any . . . ; if that should take Place in New England, thou lookedst at it as one of the horridest Acts as was ever done in New England, and would be as great a Token of God's forsaking New England as any.

Using the word "tender" in its technical Quaker sense as "spiritually prepared," he could affirm that even persecutors like Richard Bellingham and John Endicott, "whose Names and Memorials shall stink and rot . . . formerly had some Tenderness" in them. This charge of apostasy would have been vigorously denied by the Massachusetts leaders, but the general correctness of Coddington's view was strikingly confirmed by one who at the moment of decision had assumed the leadership of the opposition to Coddington and his friends. John Winthrop, on the very eve of the climax of the "antinomian controversy," recorded an earlier experience of spiritual transport which still glowed in his writing after the passage of many years:

I was now growne familiar with the Lord Jesus Christ hee would oft tell mee he loved mee. I did not doubt to believe him; if I went abroad hee went with me, when I returned hee came home with mee. I talked with him upon the way, hee lay down with me, and usually I did awake with him: and so sweet was his love to me, as I desired nothing but him in heaven or earth.

This type of devotional expression, as pointed out, was not unnatural or disruptive so long as it remained only one of several contributory factors in the Puritan evangelical faith. But the equilibrium maintained only with grave difficulty in England in the 1630's was not to be maintained at all in the new conditions of America. Here a number of factors stimulated the development of a more legalistic mentality, which in turn elicited a contrary emphasis on the centrality of the experiential element in a desperate attempt to safeguard the threatened balance in Puritan religion.

The primary factor to be considered is the compulsion, now raised to extreme heights by the realization of autonomy, toward the purity of outward forms. New England, as John Norton reminded a later and less tractable generation, was a plantation religious. In this land the opportunity to fashion a new society and church had at last arrived. The time for building by God's Word was at hand. The opportunity was particularly great not only because of freedom from hostile ecclesiastical oversight but because the experiment was being made in a new country relatively free from the limitations and rigidities normally imposed by history and tradition. The centrality of this responsibility in the mind of New England can best be seen in Winthrop's *Journal* where increasingly every doubt, however trivial, is referred to the oracle of Scripture. Construction of a biblical commonwealth, moreover, was thought of in relation to the English struggle: New England must be a "city set on a hill," the unanswerable argument of Puritanism in the debate with Anglicanism. To this duty the colonial leadership was extremely sensitive. The principle, "There is nothing done in corners here but it is openly there related," seems always to have been kept in mind. It was a concern typically voiced by Zachariah Symmes during the troubles over Anne Hutchinson: "I fear that if by any meanes this should be carried over into England . . . it will be one of the greatest Dishonors to Je:Ch: and of Reproach to thease Churches that hath bine done since we came heather." The consequence was the impulse to subordinate everything to those aspects of Puritanism by which its truth could be visibly manifested, that is, to institutional and moralistic externals.

Reinforcing this tendency was another feature of the American scene. The few tiny settlements around the Bay constituted a frontier community. This fact had both psychological and political significance. Psychologically, the enormous hardships and perils which the first settlers were called upon to endure were soon to foster an element of morbidity and emotional instability in religious life which was largely absent from English Puritanism at this time. But it was also to produce a mentality of desperation, terror, and siege in which frenzied activity to conquer and build in measurable conformity to exact scriptural prescription seemed to offer the only security. Something of the nightmare, both physical and psychological, in which the founders of the Bay Colony found themselves was conveyed by Edward Johnson:

> With eyes full of anguish, they face to the right, upon the damnable Doctrines, as so many dreadfull Engines set by Satan to intrap their poore soules; Then casting forth a left hand looke, the labour and wants accompaning a Desert, and terrible Wildernesse affright them. . . . When with thoughts of retreating, they turne their backs about, the experienced incumbrances and deep distresses of a dangerous Ocean hinders their thoughts of flight, besides the sterne looke of the Lordly Prelates, which would give them a welcome home in a famishing prison.

It is not surprising that there should have been a tendency to seek whatever psychological reassurances there might be in faithful striving toward the fulfillment of God's demands, a note naïvely evident in Johnson's own vigorous career. But this need for security existed not only in the psychological but also in the practical or political realm. In Massachusetts religious uniformity was much more of a necessity than it ever was in the England of Laud. Here was no mature society with minimal standards of order and stability already achieved, but one in which the disruptive consequences of undisciplined religious experimentation simply could not be tolerated. The outcome was an insistence on external conformity to a degree unknown in English Puritanism. Preoccupation with this problem was patent in the later judgment of the general court on Anne Hutchinson: "She walked by such a rule as cannot stand with the peace of any State; for such bottomlesse revelations . . . being above reason and Scripture, they are not subject to controll." The need for such controls was particularly great since the excitement produced by the atmosphere of innovation and experimentation in which the colony had enveloped itself was apt to get out of hand. The idea that "the Lord had more truth and light yet to break forth out of his holy Word" was as heady a mixture in Massachusetts as in Plymouth, as the early religious history of the single community of Salem amply testifies.

These factors must have been operative from the first planting, and they were slowly bringing about the subtle changes which were later to occasion Coddington's grief at the loss of tenderness in his former friends. But it is not unlikely that in the reaction to which they gave rise they also provided the initial impetus to Coddington's own spiritual pilgrimage. Hence a heightened spirituality as well as a heightened legalism was to result, and the convulsions which were to shake the infant colony in a few years' time may be regarded as the maturation of tensions which had been in incubation since the moment of arrival. And this maturation was undoubtedly hastened by the coming in 1633 of the most celebrated of English Congregational divines and the subsequent glory of New England scholarship, the Reverend John Cotton.

It is certain that Cotton unwittingly contributed much to the advance toward the theological eruption which took place three years after his arrival. The involvement of their most famous doctor in the commotions of 1637 was the scandal of Massachusetts, and in later years vigorous efforts were made to obscure his part in the development. Official histories took care to preserve Cotton's reputation. . . . Far away in England, Robert Baillie was able to smell out the truth: "With all care and study, they endeavour to save Master Cottons credit; yet let the truth of Master Cottons seduction fall from their Pens in so clear termes, as canot bee avoided." Other contemporaries like Winthrop and Thomas Shepard privately, and Roger Williams publicly, made similar accusations, while from the other side, later Quaker writers uttered lamentations over the fall of him "who in his day did know the Power of God to salvation." Even Cotton himself conceded that many thought that "such a Doctrin of Union, and evidencing of Union as was held forth by mee, was the Trojan Hourse, out of which all the erroneous Opinions and differences of the Country did issue forth."

What truth lay behind this reputation? Unfortunately, Cotton published no doctrinal work before 1641 when events had doubtless made him more cautious. All contemporary references, however, note his homiletical emphasis on the indwelling Spirit, while Coddington in his reproach to Massachusetts was able to recall the gist of a sermon delivered during the crisis:

Turn to the Light within you, wherewith you are enlightened. . . . Even Christ in you the Hope of Glory, which was declared to you by . . . John Cotton . . . on His Lecture Day . . . he magnified Grace within us, the Priests Grace without or upon them: . . . the Difference was as great (saith he) as between Light and Darkness . . . and from the Spirit of Jesus did he then declare . . . turn to the Grace of God within you, that, as in former Dayes, so in this is the Saints Teacher, then shall you never be without a Teacher.

But we are not dependent on mere hints of this sort. Even in the throes of the reaction to the "antinomian" agitation Cotton could voice misgivings as to whether God's truth had not suffered by the victory of the triumphant party, and his later works contain sufficient material to make his impact on the New England religious scene understandable.

No evidence indicates that Cotton was ever a Spirit-mystic. Rather, he is best understood as a convert of Richard Sibbes, and like Sibbes, his piety centered in an evangelical faith in which Christ both past and present found a place. Thus the leading defender of Congregational polity and the writer of *Moses, His Judicials* could also be the author of such a treatise of distilled spirituality as *Christ the Fountain of Life.* Like Sibbes, Cotton chose to emphasize a call to a warmth of piety, an ardor of devotional love, an immediate experience of Christ which transcended not only all ecclesiastical considerations but even the hope of salvation itself, and this emphasis led him to proclaim a theology of the Holy Spirit in teaching and exhortation.

Cotton's fifth sermon in *Christ the Fountain of Life* provides a good example of the preaching which must have excited the church at Boston. . . . Three quotations suffice to suggest the tone of the sermon:

There is a secret fellowship between Christ and the Spirit so that, have one and you have both, have not the Spirit of Christ, and you have none of Christ.

The spirit of God, wheresoever it is shed abroad in any member of Christ, it doth make us one with the Lord Jesus, it unites us into one fellowship of nature, a likenesse in affection and disposition, and a likenesse in all the graces of God.

The man reborn in the Spirit is but a bungler in sin now; not now learned in the law of sinne, as sometimes he hath been; but the Law of the Spirit of life hath freed him from the skill of sinne, and from the command of sinne.

The words are revealing, and Cotton's few cautionary phrases concerning the Spirit—such as "though in us it be the weaker, by reason of a spirit of corruption found in us, and not in Christ"—do not bulk large in his message.

Elsewhere Cotton gave evidence of other Spiritist accents in his teaching. Concerning the reading of prayers and signing of psalms he wrote: "Thou wilt neither pray, nor sing well upon a Book, unlesse God give thee a spirit of Grace." His treatment of sacraments was more forceful than that of Sibbes, . . . :

Hold close to the Ordinances . . . but while you enjoy them, trust not in them, nor thinke not to stand upon this, that you are blessed in regard of them; but looke at them all as losse, and drosse, and dung, that you may win Christ. . . .

And Cotton even seems hesitantly to make allowance for the witness of the Spirit *apart* from the Word. . . . Thus prayers, sacraments, Word—all were in some measure disturbed by the attention accorded to the doctrine of the Spirit.

There remains to be answered the question whether some among Cotton's hearers had already passed beyond his words. Were there in the thousands of immigrants who crossed the Atlantic in the decade of the 1630's some representatives of advanced Spiritist heresies? Evidence is slight, but certainly the rapid foliation of these ideas in the critical months of 1636–1637 leads one to suspect the catalytic action of a limited amount of fully developed Spirit-mysticism. . . . Indeed, it seems necessary to agree with the editor of the first history of the "antinomian controversy," Thomas Weld, that some came to New England "full fraught with many unsound and loose opinions," and "after a time, began to open their packs, and freely vent their wares to any that would be their customers."

This was the situation when in 1634 Anne Hutchinson, obedient to an immediate revelation, followed Cotton across the Atlantic to Massachusetts Bay.

The romantic and tragic story of Anne Hutchinson has been often told and need not be recounted here. Some futher consideration may be given, however, to her place in the Spiritist tradition and her impact on the religious development of Massachusetts.

There can be no doubt that Mistress Hutchinson had plunged deeply down the road to Spirit-mysticism by the time of her arrival in the Bay Colony in 1634. "Thease are no new Thinges, but she hath ayntientlye held them," was the judgment at her trial, and William Bartholomew testified that he had known Anne in London where she had "said that she had never had any great thing done about her but was revealed to her beforehand." But if it is certain that "this woman had learned her skil in England," it is not so certain what were the sources of her instruction. She herself was prevented by her theological commitment from admitting any influences other than divine: "I had none to open the Scripture to me, but the Lord, he must be the Prophet." In this conviction she differed in no respect from scores of later Spiritists. But, like them, she did not, in all probability, develop her views in isolation. Her early home at Alford was in the northern part of Lincolnshire where rumors of Grindletonianism must have been frequent, while the formative years of her young womanhood were spent in the equally active Puritan circles of London. After her marriage and return to Lincolnshire, she was drawn into the orbit of Cotton's preaching at Old Boston until this was brought to an end by "the Lord carrying Mr. Cotton to New England (at which I was much troubled)." In a curious reference, Hugh Peter also spoke of her admiration for a certain Woman of Elis [Elie?, i.e., Ely?], "a dayngerous Woman" who "houlds forth greewous Things, & ferfull Errors." Whatever these influences may have been, they were adequate to producing the experience which Mrs. Hutchinson so eloquently described at the climax of her trial:

> When I was in old England, I was much troubled at the constitution of the Churches there, so farre, as I was ready to have joyned to the Separation, whereupon I set apart a day for humiliation by my selfe, to seeke direction from God, and then did God discover unto me the unfaithfulnesse of the Churches, and the danger of them, and that none of those Ministers could preach the Lord Jesus aright, for he had brought to my mind, that in the 1 John 4.3. Every spirit that confesseth not, that Jesus Christ is come in the flesh, is the spirit of Antichrist; I marvelled what this should meane . . . then it was revealed to me that the Ministers of England were these Antichrists, but I knew not how to beare this, I did in my heart rise up against it . . . after I had begged this light, a twelve moneth together, at last he let me see . . . how I did turne in upon a Covenant of works and did oppose Christ Jesus.

This experience was to remain the key event of her life, and all the decisions of her later life were determined by it. In this remarkable confession were found, too, the utterances soon to appear in the conventional testimony of many Interregnum Spirit-mystics—the great weariness with the ecclesiastical problem, the terrible discovery of the apostasy of the churches and clergy with their corruption of the gospel into a covenant of works, and finally the conviction that such teachings as had been granted resulted from the direct communication of the divine Teacher. Anne felt that henceforth she must apply her own experience to what she heard from the pulpits and strive to distinguish "which was the voyce of Moses, which of John Baptist, and which of Christ." It was this faithfulness to her revelation, in fact, which caused her emigration to New England for "after our teacher Mr. Cotton, and my brother Wheelwright were put downe, there was none in England that I durst heare."

But faithfulness to her revelation also required that she should speak. There could be no greater sin than silence on the part of one in whom the Spirit pressed for articulation. . . . On being installed in New England under the protective mantle of Cotton, the compulsion to speak was intensified. In view of her strong personality, her intelligence, and the visible sincerity of her devotion, it is not surprising that soon "she had more resort to her for counsell about matter of conscience, and clearing up mens spirituall estates, then any Minister (I might say all the Elders) in the Country." She "divided" texts; she interpreted the Word; she repeated sermons. This "prophesying" was not without precedent, but her textual justification was interesting. "I will poure my Spirit upon your Daughters, and they shall prophesie," she quoted. "If God give mee a gift of Prophecy, I may use it."

According to the colony's official account, *The Short Story of the Rise, Reign, and Ruine of the Antinomians,* Anne was at first helpful and orthodox but later began "to set forth her own stuffe." Winthrop correctly condensed this teaching into two principal propositions—an affirmation of "that opinion of the indwelling of the person of the Holy Ghost, and of union with Christ" and a collateral insistence that awakening to the Spirit was primary "and that to see any work of grace (either faith or repentance &c.) before this immediate witnesse, was a Covenant of works." Her opponents never failed to conclude that this must issue in moral license and antinomianism, and allusions to the excesses of the German Anabaptists and the kingdom of Münster were made.[3] But actu-

[3] EDITOR'S NOTE: A group of religious radicals, called Anabaptists, seized control of the Westphalian city of Münster in 1532 and planned further conquests with the goal of establishing the reign of universal righteousness. The radicals believed themselves acting on direct divine orders. After a hostile army laid seige to the town, some of the Anabaptists began to think that further revelations required or permitted them to indulge in various kinds of unconventional behavior, including poly-

ally Anne's behavior was blameless and her ethic scriptural. Normally, antinomian tendencies in most Spiritist groups were balanced by a concern for keeping the soul morally pure that it might be a fit vessel of the Holy Ghost. Probably the accusations made by Anne's opponents on this score were for propaganda effect; they were much nearer the real issue in exposing the implications of her teaching for the church. The divines correctly saw that the whole theological tradition of which Anne was a part was one which drove men, invincible in their conviction of possession of the Spirit, toward transcending—and thereby destroying—existing outward forms and ordinances. In her case, this iconoclasm was manifested most clearly on the question of the ministerial office.

The enmity between Mrs. Hutchinson and the Massachusetts ministry has usually been grossly misinterpreted as a case of personal pique and slander on the one side and of outraged professionalism on the other. This is superficial. To be sure, these emotions were present, but the determining influences were theological. To Anne, her clerical enemies not only taught unsound doctrine, but were themselves false guides and impostors, pretending to teach Christ without experience of Christ. "They had not the seale of the Spirit." She told them to their faces that they were like "Christ's Disciples, and their ministery, before his ascension, and before the holy Ghost was come downe upon them." In saying this, she was merely proclaiming the distinction taught her in her first revelation and differentiating "the voyce of my beloved, from the voyce of strangers." Thus, whether she appreciated the implications or not, Mrs. Hutchinson had become committed to a ministry of the Spirit from which all marks of a ministry of external status must necessarily be expunged. Did she go beyond this? If the true ministry was a ministry of the Spirit, could it also be said that all who possessed the Spirit were themselves ministers and hence independent of all external pastoral services and functions? She never stated this position explicitly, but the logic of her theology must have impelled her toward it. Cotton implied as much when he complained to her "that her Faith was not begotten nor . . . scarce at any time strengthened, by publick Ministery, but by private Meditations, or Revelations onely." Of what use was even such a teacher as John Cotton to those whose Teacher was the Spirit?

There is no definite evidence that Anne carried this iconoclasm further, to a fearless pursuit of all the logical consequences of her cardinal

---

gamy and murder. The Anabaptist rule ended in 1535, when the city fell and the victors began a ferocious repression. But the episode was not forgotten; for years afterwards, conservative Christians alluded to it frequently as proof of the ultimate effect of belief in direct communion with the Holy Spirit.

conceptions. But her partisans undoubtedly did as her teaching precipitated a vast outpouring of popular religious speculation and experimentation. "Indeed," wrote Winthrop, "it was a wonder upon what a sudden the whole Church of Boston (some few excepted) were become her new converts . . . and many also out of the Church, and of other Churches also." The popular aspects of the movement have been too little stressed by historians dominated by the personality of the leader. The infection penetrated all classes. Among the more prominent persons whom it reached were Governor Vane, Treasurer Coddington, and magistrates like William Aspinwall, John Coggeshall, and Atherton Hough, but the most significant effects were beginning to appear at the more popular levels of society. An alarmed Captain Johnson recorded an experience which must have been common in those months:

There was a little nimble tongued Woman among them, who said she could bring me acquainted with one of her own Sex that would shew me a way, if I could attaine it, even Revelations, full of such ravishing joy that I should never have cause to be sorry for sinne, so long as I live, and as for her part shee had attained it already.

As was the case with Mrs. Hutchinson, it was in anticlericalism that the Boston population manifested the iconoclastic impulse of Spiritism most obviously. Men vilified ministers, wrote abusive letters to them, walked out of their churches, and reviled them as "legall Preachers, Baals Priests, Popish Factors, Scribes, Pharisees, and Opposers of Christ." . . .

But other characteristic positions in which Spirit-mysticism usually terminated were also exhibited in this fermentation. Praying except by the direction of the Spirit was proscribed. The authority of the Bible was much mooted. One of Wheelwright's congregation proclaimed the obsolescence of sacraments: "In the New Testament there are no signes, no not our baptisme, for the baptisme of water is of no use to us, when once wee are baptized with the Holy Ghost." Questions about "the immortality of the Soule, about the resurrection, about the morality of the Sabbath" were discussed. And pervading all this excitement was an anxious expectation of the new age of the Spirit, for "there is a great light to break forth, if men do not resist it."

Massachusetts remained in the crucible throughout the fall and winter of 1636–1637 while the struggle, projected inevitably into the political arena, raged without restraint. Then in May, 1637, Vane was defeated and Winthrop took his place in the governor's chair. It remained only to be seen how much of the Spiritist tradition would survive the reaction to follow.

The political history of the reaction—the flight of Vane, the judgments against Wheelwright and Anne Hutchinson, the exodus to Rhode Island —is a familiar story and requires no repetition. Massachusetts leaders believed that these measures were successful in effecting the purgation of the autonomous mystical element from the piety of Massachusetts, and two decades later the Barbadian Quaker, John Rous, pronounced a dirge over Boston which seemed to indicate his sorrowful concurrence in their belief. Yet this was not the whole story. At the time Rous wrote, the mystical tradition, though a suppressed and subordinate current in Massachusetts and Plymouth, was regnant in Rhode Island, and in both regions it had prepared the way for the Quaker successes of the 1650's and 1660's. The course of the development may be traced briefly.

It is clear that in Massachusetts the mass of the infected population was successfully disciplined, quieted, and rehabilitated by political and ecclesiastical authority. Apart from the banishment of the "antinomian" leaders, the reintegration of Cotton with the colonial leadership was probably of greatest importance in this achievement. This was not an easy task. Not only did Cotton resist the tremendous pressures placed upon him throughout the summer and fall of 1637, but at one time he prepared to abandon the colony entirely. Years later Cotton insisted that his intention had been to seek New Haven as a refuge, though Roger Williams' report that "he [Williams] was imployed to buy from the Savages, for the late Governour, and Master Cotton, with their followers, a proportion of Land without the English Plantation whither they might retire and live according to their own mind" presents what is at least an interesting alternative possibility. But the significant point is that Cotton at length yielded. And by doing so he greatly facilitated the task of bringing the Boston population to a genuine submission. . . .

By these methods the Bay Colony was saved for orthodoxy, but it was a somewhat altered orthodoxy. For not only had an exaggerated Spiritism been cast out, but the destructive power of the reaction had begun transforming the residual Puritanism of Massachusetts itself, bringing into uncontested prominence that preoccupation with "preparation" (for justification) which Perry Miller has identified as one of the chief marks of the New England theology.

Even in Massachusetts, however, Spiritist concepts continued a subterranean existence. There the quaintly worded judgment that errors "were so put to death, that they never have stood up in a living manner among us since, but sometimes like Wizards to peepe and mutter out of ground" was substantially correct. Even among those who genuinely conformed there must have been not a few who harbored misgivings and felt with Cotton that "in the course taken for the clensing of Gods Field . . . some truths of God fared the worse for the resemblance which the tares bared to them." Colonial authorities were alive to these dangers. When "familist" Samuel Gorton and his followers were released from imprisonment in 1644, Winthrop required their departure within two hours, though they did not leave before some Boston citizens had welcomed them joyfully into their houses. In Salem, too, a warning was sounded by John Endicott: "Assuredly both with you and with vs and in other places that heresie doeth spread." The danger from England, where radical Puritanism was now dominant, was met by an attempted quarantine, and it is not surprising to hear Roger Williams reporting in 1654 that "two of Mr. Dells books were lately burnt at the Massachusetts." Despite this vigilance, the danger still continued. In 1658 a Quaker evangelist was writing, "The Seed in Boston and Plymouth Patents is ripe," and two decades later Peter Folger was still chanting in the authentic key of the "antinomian" troubles of 1637:

> There's one thing more that I believe
> is worse than all the rest,
> They vilify the Spirit of God,
> and count School Learning Best.

In the older colonies to the north this was a minor strain, but not so in the refugee settlements at Narragansett Bay. Here Williams had already established a tradition of freedom, experimentation, and skepticism concerning externals in which the Spiritist concepts brought by the outcasts from Massachusetts could thrive. To their villages on Rhode Island, moreover, was soon added Samuel Gorton's plantation of Warwick on the west Narragansett shore as another haven of these ideas. The consequence was that continuing religious fermentation which never failed to attract the horrified gaze of the leaders at the Bay, in whose writings are found innumerable variations on the theme of "new errors daily." Though these echoes were hostile, they were not greatly distorted. . . .

Here was the fierce vindication of the liberty of the Spirit, "making a goodly piece of Preachment; among whom there were some of the female sex"; here the vigorous rejection of any intrusion of human learning into preaching by the Spirit. Here was Spiritist iconoclasm with regard to such carnal observances as Sabbath and sacraments—Randall Holden deriding the practice of the Bay in turning the "juice of a poor, silly grape, that perisheth in the use of it, into the blood of our Lord Jesus, by the cunning skill of your magicians." In some these attitudes assumed the somewhat hesitant shape of Seekerism in which the suspension of forms was grounded in the view that "there were no churches since those founded by the apostles . . . nor any pastors ordained, nor seals administered but by such, and that the church was to want these all the time she continued in the Wilderness, as yet she was." In others vivid and imminent expectation of the full dispensation of the Spirit in the hearts of men led to the adoption of an ethic in which there was no place for magistracy or sword. According to Baillie, Mrs. Hutchinson herself reached this position, and persuaded her husband to resign his office at Portsmouth.

But most revealing of all were the arrangements for corporate worship. Governed by concepts of the ministry of the Spirit and in actual fact lacking an ordained minister, these settlements gravitated naturally toward the type of meeting later to become common among the early Friends. Lechford noted that a Portsmouth meeting was composed of "men, who there teach one another, and call it Prophesie," while in 1659 a Quaker tract could rejoice that throughout Rhode Island, "the habitation of the hunted Christ, . . . none of the dumb doggs dare come so much as to lift their tongues for lucre." And no Friend ever expressed the theory of the "silent" meeting more adequately than Samuel Gorton in 1647:

[The] spirit uttereth it selfe freely without respect of Persons in all the Congregations and Assemblies of Saints, giving words for edification and comfort of the Church sometimes in one, and sometimes in another that all flesh may bee silent before him, and onely listen unto the Oracle of God by whom hee is pleased to utter it; for yee may all prophecy one by one for the edification of the Church, but if any thing bee revealed to another that sits by, let the first hold his peace.

Already the leaven of the Spirit had produced in amorphous form many of the salient features later to be given definition and permanence in the Quaker movement. And though Friends were generally reluctant to admit this, it was substantially the point made by Samuel Groome, who concluded a denunciation of the Bay Colony with the words: "The Lord raised up a Testimony in many of their Neighbours and Inhabitants of the same Country, who witnessed for the God of Heaven, against their Wayes, Doctrines, and Worships."

"In 1656 or 1657 some of the people called Quakers came to this Colony and Island," wrote John Callender, the first historian of Rhode Island, "and being persecuted and abused in the other Colonies, that together with the opinions and circumstances of the people here, gave them a very large harvest." Quakerism, the final product of the English tradition of mystical Puritanism, had now arrived on American shores. It was, as G. F. Nuttall has written, "but the carrying forward of a development already well advanced within radical Puritanism; . . . an emphasis, a fusing and a systematization of beliefs which had appeared earlier but which had then been more hesitant, sporadic, and unrelated."

Here was the ultimate form of Spirit-mysticism in which the radical completion of the spiritualization of Word, ministry, and sacraments terminated in a church exhibiting itself as a pure culture of the Holy Spirit, free from human officers and external observances. . . .

Considering the preparation which had taken place, it is not surprising that the first Quaker missionaries were received in many places as "messengers of God." Not waiting for a personal encounter, Gorton rushed off a letter of welcome: "The errand you profess you come with, into these parts, hath much taken my heart . . . we are persons who lie here as buried unto the sons of men, in a corner of the earth. . . . But our God may please to send some of his saints unto us, to speak words, which the dead hearing, shall live." Conquests were made instantly. By 1658 Newport could be referred to as one of the "strong places in this land," and Rhode Island was being affectionately set down in Quaker writings as "that Island, where we ever found a place to rest our heads when weary we have been." The Hutchinsons were dead, massacred by the Indians, but the "convincement" of Coddington, Joshua Coggeshall, the Eastons, the Scotts, the Dyers, the Clarkes, and others of the exiles of 1637 had taken place almost immediately. The words used to Richard and Catherine Scott, founders of the Providence meeting, must have been applicable to many: "When that which is good came, full ready were they to receive it, and those who brought it." By the 1670's this tide had swept Quakerism into control of the government of the colony; and beyond its boundaries, in the persecuted meetings of Lynn, Salem, Sandwich, and other towns of the older colonies, the foundations of the modest but lasting Quaker tradition of Massachusetts were being laid.

Thus, in New England as in Old England, the mystical element in Puritan religion had now come to rest in Quakerism. Did contemporaries see this succession? That it was discernible seems certain. But just as leaders of the Bay Colony wished to avoid paternity of New England Quakerism and to bestow upon it a more impressive pedigree derived from heresies of antiquity and the German Reformation, so the early "publishers of Truth" were concerned to vindicate the uniqueness of the revelation which had come to George Fox. Yet there were exceptions. A simple soldier like Captain Roger Clap knew that the Hutchinson party in 1637 had been "much like the Quakers." "They would talk of the Spirit," he continued, "and of revelations by the Spirit without the Word, as the Quakers do talk of the Light within them, rejecting the holy Scriptures." And on the other side, the Quaker tract called *The Secret Works,* George Bishop, Samuel Groome, and Humphrey Norton all touched on how Anne "had seen the end and emptiness of all their Ceremonies." But the most eloquent testimony was to come from William

Coddington in a message to his former friend, Governor Richard Bellingham of Massachusetts, in which his mind returned again to the origins of that spiritual pilgrimage of New England piety which his own life had so clearly portrayed: "Forty five Years past, thou didst own such a suffering People, that now thou dost persecute; they were against Bishops and Ceremonies, and the conformable Priests; they were the Seed of God that did serve him in Spirit, then called Puritans, now called Quakers."

From Diversity to Orthodoxy in the Massachusetts Churches

DARRETT B. RUTMAN

Perry Miller's interpretation of the founding of Massachusetts—that non-separatist Congregationalist Puritans who supported the covenant theology planned and executed it—has come under criticism. Two critics, Edmund S. Morgan and Darrett B. Rutman, have reviewed the events of the early decades to show an absence of preconcerted plans. Morgan in *Visible Saints* (1963) has proposed extensive revisions of Miller's views on the purposes of the Massachusetts Bay Company leaders, the importance of some early decisions on ecclesiastical regulations, and the significance of making church membership a prerequisite for full political rights. Morgan did all this by way of a disarmingly modest inquiry into requirements for church membership, which showed that the Puritan congregations changed near the end of the 1630s from standards that admitted many candidates to standards that admitted few. Rutman, who earned a doctorate at the University of Virginia and teaches history at the University of Minnesota, has been attentive to the details of institutional life on a much broader scale. His study, *Winthrop's Boston* (1965), while focused on the Massachusetts capital, covers many colony-wide matters both directly and by implication. In ecclesiastical affairs, he accepted Morgan's findings and went further in explaining the change in the nature of the churches which included the alteration of requirements for membership.

THE BASIC STRUCTURE OF THE MASSACHUSETTS CHURCHES CONformed to God's truth as the ministers saw it, but the surface unity which had been achieved by the laymen displayed too many half-hidden disparities for their tastes. Too many "of weake Judgments" had found their way into the churches, a correspondent in England wrote in March 1633: "I verilie perswade my self you have many . . . amongst you, on whome it were good your ministers took a little paines, that they might be rectified." Cotton perforce agreed. Noting the lack of ministerial direction, he wrote on behalf of himself and Thomas Hooker that their work in the Bay was "enough, and more than enough to fill both our handes, yea and the hands of many brethren more." This was the case even in regard to the general polity of the Bay, for not all the churches of the commonwealth had come to the same conclusions with regard to various problems. Before the end of 1633, the ministers began to meet periodically "at one of their houses by course" to debate and presumably establish a common position on "some question of moment." Orthodoxy was in the making, for although the ministers maintained that "no church or person can have power over another church" and that they did not "exercise any jurisdiction" by virtue of their meetings, the fears of Roger Williams and Samuel Skelton that "it might grow in time to a presbytery or superintendency to the prejudice of the churches' liberties" were to prove prophetic.

Yet orthodoxy was not to be established overnight, nor disparity to disappear. The latter was still rampant in 1635, when the General Court entreated "the elders and brethren of every church" to "consult and advise of one uniforme order of discipline in the churches, agreeable to the Scriptures, and then to consider howe farr the magistrates" might act "for the preservacion of that uniformity and peace of the churches." The newly arrived Hugh Peter noted it a year later, when, before the Boston church, he suggested that Cotton go through the Bible "and raise marginal notes upon all the knotty places of the scriptures" and that "a form of church government might be drawn according to the scriptures."

Neither plea could be acted upon at the moment. The ministers were in actuality not of a single mind as to God's truth, and while they sought unity they regularly introduced dissent among themselves. The English correspondent of March 1633 had noted this, as well as the "weake Judgments" among the laymen: "I have heard . . . that your ministers preach one against anothers doctrine; which I conceive to be a great scandall to your societieis, and if not reformed in tyme, may prove . . . fatall." The case of Roger Williams is familiar, the brash young separatist lighting fires of dissent everywhere he passed, challenging the validity of the charter, the authority of the magistrates in questions of morals, the advising of one church by another, the presence of unregenerates at church services. John Eliot at Roxbury questioned the validity of the ministers' part in negotiating an Indian treaty and had to be brought "to acknowledge his error in that he had mistaken the ground of his doctrine." In Charlestown, the Reverend Mr. James and his congregation fell to squabbling, and it grew "to such a principle of conscience among them" that the other ministers were asked to give their advice; after two meetings the ministers themselves were divided.

And it was not only the ministers. Much of the fiery controversy was emerging from the congregations, for the conversion and edification which Winthrop commented upon following Cotton's installation in Boston was but a part of a religious enthusiasm running rampant through the commonwealth. In Salem, the congregation turned on the "King's colors," defacing them on the grounds that "the red cross was given to the king of England by the pope, as an ensign of victory, and so a superstitious thing, and a relique of antichrist." In Dorchester, a church was to be gathered to replace that which had left the commonwealth for the Connecticut River, but it was forestalled when it was found that some of the would-be members "had builded their comfort of salvation" upon "dreams and ravishes of spirits by fits; others upon the reformation of their lives; others upon duties and performances."

It was in Boston, however, that both dissent among the ministers and popular enthusiasm reached their highest peak. The first was presaged early in 1636 when the Reverend Thomas Shepard, having attended Cotton's Thursday lecture, returned home to Newtown in consternation. Cotton had spoken of faith and sanctification in terms which seemed to contradict Shepard's teachings, and Shepard wrote to ask a series of questions: "It is the earnest desire not only of my selfe, but of diverse of our members, whose harts are much endeared to you, that for the further clearing up of the truth, you would be pleased to give us Satisfaction by way of writing rather than by speech for this one time to these particulars. . . . I have plainly writ my hart unto you, being perswaded that in the spirit of meeknes, you will not thinke I have thus writ to begin or breed a quarrell; but to still and quiet those which are secretly begun." Cotton had responded in kind: "As for difference, and Jarres, it is my unfeigned desire to avoide them with all men especially with Brethren; but I doe not know, I assure you, any difference, much less Jarres between me, and any of my Brethren in our Publique Ministery." Yet he was in error. There was a fundamental difference.

To such as Shepard, the holy church of Christ as an institution among men was all important, and feeling that sanctification—the moral behavior of the individual—was the principal sign by which man and the churches could hope to recognize God's elect, they were content to build their churches upon visible morality, calling their listeners to a reformation of their lives and inviting those of moral appearance to apply for church membership. True, the reprobate could not be transformed into a saint, nor could a man profit by his good works, storing up credits in heaven which would be counted in his favor at the Judgment, for those whom God would save were already known to Him. But the saint, living in sin, could be awakened (if it were God's will) to follow his duty toward God, while a man who could look upon his total life and say "I have lived as God would have me live according to His revealed word" could take comfort in the possibility that he was of the elect, for God's saints (by virtue of their election) would abide by God's commandments and ally themselves with the true church.

Cotton, concerned more with the individual than the institution, more with salvation than morality, would go further. He had earlier introduced the idea that admission to the church should be dependent not merely on the outward behavior and knowledge of the faith of the applicant, but on the church's evalution of the applicant's profession of the working of Christ within him—a subtle but profound change in the admission procedure, in time transforming the church from a gathering of the professedly godly to a gathering of the professed visible saints. Other churches in Massachusetts were adopting the profession of grace as part of the admissions procedure, the would-be members being required to acknowledge "the great mercy and grace of God, in receiving them to his grace: and changing their heart and life by such or such means." But in most it remained secondary to the formal confession of knowledge of the faith and the evidence of good conduct; that the profession of grace was "weakely" and "briefly done . . . mindes not," a 1637 statement of admission procedures stipulated.

For Cotton, however, the profession of grace was cardinal. It was not enough, however. Like any other minister he sought to join men to the church, urging them to accept (and declare to the congregation) what they felt to be God's help in renouncing their sins and embarking upon a reformed life. The number of conversions in the years immediately after his arrival indicates a great response to his appeal. But membership in the church was only an outward indication or, as he termed it, a "seal" of the individual's saved condition, and a slight one at that. Cotton sought to move his communicants into a pitiless self-examination, a never-ending search for a second and true seal, driving his words into the very entrails of his hearers. "It is the desire of my heart by the grace of Christ," he wrote, "to provoke Christians (in this countrye of universal professein) not to rest in any changes of graces, Deutyes or Ordinances (as Church-fellowship etc.)." "I would not wish christians to build the signes of their Adoption [by Christ] upon any sanctification, but such as floweth from faith in Christ Jesus; for all other holynesse, and righteousness . . . may be . . . mortall seede, and fall short of perseverance: whereas the least seede of fayth, and of that holynes which floweth from it abideth for ever." Take comfort in the true ordinances of the church, but "while you enjoy them, trust not in them, nor thinke not to stand upon this. that you are blessed in regard of them." Take comfort, too, in the Word and in following its commandments, but do not let it close your eyes to the nearness of God Himself, "for it is not all the *promises* in Scripture, that have at any time wrought any gracious changes in any soul, or are able to beget the faith of *Gods Elect.*" Only true faith—faith emanating directly from God, faith in the absolute perfection of God's will and the utter desirability of "closing" with God, faith that leads one to say "here am I as you have created me, weak, abject, yearning for your comfort yet comforted only as it befits your will"—only such faith is "the Witnesse of the Spirit it selfe, as it is distinguished from our Spirit." And it was such a witness of the holy spirit within for which he would have his hearers search. "God giveth us his sonne and his Spirit in a promise of grace, when he giveth Faith to the soule," he wrote; it infuses with a perfect and irrevocable promise of salvation, and all other signs of justification, while encouraging to the individual, should not assure him of God's intention.

As abstract theology, Cotton's doctrine was not dangerous. But transferred through his teaching to the public mind there was danger indeed, and this was what worried Shepard. To stress to such an extent the personal quest for evidence of God's grace, to dismiss the ordinances of the church as comforting but ineffectual, to preach God's spirit rather than the moral law, absolute faith rather than conduct, was to unleash an individual approach to God undermining all formal religion.

This was what Cotton was doing in Boston, first among those who had followed him from old Boston to new—the Leveretts, Haughs, Hibbenses, Heatons, Hutchinsons, Coddingtons, Quincys—then spreading through the town. Anne Hutchinson, who had followed her beloved teacher to the New World, was a logical vehicle for translating the teacher's doctrine into language which the everyday townspeople could understand. . . .

[Mrs. Hutchinson held meetings to discuss Cotton's sermons; by 1636 she was interpreting him to mean that "The person of the Holy Ghost dwells" in the person chosen for salvation and that everyone else "remains dead to every spiritual action and hath no gift or graces." She and her disciples further twisted his teachings to mean that the presence of the spirit alone, not virtuous conduct or even faith, was the sign of election. They regarded all the ministers except Cotton and John Wheelwright as lacking the holy spirit and hence as being "legal teachers" whose doctrine and authority should be rejected. The Hutchinsonians accordingly stood poised to oppose traditional religious learning as well as all authority in church and state; they heckled Cotton's colleague in the Boston pulpit, John Wilson, and spoke darkly of resisting the "enymies to the truth." Winthrop and other colony leaders stopped the Hutchinsonian menace by sharp blows at its leaders—exiling some, removing some from office, disfranchising others, or in the case of Cotton, severing him from his unscrupulous admirers at a conference of ministers. The bulk of the Hutchinsonians, disfranchised, disarmed, or under threat of these penalties, had to recant or leave Boston in 1638.]*

Religious enthusiasm had given rise to the disturbances of 1637 and 1638; a statement of religious orthodoxy was to emerge from it as the ministers combined to declare truth and the magistrates sought to uphold it. Yet orthodoxy in Massachusetts was to be a curious thing. It involved no great statement of creed or belief. Truth in such matters was defined in negative terms by virtue of the condemnation of Anne's multitude of errors: Thou shalt not believe "that those . . . that are united to Ch[rist] have 2 Bodies, . . . [Christ's] and a new Body"; "That the first Thinge we receave for our Assurance is our Election," that revelations "are to be beleeved as well as Scripture because the same holy Ghost did indite both." But what one should believe as credo was left unstated.

Undoubtedly there was no other way to unite the ministers against the challenge of enthusiasm except through such a negative approach. Cotton, meek and loving, "yet one that held his owne stoutly . . . what himselfe judged to be the truth," had not been brought to see error in himself, only error in his followers. "The difference of judgment and Profession" between himself and the other ministers of the Bay was "still the same," he wrote to one of the exiles who accused him of acting Samson for the ministers' Delilah. "If you thinke I condescende to the opposite part, because I beare Witnesse against a more opposite Part (to wit against our [brethren]) . . . I wish you a better Spirit of Discerning." "It is one thing to Invert a Branch or [twig] of the [Covenant] of Grace (by letting the Light of [Works] before the Light of Christ:)" —an allusion to the stressing of good conduct by the majority of Massachusetts' ministers. It is a more reprehensible thing "to subvert the Covenant of Grace, by blotting out the [moral] Law written in our hearts and bring in (instead thereof) the . . . life of the Sonne of God . . . and so make all New Creatures" as the Hutchinsonians had done.

Thomas Shepard realized that "Mr. Cotton: repents not: but is hid only . . . he doth stiffly hold the revelation of our good estate still, without any sight of woord or woorke." John Eliot knew it too, and went to great pains to translate Cotton's doctrine into one more palatable to himself and suitable for his Roxbury congregation. When Cotton

* The paragraph enclosed in brackets is my précis of Darrett B. Rutman's account of the Hutchinsonian disturbance in *Winthrop's Boston, pp.* 117–124.—EDITOR.

taught that "the spirite of God . . . Declareth and wittnyseth to me the grace and favour of God in Christ Jesus," Eliot carefully explained that the spirit acted through the ministry, "for ministers are witnesses of Christ." The ministers being rational and learned men, reasonable disagreement between them could be tolerated, indeed had to be tolerated if such as Cotton were not to leave the commonwealth. But the congregations, in their enthusiastic outbursts at Salem, Dorchester, and, climactically, Boston, had proved irrational and unlearned. They had seized upon a direct and individual communion with God and rejected man's institutions, threatening the very foundations of society. Challenging magistrates and ministers alike, they had opened the door to a thrusting aside of all distinctions of birth, wealth, education. To the internal peril they had added an external danger, for they had made it more difficult to present a united front to renewed English criticism; at the very height of the Hutchinsonian struggle a group of English ministers had written to their New England brothers accusing them of having "embraced Certaine new opinions" since their removal overseas, separatist opinions "such as you disliked formerly." Similarly, the religious upheaval had endangered the settlements at a time of Indian peril, for while the dispute raged, war had broken out with the Pequots of Connecticut, and the Bostonians, called to serve in an expedition into Pequot country, at first refused to comply on the grounds that Pastor Wilson was to go as chaplain to the force.

The congregations, therefore, not the ministers, were to be curbed by an orthodoxy asserting that the minister's voice within the church was the voice of God. . . .

The Government of the Massachusetts Bay Colony, 1630–1650

GEORGE LEE HASKINS

George Lee Haskins, Professor of Law at the University of Pennsylvania, brought to the study of early New England an extraordinary combination of talents and training. Having studied history, government, and economics at Harvard and Oxford, he also earned a law degree at Harvard and went on to become an expert in English and American legal history. As a result, he was prepared to make what is currently the most authoritative analysis of the way in which government and laws were set up in Massachusetts Bay. While he accepted Perry Miller's interpretation of Puritan beliefs, Haskins did not find in them a sufficient explanation for the governmental decisions made in early Massachusetts. (In this respect he figures as a critic of the Harvard school.) Rather, he found a mixture of sources for these decisions—notably English practices of various sorts, Scripture, Puritan ideas, and rational innovation—as well as evidence of widespread opposition to the Puritan views of the leadership. Haskins' discoveries should explode forever simple-minded notions of a "Bible Commonwealth," even if his conclusions themselves do not remain the final word. His most original work in *Law and Authority in Early Massachusetts* (1960) was on the contents of statute law and its enforcement. The passages presented here, containing part of his preliminary description of the establishment of organs of government and the controversy over making law fixed and explicit, deal with more familiar topics, but have been chosen for their merit and to show how he put the role of Puritanism into perspective.

ALMOST THE FIRST TASK THAT FACED THE COLONY LEADERS UPON their arrival in Massachusetts was the adaptation of the machinery of a simple business organism[1] to the requirements of a body politic. As they viewed the task, it involved the institution of legal and political arrangements which would most effectually control and shape the social

Reprinted with permission of The Macmillan Company from *Law and Authority in Early Massachusetts; A Study in Tradition and Design* by George Lee Haskins. The passages reprinted are pp. 25–57, 60–65, without footnotes and with deletions where indicated.

[1] EDITOR'S NOTE: The "simple business organism" was the Massachusetts Bay Company, a joint-stock trading company created by royal charter in March, 1629.

and religious life of the colonists in accordance with the purposes for which the enterprise had been undertaken. That those purposes were primarily social and religious, rather than commercial, is clear not only from the creeds in which their hopes were sown but from the courses of action upon which they immediately embarked.

From the outset, for example, the new government adopted land and trading policies which were entirely different from those usual in trading companies of the day. By the time of Winthrop's arrival, the company had ceased to act as an organization seeking profit from its landholdings. It began at once to grant land to the various communities as they were established, and these in turn distributed allotments to individual colonists. Trade, likewise, was encouraged on a private and individual, rather than on a corporate, basis, so that by the close of 1630 the commercial element in the enterprise had virtually disappeared. Moreover, within a matter of months the admission of new freemen into the company came to be based on religious qualifications rather than on a capacity and willingness to pay for shares in the enterprise. These radical departures from normal trading-company practice demonstrate that the leaders viewed the enterprise as anything but commercial in character. Above all, however, the organization of the colony government, developed in association with the churches, provides objective proof that the chief aim of the undertaking, as declared by Winthrop, was to build "a Citty vpon a Hill" where it would be possible not only to worship and live as Christians but to set the world an example of godliness.

The most striking feature of the organization of Massachusetts government during the first two decades of its history was the "concentration of influence, power, offices, functions of every kind, in a small and compact group of leaders." . . . [T]he charter had placed the general management of the company in the hands of the General Court, consisting of the freemen, or stockholders, and of the officers and assistants. However, it appears that although the company consisted of something over a hundred freemen, practically none of them who was not also an assistant or an officer emigrated to the colony, and of these there were no more than ten or eleven in Massachusetts in 1630. From the standpoint of composition, therefore, the General Court and the Court of Assistants were virtually identical at this date, and hence from that

---

Like other trading companies, it was given a grant of land in which to operate, and it was expected to maintain its headquarters in England while sending over settlers under a local government. As the charter did not specify the location of the headquarters, the leaders decided they could transfer the offices of the company to Massachusetts and govern the settlement directly.

standpoint it made little practical difference by which body the affairs of the company were managed. However, since seven of the assistants constituted a quorum under the charter, and since a majority of those seven were empowered to act, it was obviously advantageous that the governing body should be the Court of Assistants rather than the General Court, in which the concurrence of the governor and at least six assistants was essential to action.

It may be inferred with some confidence that it was partly for this reason that the General Court, at its first meeting of only eight members in October, 1630, gave to the assistants the power to select the governor and deputy-governor from among themselves, to make laws and to select officers for carrying them out. A more compelling reason was the likelihood that a number of the colonists would, in due course, be admitted as freemen, and that, consequently, the assistants would be in a better position to control the life of the colony if the power of legislation were entirely in their hands. To this first meeting of the General Court the assistants, as the constituent members, invited a large number of the colonists. Although none of the latter was a freeman and entitled to participate in the proceedings, Winthrop and his colleagues undoubtedly perceived that their power would be strengthened if existing as well as future arrangements had the approval of those who were to be governed thereunder. Probably this consideration explains why so many of the inhabitants were invited to the meeting. In any event, the advisability of the transfer of the General Court's functions was put to the assemblage, which assented thereto by "ereccion of hands."

At the first meeting of the Court of Assistants, held two months before, that body had conferred upon six of its members the powers of English justices of the peace. Hence, the effect of the October meeting of the General Court was to concentrate in the hands of the "magistrates" (as all members of the Court of Assistants were hereafter referred to) all legislative, judicial, and executive powers of the government. It seems not to have concerned these few men that the assumption of the powers of the General Court was a clear violation of the charter. If pressed, they might have agreed with Milton that "Men of most renowned virtue have sometimes by transgressing most truly kept the law."

Among the powers which the charter had conferred on the General Court was the power:

from tyme to tyme to make, ordeine, and establishe all manner of wholesome and reasonable orders, lawes, statutes, and ordinances, direccions, and instruccions not contrarie to the lawes of this our realme of England, aswell for setling of the formes and ceremonies of government and magistracy fitt and necessary for the said plantacion and the inhabitantes there, and for nameing and stiling of all sortes of officers, both superior and inferior, which they shall finde needefull for that government and plantacion, and the distinguishing and setting forth of the severall duties, powers, and lymyttes of every such office and place, . . . and for imposicions of lawfull fynes, mulctes, imprisonment, or other lawfull correccion, according to the course of other corporacions in this our realme of England. . . .

Pursuant to these powers, now transferred to the Court of Assistants, the latter proceeded to grant lands, establish town boundaries, vote taxes, appoint officers, and issue orders designed to supervise and control the social, political, and religious life of the settlers. In September, 1630, they ordered that no one should settle within the limits of the patent without their consent. . . . The assistants also proceeded to regulate trade and industry by fixing prices and wages, as well as to deal judicially with such matters as manslaughter, theft, fraud, breach of contract, and the administration of estates. Orders reflecting typically Puritan concern about personal conduct were issued to punish idleness, to exact fines for drunkenness, and to proscribe tobacco, dice, and cards.

This concentration of all governmental power in the hands of a dozen or less men substantially endured until 1634. Prior thereto, several efforts on the part of some of the colonists to limit that power and to obtain a share in the government made little headway, largely because of the keen political insight of Governor Winthrop, who, like the other magistrates, had no wish to see the colony's objectives jeopardized by allowing its management to fall into the hands of those who might not be sympathetic with the leaders' views. However, at the October, 1630, meeting of the General Court above referred to, about a hundred colonists expressed a desire (whether by invitation or otherwise is not clear) to be admitted as freemen, presumably in order to obtain some voice in the conduct of colony affairs. . . . Whether a formal demand, political expediency, or even the Puritan conception of the social compact explains the step, Winthrop and his colleagues nevertheless decided to admit as freemen a substantial number of colonists in the spring of 1631. As a result, the membership of the General Court and the Court of Assistants ceased to be substantially identical.

At the same session in 1631, an order of far-reaching implications provided that thereafter no one should be admitted as a freeman unless a member of one of the colony churches. Since only a portion even of those who were devout Puritans could qualify for church membership, the order imposed a drastic limitation on the franchise and constituted another flagrant violation of the charter, which neither authorized nor contemplated any religious or political qualification for membership in the General Court. The significance of the order becomes clear when it is realized that between 1631 and 1641 only about thirteen hundred adult males are listed as having become freemen. Assuming that the total population by 1641 was about fifteen thousand, the proportion of those who had any voice in the colony government cannot, even by that date, have been much more than 7 or 8 per cent. The effect of the 1631 order was thus to put the colony government on a narrow religious basis and to ensure that the composition of the General Court, as now enlarged, should be limited to those "visible saints" who were members of the churches and shared the views of their leaders as to the dominantly religious purposes of the enterprise. Since the General Court began forthwith to elect the assistants and, after 1632, the governor and deputy-governor as well, and since in 1634 it also assumed from the latter their legislative functions, it is plain that the order was one of the foundation stones upon which the new commonwealth was built. Yet, narrow and oligarchical as the basis of the government may appear, it was hardly more so than the government of an English chartered borough in which, typically, only a small, although differently selected, portion of the inhabitants participated.

The movement on the part of the colonists to obtain a stronger voice in the government, and to restrict the power of the governor and assistants, continued to express itself in various ways and with varying degrees of success throughout most of the first twenty years of the colony's existence. In 1632 the levy of a tax by the Court of Assistants met with resistance when the minister of the church at Watertown assembled his flock and warned them that it was not safe to pay taxes to which they had not consented, lest they bring themselves and posterity into bondage. It may be observed that the charter had no more given to the Court of Assistants power to levy taxes and assessments on nonfreemen than it had given the General Court power to delegate legislation to the assistants. Yet the protestants were summoned before Winthrop for admonishment, and they confessed their error, and submitted. Winthrop counseled that the government of the colony was not like that of a corporation but was "in the nature of a parliament" in which the assistants, now the elected representatives of the freemen, had full power both to legislate and to levy taxes. Nevertheless, the government apparently felt obliged to concede that thereafter two from every town should be appointed "to advise with the governor and assistants about the raising of a public stock, so as what they should agree upon should bind all, etc."

The Watertown protest thus had an important result in that it led to the institution of representative government for the limited purpose of taxation. Two years later, however, the principle was extended, and brought about what amounted to a constitutional revolution. In the spring of 1634, the freemen appointed two deputies from each town to consider what matters might be brought before the May meeting of the General Court. An important result of their discussions was a request to see the charter, from which they learned that all laws were to be made in the General Court. Forthwith they repaired to Winthrop, who had no choice but to concede that this was so. However, he told them, the freemen were now so numerous that "it was not possible for them to make or execute laws, but they must choose others for that purpose." Accordingly, deputies from the towns appeared at the May meeting of the court, but they proceeded to pass resolutions which went far beyond the limited purposes envisaged by Winthrop in his conference and voted that only the General Court should have the power to admit freemen, the power to make laws, and the power to dispose of lands. At the same session the establishment of a general representative system was ordered: those in each town who had become freemen were empowered to choose two or three representatives to prepare business for the General Court and so act therein on behalf of all the freemen in the making of laws, the granting of lands, and in dealing with "all other affaires of the commonwealth wherein the freemen haue to doe," elections excepted. The General Court thereby became a wholly elective body, which thereafter consisted typically of some twenty or so deputies in addition to the governor and the deputy-governor and the assistants. The order applied to only three of the four yearly sessions of the General Court. At the fourth, or election, session every freeman was expected to be present and to "gyve his owne voyce."

As a result of this session, the General Court resumed the powers granted to it under the charter and displaced the Court of Assistants as the chief organ of the governmental system. Its activities were not limited to legislation, but included judicial and administrative functions as well; indeed, in conformity with ideas then current, little distinction was perceived between those functions. Much business came before it through petitions, many of which were of a public character and resulted in legislative or executive orders. Others were of a private nature—requests for licenses, for grants of land, for remission of fines—so that the action required was essentially judicial or administrative.

The task of dealing with these various matters was now shared in the General Court by the deputies and assistants, but the latter still retained extensive powers when meeting separately either as the Court of Assistants or as an executive board during the recess of the General Court. . . . Indeed, as Osgood says, the "continuous executive work of the colony was done as fully by the governor and assistants . . . as it was by the king and council in England."

The judicial powers of the governor and the assistants were in many ways more extensive than the legislative and other functions which they exercised. Not only did they have, individually, wide summary jurisdiction, but they sat in, or controlled appointments to, every court in the colony. Thus, most of the cases that arose during the early years of the colony's existence were decided by them, in one capacity or another. . . . Sitting together as the Court of Assistants, the magistrates exercised judicial powers which initially were as broad as those of the three great English common-law courts, as well as of Chancery, the High Commission, and the Court of Star Chamber. Subsequently, the jurisdiction of the Court of Assistants was narrowed as a result of the creation of new courts of first instance.

These new courts were established in 1636. In March of that year it was ordered that the assistants should hold four judicial sessions annually at Boston. This provision was made necessary partly by the pressure of judicial business consequent on the increase in population and partly by a recognition that the General Court, which by then included deputies of the towns, was ill suited in composition to determine judicial matters. These new judicial sessions of the assistants were known as Great Quarter Courts. The concurrent establishment of four Inferior Courts for Ipswich, Salem, Newtowne (Cambridge), and Boston, which were likewise to be held every quarter, also reflected the increase in the number of suits and at the same time presaged the division of the colony into counties. That division was accomplished in 1643, and shortly thereafter it became customary to refer to the Inferior Quarter Courts as the County Courts. The establishment of these lower courts had the effect of limiting the number of cases heard in the first instance by the Court of Assistants, whose original jurisdiction thereafter was limited to civil suits involving more than £10, to cases of divorce, and to all capital and criminal cases extending to life, member, or banishment. The Court of Assistants also heard appeals from the County Courts, and concurrent jurisdiction of the two courts was authorized in certain types of suits. In 1649 it was expressly ordered that the Court of Assistants should take cognizance of no case triable in the County Court except by appeal.

. . . Like the Court of Assistants, the County Courts normally employed jury trial for questions of fact. They also had extensive administrative jurisdiction, broadly summarized as follows:

> . . . They appointed . . . persons to lay out highways, . . . searchers of money, and viewers of fish. They confirmed the nomination of military officers, apportioned charges for the repair of bridges; they licensed innkeepers, and packers of sturgeon, and punished violation of licenses; they ordered the removal of obstructions on highways, punished idle persons, punished excess of apparel, compelled restitution of overcharge by merchants, determined

rates of wages in case of dispute, provided for the poor; . . . fixed ministers' allowances, saw that they were paid, inquired into the publication of heretical doctrines, . . . saw that Indians were civilized and received religious instruction, did all varieties of probate business, punished those who carried on unlicensed trade with the Indians.

Two other sets of courts supplemented the work of these courts of first jurisdiction—Commissioners' Courts and Strangers' Courts. In 1638 it was enacted that in towns where no magistrate lived, the General Court might appoint three freemen to hear and determine suits in which the debt or damage involved did not exceed twenty shillings. Later, the County Courts and the Court of Assistants were given this appointive power. Commissioners were empowered to send for parties and witnesses by summons or attachment and to administer oaths; but they had no power to commit to prison, and, when a party refused to give bond for satisfaction and had no property in the town, the case was remitted to a magistrate or to the County Court. The jurisdiction of the Commissioners' Courts was therefore less extensive, particularly in criminal matters, than that of the single magistrate. The several towns had no courts of their own other than the Commissioners' Courts, but the town selectmen usually had power to punish offenses against the town bylaws, and under specified circumstances they were required to determine "small causes" and to enforce certain of the colony laws.

Strangers' Courts were instituted by an act of 1639. Strangers who could not conveniently await the next session of the County Court were entitled to have summoned a special court consisting of the governor or deputy-governor, together with any two magistrates, who were empowered to try any civil or criminal cause triable in the County Court by jury or otherwise. . . .

For a supposedly simple frontier community, the colony's judicial system was both elaborate and comprehensive. The numerous courts made justice conveniently accessible to litigants. Procedures were simple compared with those of the English courts of common law, but they afforded the parties involved adequate notice, hearing, trial, and appeal. Although the magistrates controlled the judicial process, several were legally trained or had had experience as justices of the peace in the English quarter sessions. The judicial system, like the political system, was thus developed largely out of traditional ideas and practices.

Notwithstanding the union of the deputies and assistants in the General Court, the embers of earlier discontent flared up from time to time into open conflicts between those component parts. Essentially, the cause of these conflicts was the determination of the magistrates to retain in their hands a maximum amount of governmental power in order to promote and ensure the success of the colony mission as they conceived it. Three of those conflicts deserve special emphasis: the question of the magistrates' exercise of discretionary justice, the question of their final or "negative" vote in the General Court, and the question of the extent of their executive powers.

An early and persistent source of complaint against the magistrates was the wide discretion which they exercised in the courts in the imposition of punishments. The freemen were dissatisfied with the manner in which penalties for similar crimes varied from case to case, and they did not believe that the magistrates could be counted upon to do justice in particular situations unless penalties were openly fixed by law. Both the magistrates and the clergy were, as a group, opposed to having penalties so fixed. "I would knowe," asked Winthrop, "by what Rule we may take vpon vs to prescribe penaltyes, where God prescribes none." Nevertheless, objections to discretionary justice were voiced with increasing insistence, and they not only brought about the prescription of clearly defined punishments for certain types of crime, but, more importantly, they stimulated a movement to reduce the colony laws to writing.

As early as 1635 Winthrop noted that the deputies were fearful of the dangers which could result from the "want of positive laws" whereby the magistrates "in many cases, might proceed according to their discretions," and he went on to say that it was therefore agreed by the General Court that "some men should be appointed to frame a body of grounds of laws, in resemblance to a Magna Charta, which . . . should be received for fundamental laws." In the following year the court "intreated" Winthrop, Dudley, and others "to make a draught of lawes agreeable to the word of God, which may be the Fundamentalls of this commonwealth. . . . And . . . in the meane tyme the magistrates & their assosiates shall proceede in the courts to heare & determine all causes according to the lawes nowe established, & where there is noe law, then as neere the law of God as they can." These excerpts clearly attest the deputies' desire to limit the magistrates' judicial powers through a written constitution, but they also bring out the standards to which the magistrates were expected to adhere: on the one hand, the traditional and fundamental rights of Englishmen, as embodied in Magna Carta and the common law; on the other hand, the clear and unamendable word of God as embodied in the Bible.

The magistrates, however, were opposed to having the laws reduced to writing, partly because they believed that to do so would call to the attention of the crown colonial divergences from English law, but more particularly because a written code would put a bridle upon their own power and discretionary authority, which they regarded as necessary for the accomplishment of their tasks and as belonging to them by virtue of their office. Nevertheless, despite their opposition and continued resistance, the movement for written laws gradually made headway. By 1641 an extensive bill of rights, known as the Body of Liberties, had been prepared and published. Its provisions contained important constitutional rules and standards, many of which were intended to inhibit the exercise of arbitrary justice, but the deputies were not content. They wanted a complete codification of the colony laws, including, particularly, precise statements of punishments and penalties. This the Body of Liberties had not accomplished for any but the capital crimes, and hence it failed to meet a primary ground of complaint against the magistrates. Accordingly, the preparation of a complete code was soon consigned to a series of committees, and at the same time the whole problem of discretionary justice was again brought before the General Court as one of a number of broad issues relating to the powers of the magistrates in the colony.

During the summer of 1644, and in anticipation of the differences which were certain to arise between the magistrates and the deputies at the autumn meeting of the General Court, Winthrop prepared a "Discourse on Arbitrary Government." In it he argued for flexible penalties, partly on the basis of the discretion permitted English judges and juries in certain types of cases, but principally on the ground that the Bible prescribed few fixed penalties except for capital crimes. He also argued that, since the magistrates resorted to God's word as the guide for their decisions, the administration of justice could not be arbitrary. The issue of discretionary justice was submitted to the clergy, who substantially supported the magistrates' position but who nevertheless set forth with care and finality the circumstances under which latitude and discretion were properly to be exercised. At the end of the session, it was resolved that certain penalties ought to be prescribed, and that such as were prescribed might not be departed from without the consent of the General Court. In other situations, it must be presumed *a silentio* that the magistrates' discretion was to remain unimpaired. After this session of the Court, the work of codification again proceeded, and it was accompanied by extensive revision and elaboration of the existing laws, including those which prescribed penalties. By 1648 the long-awaited comprehensive code of laws had been completed and was approved by the General Court.

The second phase of the controversy between the deputies and the magistrates related to the latter's right to exercise, through the standing council which had been established in 1636, executive and consultative powers when the General Court was not sitting. In the spring of 1644, a bill was carried through the deputies empowering a committee consisting of seven magistrates and three deputies to order the affairs of the colony during the approaching recess of the Court. . . . The scheme was temporarily defeated by the refusal of the named magistrates to serve; but the question was again raised in the autumn meeting of the Court, the same session at which the question of discretionary justice was taken up. In this matter, too, the clergy were called upon for advice, and struck hard at the assertion of the deputies that the General Court was by itself the supreme power in the colony. Again, as in the resolution of the question of penalties, Winthrop's discourse on arbitrary government undoubtedly carried great weight. In any event, as Osgood says, "the position of the assistants as an executive board was never again questioned."

A third, though chronologically second, phase of the struggle between the magistrates and the deputies was the attack on the magistrates' asserted right to exercise a "negative vote" in assenting to or rejecting all matters—judicial as well as legislative—brought before the General Court. . . . [T]he question was resolved, for a few years, by an act of 1644 providing for the separation of the assistants and the deputies into two bodies and for the concurrence of both in the adoption or resolution of any measure. Although the issue at the time was that of ultimate judicial authority, the 1644 act had important consequences in other directions in that it resulted in establishing a bicameral legislature in Massachusetts.

These conflicts were all aspects of the same source of difference between the deputies and the magistrates, namely, the problem of the basis of political power and of the allocation of spheres of authority within the colony. Underlying the position of the deputies, and of the two or three assistants who from time to time sided with them, was the belief that the composition of the General Court as a representative body made it supreme in the colony, whereas Winthrop and a majority of the magistrates took the position that under the charter, and in accordance with contemporary political thinking, the magistrates had final authority in all matters. The issue was raised in final and dramatic form in 1645 in a case involving the propriety of Winthrop's having committed and bound over for trial two defendants who had slighted the authority of the colony government in the course of a dispute over confirming the lieutenant of the militia at Hingham. A majority of the deputies were of the opinion that the excessive power of the magistrates was jeopardizing the liberties of the freemen. The remainder of the deputies, along with the magistrates, saw in the issue the danger that, unless the authority of the magistrates was sustained, the government would fast degenerate into a popular democracy. The deadlock lasted for several months, and the issue became primarily political. Those who had been thwarted in the issue of the "negative vote" and in their wish to see an early enactment of written laws, appear to have resolved to make an example of Winthrop. The latter was determined that the issue of censure or acquittal be squarely faced, and a majority of the magistrates thereupon decided to refer the matter to the arbitration of the clergy—always their strong supporters. At that point, the opposing deputies, "finding themselves now at the wall," gave in and agreed that Winthrop should be publicly exculpated. When the sentence of acquittal had been pronounced in the General Court, Winthrop delivered himself of a "little speech" which is one of the clearest and most concise statements ever made of the magistrates' position as to the foundations of power in the colony government:

The great questions that have troubled the country, are about the authority of the magistrates and the liberty of the people. It is yourselves who have called us to this office, and being called by you, we have our authority from God. . . . I entreat you to consider, that when you choose magistrates, you take them from among yourselves. . . . Therefore when you see infirmities in us, you should reflect upon your own . . . when you have continual experience of the like infirmities in yourselves and others. We account him a good servant, who breaks not his covenant. The covenant between you and us is the oath you have taken of us . . . that we shall govern you and judge your causes by the rules of God's laws and our own, according to our best skill . . . when you call one to be a magistrate . . . you must run the hazard of his skill and ability. . . .

Concerning liberty, . . . There is a twofold liberty, natural . . . and civil or federal. The first is common to man with beasts and other creatures. By this, man . . . hath liberty to do what he lists; it is a liberty to evil as well as to good. This liberty is incompatible and inconsistent with authority. The exercise and maintaining of this liberty makes men grow more evil . . . The other kind of liberty I call civil or federal, it may also be termed moral. . . . This liberty is the proper end and object of authority, and cannot subsist without it; and it is a liberty to that only which is good, just, and honest. This liberty you are to stand for, with the hazard (not only of your goods, but) of your lives, if need be. Whatsoever crosseth this, is not authority, but a distemper therof. This liberty is maintained and exercised in a way of subjection to authority; it is of the same kind of liberty wherewith Christ hath made us free. . . . [S]o shall your liberties be preserved, in upholding the honor and power of authority amongst you.

Here Winthrop was going beyond the accepted seventeenth century doctrine that men must submit to their rulers because God orders them to submit. He was making the further point that by joining in a covenant men renounce their liberty to do anything but that which has been agreed to, and, further, that the duty to do that which is "good, just and honest" extends beyond the field of moral law and is the basis of political authority in the state. In other words, none might have the benefit of the law except those who subject themselves to it, and none have the protection of authority except those who obey it.

These conceptions of law and government were cornerstones upon which the political institutions of the colony had been built, and the freemen were continually reminded of them not only by the exhortations of the magistrates and the clergy but by the oath in which all freemen—including even the magistrates—undertook to support the commonwealth and to submit themselves "to the wholesome lawes & orders made & established by the same."

Thus, despite the broadening of the basis of government through the extension of the franchise, the management of the colony government remained, and in several respects became more strongly entrenched, in the governor, the deputy-governor, and the assistants. The right of the magistrates to exercise the broad powers which they had arrogated to themselves in 1630 and in the years immediately following had been effectively challenged and to some extent curtailed; but they had been successful in limiting the franchise to church members who subscribed to their own creeds and platforms. The magistrates had also succeeded in resolving the controversy over the "negative vote" in a way that made them supreme in legislative and, temporarily at least, judicial matters. When their executive and consultative powers had come under fire, they had again emerged triumphant.

For two decades, and more, the Massachusetts system worked, and it worked well. In the first place, the magistrates, to whom ultimate power was entrusted, were as a group united in their outlook and purpose and energetic in their leadership. Composed though that group was of men of strong personalities and differing temperaments, there was remarkably little dissension among them as to the policies to be pursued. Another reason the system worked well was that the freemen who shared political power with the magistrates were essentially in agreement with them as to the basic mission of the colony. Moreover, as will appear, many of the institutions of government established to carry out that mission were, to a subtantial extent, reproductions or adaptations of what the colonists had known in England. Hence the system also worked because little violence was done to their inherited sentiments and traditions.

The foundations of power in the government of Massachusetts Bay did not rest, and could not have rested, solely on its civil institutions and on the political arrangements which were established in the course of the first twenty years. Religious doctrine, political theory, church organization, social institutions, community sentiment and, above all, the substantive law were the principal strands which held together the web of government.

The preceding sketch of the Massachusetts civil government during the first two decades of its history reveals that, despite the development of a system of representative government, the dominating influence which shaped the course of colonial life was that of the magistrates. More importantly, it discloses how religious doctrine was translated into action through political and legal institutions. That translation had been a primary purpose of the migration, and credit for its successful accomplishment belongs to the colony leaders who inspired and directed its course. Inevitably, the Puritan conception of the enterprise determined their political thinking and hence the form and structure of the government. However, as already explained, Puritanism itself had emerged from and built upon traditional English political ideas, and those ideas had not been forgotten. Among them were the beliefs that government exists to regulate man's corruption, that civil rulers must be obeyed, and that the welfare of the whole is more important than that of the individual. Out of these older ideas there was evolved a new political theory in which the conception of covenant was used to strengthen the authority of the state. Under that conception, government was viewed as originating in a compact among the people, but the government which they had joined in creating was one to whose authority they must submit not only because of the terms of their compact but because it was a Christian government conforming to what God had decreed. Thus, in subjecting themselves to a state that was divinely approved, the people also subjected themselves to obedience to God. Although they might choose their rulers, the office to which the latter were elected was ordained by God. Once chosen, the magistrates were thus the essence of lawfully and divinely constituted authority to which the people must submit in order that the covenant be kept. Hence Winthrop could state that magistrates "are Gods vpon earthe."

Carried into practice in Massachusetts, these doctrines resulted in a government in which authority was jealously held by the magistrates, intent upon carrying out the holy purposes of God's word as expressed in the Bible. To that end, they determined that society must be regimented. Insistence upon religious orthodox and uniformity emerged from the realm of theological doctrine and was prescribed as a civil necessity. Concentration of power, and the freedom to use it, were axiomatic principles to the magistrates, who were convinced that the state should be "an active instrument of leadership, discipline, and, wherever necessary, of coercion." Hence the colony government undertook not merely to regulate misconduct but "to inspire and direct all conduct." Its leaders were not concerned that the major part of the colonists had no political rights, for not only were the latter outside the covenant and the engagements represented by the freeman's oath, but, as the Code of 1648 recites, those coming into the colony "doe tacitly submit to this Government and to all the wholesome lawes thereof." Moreover, every nonfreeman was required to take a special oath acknowledging himself lawfully subject to the authority of the colony government and submitting his person, family, and estate to the laws, orders, sentences, and decrees published or to be published for the welfare of "this body pollitique." The government of Massachusetts was thus a dictatorship of a small minority who were unhesitatingly prepared to coerce the unwilling to serve the purposes of society as they conceived it.

These ideas and practices can hardly be described as democratic in a modern sense, but Puritan doctrine, like that of the mediaeval Church from which it ultimately derived, was little concerned about the equality of men. Even Roger Williams, always a liberal in theological matters, believed that anarchy would result if all were politically equal. In the eyes of the Massachusetts leaders, not only was the right to share in the government restricted to those few "visible saints" who were the proven elect, but the supreme power in that government belonged only to the magistrates. The latter accordingly objected to the concessions wrung from them by the "people," for they viewed them as evidence of an unfortunate "democraticall spirit." . . .

. . . The magistrates conceded that political power must be shared, yet they were determined that it should not be divided equally but on a basis appropriate to the superior and inferior conditions, respectively, of the magistrates and the deputies. John Norton, writing in support of the magistrates, declared that it was "not an Arithmetical equality but a Geometricall that is to be attended to; that is, not the equality of number, but of vertue."

The magistrates' views as to the ends and purposes of government were not merely siphoned out of arid political and theological tracts. They were living ideals, translated into viable political and legal institutions in the light of what were conceived to be the colony's needs. From the outset, Winthrop, who was a political realist, recognized the importance of patience and flexibility in the process. Repeatedly, when confronted with crises which threatened to tear the colony asunder, he dealt with them by negotiation and persuasion, always recognizing that harsher measures would have been self-defeating in terms of preserving community solidarity. Largely because of his personal influence, the colony authorities, with few exceptions, displayed a distinct and politic reluctance to make martyrs of the dissident. They preferred to exact obedience and enforce standards of conduct by persuading the recalcitrant elements not only that the course of the magistrates was right and honest in itself but that, by entering into the covenant, everyone had voluntarily bound himself to accept their rule. Reform and regeneration were among the magistrates' chief objectives, but when neither appeared possible they did not hesitate to apply the most serious sanctions at their command.

Winthrop's instinctively pragmatic bent was encouraged by his personal success in dealing with various crises on an *ad hoc* basis, and his capability in this direction helps to explain why he consistently advocated that the magistrates be vested with wide discretionary powers. Although that position could be justified on the basis of expediency, it conformed, as has been pointed out, with Puritan beliefs about the social covenant, Christian calling, and divine providence. If God was pleased, through the agency of the social covenant, to call a man to rule over His people, He would afford him the judgment and insight needed to understand the divine purpose. Thus the magistrate, in Puritan thinking, could be assured of arriving by logical processes at the "matter of the scripture," which, in Winthrop's words, "be always a Rule to vs, yet not the phrase."

The principal illustrations of the regimentation of society in accordance with God's revealed purposes are to be found in the government's insistence on religious orthodoxy and in its regulation of personal conduct. With respect to the first, it should be pointed out that, from the beginning, a chief source of danger to the new colony was the Separatist tendencies inherent in Puritanism, particularly in its Congregational form, which prescribed that the churches were not subject to external supervision and that each was wholly independent of the others. The danger was twofold. On the one hand, there was the possibility that the principle of independence would result in splintering the colony into a number of separate holy communities, each convinced of the sanctity of its own form of doctrine, so that the unity of the colony would be shattered. On the other hand, there was the related danger that even if the unity of the churches were maintained, the same principle could lead to an open separation of the Massachusetts churches from the Church of England and thus bring down upon the colony government the wrath of Archbishop Laud and the English crown.

As explained earlier, it was the intention of the Massachusetts leaders to find a middle way whereby doctrinal and other reforms could be accomplished without open separation. To this end, it was imperative that their own brand of religious orthodoxy be strictly enforced and maintained. Ordinarily, argument and admonition on the part of the magistrates and the ministers sufficed to cause errant strays to see the folly of their ways. However, the celebrated cases of Roger Williams and Anne Hutchinson vividly illustrate not only the firmness with which the colonial government was prepared to meet departures from orthodoxy, when the situation required, but the rapidity with which the churches could be aroused by an attack on the civil power.

Williams was a stubborn man, but courageous. He was an avowed Separatist who believed, and taught, that the New England churches should separate completely from the English Church, defiled as it was with the corruption of "whores and drunkards." He preached that a truly reformed group, such as the Massachusetts Puritans professed to be, should express repentance for ever having had connection with the Church of England, and he specifically counseled the Salem church to withdraw from the other Massachusetts churches. As Williams' zeal increased, he went even further and denied that the magistrates had any authority in religious matters. Earlier, he had been rash enough to question the legality of the land titles in Massachusetts and to pronounce that the king's authority to grant land to the company rested on "a solemn public lie." Present-day admiration for the proponent of religious toleration, which Williams later became, must not be permitted to obscure the fact that he presented an obvious and dangerous threat to the non-Separatist principles on which the colony churches were founded and consequently to the whole foundation of the colony's existence. The authorities therefore felt compelled to bring him to heel. Immune to persuasion, spurning all opportunities to recant, he was finally banished from the colony by the General Court in 1635.

The Hutchinson affair was far more serious than that of Roger Williams because, although it began as a theological dispute, it developed into the political issue known as the Antinomian controversy, which came close to splitting the colony asunder. Anne Hutchinson began her short and brilliant career in Boston by teaching the doctrines of Antinomianism, which not only fostered egalitarianism but embraced the belief that man's conduct in this world is no proof of what he may expect in the next. In proclaiming the truth of these doctrines, and in announcing to her disciples that most of the Massachusetts clergy were not under a "covenant of grace" and hence unable properly to interpret or expound the Bible, she struck a deep blow at principles upon which both the Massachusetts churches and the civil government were based. After prolonged debates among the magistrates and the clergy, she was charged before the General Court with "traduceing the ministers." At the legislative hearing, she so handled her defense that, despite solicitous statements made on her behalf, she antagonized the entire Court, magistrates and deputies alike. In her supreme self-assurance, she flung out a challenge which, on top of the Williams affair, posed the gravest of threats to God's special commission to Massachusetts. "For this you goe about to doe to me," she proclaimed, "God will ruine you and your posterity, and this whole State." The sentence of banishment was pronounced upon her as "a woman not fit for our society." Shortly afterward, in 1638, she was brought to trial before the Boston church, by which she was also convicted and solemnly excommunicated. . . .

Criticisms of the Massachusetts leaders for their conduct of the Hutchinson trial tend to be unduly harsh because their actions have commonly been judged by modern rather than by contemporary standards. Seventeenth century English law provided few of the safeguards that are presently regarded as essential to the fair conduct of a criminal trial. . . . In criminal trials generally, but particularly in trials of persons accused of offenses threatening the safety of the state, the accused had "a very slender opportunity of making an effective defence." By contrast, Mrs. Hutchinson, whose heresies threatened everything that her judges and accusers held most dear, was in fact allowed considerable freedom in making her defense. If the heated disputation that permeates the Hutchinson trial is shocking to modern notions of proper judicial demeanor, it should be emphasized that in the early seventeenth century, no less than in the sixteenth, the ordinary English criminal trial was basically "an altercation between the accused, and the prosecutor and his witnesses." In state trials, such as that of Sir Walter Raleigh for treason, the "altercation" was typically between the prisoner, the court, and king's counsel. Not only was the prisoner at a disadvantage from the standpoint of procedure; he was often subjected to vilification and abuse by the court and the prosecutor. If Winthrop and the other magistrates were occasionally peremptory in their questioning, and if, thwarted by the astuteness of Mrs. Hutchinson's answers, they displayed their anger, her trial did not involve anything like the judicial badgering that often characterized the English state trial.

To accuse the colony government of religious intolerance because of its handling of the Williams and Hutchinson affairs is idle. The mind rebels at the lack of historic sense in accusations that in the Bay Colony free speech and free inquiry were suppressed and that the voices pleading for toleration and civil liberty were silenced. In the first place, the idea of toleration was hardly known, certainly not understood, in England or Europe at this time; indeed, it ran counter to those mediaeval principles of unity and uniformity which were accepted nearly everywhere. . . . In the second place, if the Massachusetts leaders were deaf to the "new voices being raised on behalf of justice and humanity," it may be remarked that separation and departures from orthodoxy were utterly subversive of the whole purpose for which the Winthrop group had come to New England. The extirpation of any dissent was essential to the survival of the enterprise. Indeed, the royal charter had expressly authorized the colony government to expel any who might endanger the undertaking, and banishment from the country was a regularly employed penalty in seventeenth century England. Winthrop, as a political scientist, unquestionably understood that, if any element in a community persists in opposing the basic premises of government and its purposes, the psychological attitudes on which its effectiveness as an agency of social control depends are broken down.

The magistrates, as well as the ministers, were convinced that to tolerate many religions in a state would destroy the peace of the churches and dissolve the continuity of the state. Hence they were forced to brand competing religions as heresies. Nearly everyone in the colony government was in agreement with Winthrop when he said that the cause against Anne Hutchinson was "not their cause but the cause of the whole country." Thomas Weld, the eminent divine, wrote that if the New England Way were *"our way* and not Christs," suppression would be "our great sinne." This view was to their minds merciful as well as necessary, for it was firmly believed that the faithful would be corrupted and destroyed by the toleration of other groups. "It is a mercilesse mercy," wrote John Cotton, "to pitty such as are incureably contagious, and mischeivous, and not to pitty many scores or hundred of the soules of such, as will be infected and destroyed by the toleration of the other." Weld was not alone in proclaiming that "to forebeare giving priviledges to such as submit not to the rules of participation, is no rigour, but such a thing as Christ himselfe would doe if in our places. . . . It is no more than all other societies in the world doe, who first require conformity before they permit to any the injoyment of their liberties."

The colony government's supervision of the moral welfare of the community was not confined to the prescription of religious orthodoxy, but extended to countless aspects of personal conduct and behavior. Wages and prices were fixed, gaming for money was proscribed, and heavy penalties were imposed for excesses in dress and for idleness, disobedience, tippling, drunkenness, profanity, and the telling of lies. Puritanism, it will be recalled, was a way of life, prescribing strictness of living as well as of worship, and God must be worshiped by outward as well as by inner conduct. Moreover, the world was viewed as the scene of open and actual warfare between God and the devil, and the magistrates therefore conceived that, as divinely appointed agents of God, it was their duty to shield the colonists from the temptations of greed and idleness, for "Where God hath a Temple, the Devil will have a chapel." If the divine commission was fully to be carried out, sin in all its forms must be sought out and strictly punished so that the community might remain pure and undefiled by human waywardness.

It is therefore idle to castigate the Massachusetts Puritans for the restrictions which they imposed on personal liberty. The regulation of prices and wages was not only imperative under conditions of scarcity in the colony but entirely consonant both with currently accepted theories with respect to the "just price" and with the Puritan belief that high wages promoted "vaine and idle wast of much precious tyme." Extensive regulation of economic life was also a well recognized feature of contemporary England, which demanded that activities affected with a public interest be supervised and that deceits and abuses in manufacturing be stamped out. Moreover, Puritan ideas as to the realization of God's bounty meant that the production of wealth could not be left to man's volition but must be controlled by government in accordance with social and religious standards. The same kind of paternalism, also reflective of English practices but strongly infected with religious ideals, is apparent in the regulation of personal conduct. Thus, if the community was to function as a unit and carry out the precepts of God's word, it was essential that human conduct in all its aspects be regulated in the interest of promoting the welfare of the whole community.

It would be a mistake, and a grave one, to suppose that the control exercised by the magistrates over the affairs of the colony and its inhabitants was either arbitrary or despotic. It is frequently overlooked that the charter had not only given the company broad powers to determine the form of the colony government but, as emphasized above, had authorized them to expel any persons who proved a source of annoyance. Although at the outset the magistrates assumed certain powers for which there was no warrant in the charter, most of those that they subsequently exercised or acquired were confirmed to them, or conferred upon them, by orders of the General Court in which the freemen of the colony participated. Designated freemen regularly sat with the magistrates in the County Courts and, through committees of their deputies, participated in assembling the colony laws in the Code of 1648.

Despite sporadic efforts to narrow the extent of certain of the magistrates' powers, there can be little doubt that the freemen of the colony reposed great confidence in the small group of magistrates whom, year after year, they returned to office. Political authority, writes John Dickinson, "rests on obedience, whether produced by reverence, habit, rational conviction, or the fear of compulsory sanctions. . . . [T]he use of force against recalcitrant individuals will not be effective unless acquiesced in, and if need be supported, by the preponderance of the impartial elements in the community not directly concerned with the controversy." In

Massachusetts the magistrates had to go before the voters once a year, and this requirement provided a potential check on their exercise of arbitrary power. Yet the check was seldom applied. . . .

The confidence displayed in these few men was, generally speaking, continuous despite the fact that the colony population, numbering scarcely more than a thousand at the outset, grew to something in the neighborhood of fifteen thousand within approximately ten years. That confidence resulted in part from the magistrates' conspicuous qualities of leadership and of sound judgment in handling colony affairs; but it also resulted from their political astuteness, for they took advantage of every opportunity to consolidate their power and to justify its exercise—often after the fact—by ingenious and frequently dialectical arguments. Their casuistry, however, was not attended by a cynical rejection of moral values but resulted from a conscientious effort to relate fundamental tenets of Puritan theology to political realities.

The magistrates enjoyed the advantages that accrue to a clique in power, and their individual temperaments and sense of invincible rectitude were such that they exercised that power without hesitation. All of those who served as governor during the early years were born commanders or trained to a kind of leadership that the colonists were willing to accept. . . .

Government normally enlists obedience by deriving its purposes and the standards it applies from forces and tendencies at work within the community. Much of the strength of the magistrates' position was therefore a consequence of the fact that the Puritan elements were in general agreement as to the colony's mission, which it was realized must be carried out through forceful and centralized leadership. To men of that time a primary concern of government was thought to be the effective maintenance of order in the community, and general acceptance of the basic postulates of contemporary English political thought, which viewed government as a power existing independently of the people, clearly reinforced the magistrates' power. Moreover, it was an age in which the mediaeval belief was still current that men are appointed by God to different stations in life and have a duty to cleave to those stations and carry out the responsibilities attaching thereto. Hence in orthodox Puritan thinking the "rights of the people" were far less important than were the advancement of God's glory and the achievement of true liberty through fulfilling the ordinances of Christ. . . .

The rigor of the rule of the magistrates was tempered, however, by certain doctrines which were deeply rooted in English political tradition and which helped to prevent the government from becoming a tyranny. Chief among them was one which had been given special impetus in the seventeenth century and which the colonists were hardly likely to forget. This was the ancient principle that the government of kings and civil rulers is limited by the concept of a "fundamental law," made up of immemorial usages which, through lapse of time, had acquired a character of permanence and inviolability. This view of law gave it a transcendental force from which emanated a protective power existing independently of any human agency and immune from interference either by men or their civil rulers. With this concept of fundamental law many of the Massachusetts colonists were entirely familiar, and among the principal safeguards which it was thought to provide were long-accepted judicial procedures that protected the people from arbitrary governmental acts. Indeed, the freemen's concern about such safeguards was a primary reason for their wish to have prepared a declaration of rights "in resemblance to a Magna Charta," which resulted in the constitutional guarantees of the Body of Liberties.

Although the freemen accepted the Puritan premise as to the force of the law of God, to them the "Fundamentalls" of the commonwealth also included the traditional rights and liberties of Englishmen. Indeed, the charter had expressly assured that all the colonists "and every of their children which shall happen to be borne there . . . shall have and enioy all liberties and immunities of free and naturall subiects . . . as yf they and everie of them were borne within the realme of England." . . .

Probably the most important single force contributing to the solidification of the power of the magistrates in the government and in the life of the colony was the influence of the clergy. From its inception, the Massachusetts enterprise was characterized by the active cooperation of lay and ecclesiastical elements; indeed, without the close union that developed, the oligarchy that constituted the Massachusetts civil government might well have failed. The teachings of Calvin had emphasized the mediaeval belief in the organic relation between church and state, and, as interpreted by the Massachusetts Puritans, it was the duty of both to create and foster a perfect Christian society. The ministers continually gave direct support to the policies of the magistrates, and, through their sermons and otherwise, they regularly exhorted their congregations to keep the magistrates in office and likewise to support those policies. The handling of the controversies with Roger Williams and Anne Hutchinson provides two notable instances of the cooperation of church and state. In these as in other controversies the influence of individual ministers, such as Hooker, Cotton, and Shepard, was very great, and they could be counted on to form public opinion by explaining and justifying to their congregations important issues of policy. As Winthrop said, the "Ministers have great power with the people, wherby throughe the good correspondency between the magistrates and them, they are the more easyly gouerned." The efficient functioning of the system was virtually guaranteed by the requirement that the electorate be members of the churches.

Thus the churches were important agencies of social control not only because they fostered solidarity within the community but because they had extensive powers over individual conduct and behavior. As a group, moreover, the ministers performed an especially valuable function in the resolution of difficult public questions, especially those which related to the allocation of power between the magistrates and the deputies. When such questions were submitted to the clergy for advice, their responses were nearly always favorable to the magistrates' position. In fact, the clergy acted as a kind of board of referees or supreme court on constitutional issues. In their turn, the magistrates as "nursing fathers" of the churches were expected to, and did, support the ministers in the rigorous enforcement of punishments for moral and religious offenses.

In principle, the partnership between the magistrates and the clergy was an equal one. The civil government and the churches were planted and grew up together "like two twinnes." Both had the same general objective—the establishment and maintenance of a divinely ordered commonwealth—and through both it was achieved. In 1640 Thomas Lechford wrote that "The Magistrates, and Church-leaders, labour for a just and equall correspondence in jurisdictions, not to intrench one on the other." Thus, although the magistrates were under a duty to reform corrupt worship, they had in theory no authority to interfere with the election of church officers, to perform any ecclesiastical function, or to establish any but a "pure" form of worship. In practice, however, although they continually supplemented one another's efforts, the civil arm was the superior of the two. For example, the magistrates were able to uphold Winthrop's belief in their immunity from church censure contrary as this position was to Puritan thinking of the time. After 1636 permission to establish new churches had to be obtained from the magistrates, and the prospective members were examined by them for proof of the work of God's grace. Similarly, approval of the selection of church officers by the magistrates was customary, and ministers whose remarks displeased the magistrates were subject to censure and rebuke. Even the ministers took the position that any limitation of the magistrates' jurisdiction to nonreligious questions was sinful as well as dangerous. . . .

. . . In Massachusetts, church and state were separate, however much the two strove for the same goals, and the final voice was not in the clergy. No church could depose a man from public office, and excommunication, though a powerful sanction, did not result in civil disabilities.

It should also be noted that in Massachusetts the civil authorities assumed jurisdiction over many matters which in contemporary England were within the province of ecclesiastical authority, for example, the recording of births, marriages, and deaths, the performance of the marriage ceremony, and the granting of divorces. . . .

Within the first two decades of its history, the Bay Colony had assumed the form which it was substantially to retain for the greater part of the seventeenth century. The structure of its civil government, its ecclesiastical organization, as well as the relationship between the two, had been formed and settled in a way that seemed to assure for posterity the fulfillment of the mission for which the enterprise had been undertaken. Orthodoxy in civil and ecclesiastical affairs was the central characteristic of this community in which religion was a living, emotional force. Every phase of political and social life was made to contribute to the maintenance of the Puritan system of belief. The electorate had been narrowed to church members who could be expected to support their leaders' policies. Heresies and even differences of opinion were quickly and sharply repressed. Outsiders were discouraged or denied permission to settle. Relations with other colonies were determined by the colonists' growing sense of self-righteousness and their fear of contamination by nonbelievers. Winthrop, for example, did not scruple to calumniate Virginia as a place where drunkenness customarily prevailed. "These people," wrote the Dutch De Vries of the Bay colonists, "Give out that they are Israelites, and that we at our colony are Egyptians." At the same time, the Massachusetts government did not hesitate to bring under its jurisdiction new territory to the north and also to attempt to dominate the neighboring Puritan colonies.

Outwardly the Massachusetts colonists professed that they remained loyal to the Established Church and to the royal government in England. At the outset the leaders were sensitive both to accusations of Separatism and to any expression of hostility on the part of the English government. It was partly for this reason that they were reluctant either to publish a code of their laws or to frame a written statement of church discipline. Any aspersion on the royal grant, wrote Winthrop, might "have provoked our Kinge against vs, and putt a sworde into his hande to destroy vs." Yet slowly and unobtrusively, and aided by geographical isolation, they set about establishing the New England Way. . . .

The onset of the English Civil War in 1642 removed much of the necessity for continued lip service to the English Church and state, and the colony thereafter began to express its independence more openly. Even the intimacy of accord and understanding which had characterized the relationship between the Massachusetts and the English Puritans disappeared, and the Puritan leaders in England became "almost as hostile to the ruling oligarchy in Massachusetts as were King Charles and Archbishop Laud." Ancient bonds were dissolved, and the force of English ways lessened as orthodoxy became more deeply entrenched and isolationism more pronounced. Dogmatic, self-confident, and completely convinced of the rightness of their mission, fiercely intolerant of opposition from within and without, the colony leaders were prepared to, and did, take every step necessary through the instruments of government and otherwise to guarantee the success of their enterprise. This was the Massachusetts commonwealth established under a "due forme of Goverment both ciuill and ecclesiasticall."

Puritanism and New England Merchants

BERNARD BAILYN

Though it would be convenient to think of Puritanism as a fixed body of beliefs and attitudes, it kept changing and producing subvarieties. Miller found in the covenant theology a system of ideas that remained largely unaltered during the first century of Massachusetts and Connecticut, but he made no claim that the ideas had a static relationship with Puritan culture as a whole. Like many other historians, he insisted that Puritanism underwent constant change from its beginnings in the Elizabethan age to its extinction as an identifiable movement in the eighteenth century. Even by the time that Boston was established, the original religious fervor had come to terms with daily life—some would say it had cooled—and Puritans were deliberating on how to arrange institutions to perpetuate their religion and guard it against corruption (i.e., further change), how to use governmental power for religious ends, how to prescribe in detail the applications of religious standards to economic and individual behavior in all respects.

Reducing piety to a code of conduct unavoidably provoked controversy and brought religion into new clashes with the world. Bernard Bailyn, Professor of History at Harvard University, analyzed the fate of Puritan ideals in the mercantile world which the New Englanders faced. As Haskins found English law and tradition guiding Massachusetts legislators just as much as did theology, so Bailyn found mundane circumstances guiding Massachusetts merchants just as much as Puritan ethics. Haskins described a predominantly successful amalgamation of the several sources of Massachusetts law and government, but Bailyn discovered an irreconcilable opposition between the morality and the conditions of success in the colony's trade.

In the selection which follows, Bailyn explains the Puritan code of economic ethics, some considerations that led merchants to disregard it, and the conflict that resulted. Though the merchants accepted Puritan precepts, and the magistrates and ministers accepted the need for commerce for the good of the community, the merchants in spite of themselves could not follow their own standards or abide by the regulations designed to enforce them. The code forced the merchants to ignore it from the outset, for it gave them no guidance when they confronted their basic problems: discovering commodities that could profitably be exchanged, and finding reliable men to trade with in distant markets. Inexorably, Puritan merchants became participants like any others in the English Atlantic trading world, not servants of a Puritan community. They solved their problems so well that they outgrew the rank originally assigned to them by Puritan ethics and demanded that the community readjust its regulations to their needs and desires.

Bailyn's discussion of the fate of Puritan ideals in New England commercial life, striking though it is, has greater significance when read as part of his brilliant study, *The New England Merchants in the Seventeenth Century.* Put briefly, Puritanism in this context figures as an intrusion, doomed to fail, in a process of colonial development which was not controlled by religion. In effect, this process, rather than Puritanism, connects seventeenth-century New England to the whole of American history. In this respect Bailyn differs markedly from Miller.

INTO THE COMMERCIAL SITUATION OF NEW ENGLAND IN 1630 THE great Puritan Migration brought the first of the permanent merchants. Though clearly distinguishable from the interlopers, servants of English merchants, and Pilgrims who had preceded them in trade, they were not men of uniform background or training. Some whose origins lay in the lower levels of London's commercial populace were experienced tradesmen who put their skills to good use in the New World. Others, gentlemen and yeomen of rural England, found in the New World inducements to enter business for the first time.

Despite such differences all of the first generation Puritan merchants agreed that religious considerations were highly relevant to the conduct of trade, that commerce, being one of the many forms of human intercourse, required control by moral laws. But some of the newly arrived merchants, as they assumed power over the exchange of goods, felt the restrictive effect of these ideas when acted upon by a determined ministry and magistracy. In their confused reaction to ethical control as well as in the progress of their business enterprises lay seeds of social change. . . .

The ethical keystone of the great edifice of Calvinism was the conviction that all men were totally responsible for their behavior. The heart of the question, as a sixteenth-century writer put it, is not the quantity of sin but the fact that God's majesty is offended at all; ". . . be the thing never so little, yet the breach of his Commandment deserveth death."

To men for whom life was moral experience, no actions were more relevant to the overwhelming consideration of salvation than those touching the welfare of one's fellow men. For, however discouraging to those who found a righteous life a simpler matter when lived in solitude, the Puritan's obligation to live intensively as a social being was nothing less than God's will. Society was an organism functioning for the good of all its members. Each component sought its own welfare, yet contributed and was subordinated to the whole. In a world of sinful men seeking salvation, a compact society had the advantage of a readier discipline exerted by those in authority. This fact was of first importance, for men in positions of political power were, in their official capacities, limited agents of God. Those you have called to public office, Winthrop told a bumptious General Court, "have our authority from God, in way of an ordinance, such as hath the image of God eminently stamped upon it, the contempt and violation whereof hath been vindicated with examples of divine vengeance." Leaders, once selected, were to whip the moral sluggards into line, for their own good, for the welfare of society, and for the glory of God.

The variety of men's occupations made it possible for each individual to find the work in which he could best acquit himself of his obligations. But it also meant that some men were more exposed to temptation than others. Those whose work bore broadly on the welfare of others were called upon to exert a scrupulousness in their transactions commensurate with the temptation to sin. Of all private occupations trade was morally the most dangerous.

The soul of the merchant was constantly exposed to sin by virtue of his control of goods necessary to other people. Since proof of the diligence he applied in his calling was in the profits he made from precisely such exchanges, could a line be drawn between industry and avarice? The Puritans answered, as had Catholics for half a millennium, that it could, and they designated this line the "just price."

They assumed that there existed an ideal standard of valuation applicable to every situation. An unjust figure was the result not so much of the mechanical operation of an impersonal market as of some individual's gluttony. A just charge was one willingly paid by a person experienced in such matters and in need of the article but under no undue compulsion to buy. The Reverend John Cotton laid out the principles clearly: "A man may not sell above the current price, i.e., such a price as is usual in the time and place, and as another (who knows the worth of the commodity) would give for it, if he had occasion to use it. . . ." A merchant's personal losses or misfortunes ought never to be reflected in an increased valuation, "but where there is a scarcity of the commodity," Cotton wrote, "there men may raise their price; for now it is a hand of God upon the commodity, and not the person." As for the particular determination of the price, in case private men cannot agree on a common estimate, "the governor, with one or more of the councell" or perhaps "certaine select men" will be able to make the matter clear. Convinced that justice could be reached, the Puritans sought only the detailed figures in concrete situations.

Equally treacherous to the soul of the businessman and the good of the public was the fact that the merchants came into control of the available supply of money and charged interest on debts. One who controlled supplies of cash or credit held a knife over a vital vein in the social body. Such a power had for centuries required the closest regulation, which it had duly received along with its rationalization in the literature on usury. But in the sixteenth century the medieval excoriation of all interest-bearing loans had given way to a qualified acceptance of interest within the limits of justice and official determination. The New England Puritans took over the continental Calvinist phrasing of this acceptance. The principle was clear. "What rule must wee observe in lending?" asked Winthrop rhetorically.

ANS: Thou must observe whether thy brother hath present or probable, or possible meanes of repayeing thee, if ther be none of these, thou must give him according to his necessity, rather than lend him as hee requires; if he hath present meanes of repayeing thee, thou art to looke at him, not as an Act of mercy, but by way of Commerce, wherein thou arte to walke by the rule of Justice. . . . If any of thy brethren be poore etc. thou shalt lend him sufficient that men might not shift off this duty by the apparent hazzard. . . . From him that would borrow of thee turne not away.

QUEST: What rule must wee observe in forgiveing?

ANS: Whether thou didst lend by way of Commerce or in mercy, if he have noething to pay thee [thou] must forgive him (except in cause where thou hast a surety or a lawfull pleadge) Deut. 15.2.

John Cotton, flourishing "*Exo.* 22. 25. *Lev.* 25. 35, 36," asserted quite simply: "Noe increase to be taken of a poore brother or neighbour for anything lent unto him."

Though church and state in New England most readily impinged on the professional life of the merchant in regard to just price and usury, the assumption of justified control of economic life had a far wider applicability. If prices came under the aegis of authority so also did wages. Encouragement, even direct subsidization of economic activity, no less than restriction, flowed from the same obligation to manipulate material life for spiritual ends.

Such precepts had a special appeal to a predominantly agricultural people whose emigration was at least in part due to economic distress. Many settlers had lost their stability in a rapidly changing world where "trades are carried soe deceiptfully and unrightusly as that is almost inpossible for a good upright man to maynteyne his charge and to live comfortably in his profession." The Reverend John White, who had inspired the founding of two commercial companies, voiced a typical thought in writing to Winthrop,

I heare shopkeeping begins to growe into request amongst you. In former age all kinde of retailing wares (which I confess is necessary for mens more convenient supply) was but an appendixe to some handicraft and to that I should reduce it if I were to advise in the government. Superfluity of Shopkeepers Inholders etc. are great burthens to any place. We in this Towne where I live . . . are of my knowledg at Charge 1000*li* per annum in maintaining several familys in that Condition, which we might well spare for better employments wherein their labours might produce something for the common good which is not furthered by such as drawe only one from another and consequently live by the sweat of other mens brows, producing nothing themselves by their owne endevours.

At a time when mercantilism in Europe made the needs of trade a reason of state, some of these ideas of the New England leaders were archaic. Yet they were able to survive and even to flourish because the governing Fathers, being, in John Hull's phrase, "no babes nor windy-headed men," understood the necessity to found their society on a solid economic base. They merely insisted that the life of business be placed within a structure whose proportions had been drawn by the hand of God.

These ideas were put into use in the very first years of the Puritan settlements and helped shape the development of institutions and traditions from the start. Nowhere else did Calvinist doctrines of social ethics find such full application. In Geneva, Scotland, and the Netherlands theory had always to be qualified to some extent by pre-Calvinist practices. In New England, doctrine literally preceded practice. . . .

Whatever its danger to the purity of men's souls or to the independence of the Puritan Commonwealths, overseas trade alone could furnish the settlers with the materials needed for maintaining reasonably comfortable lives. Yet the governments . . . could do little to further the development of commerce. This was left to the individual enterprise of the transplanted London tradesmen who had imported and distributed goods from England during the first decade. Though these men participated in the expansion of the fur trade and in the attempts to start manufactures, their main efforts after 1640 went toward creating a type of commerce capable of continuing the flow of goods from England. They assumed that since, once the furs were gone, the natural goods of New England largely duplicated the produce of England, exchanges were to be made in places outside of England and profits translated into credits in England. Finding the markets and actually launching the trade was a difficult matter, however, attended by disappointments and losses. But within twenty years this form of commerce had been established and had become the dynamic economic force in New England. Such it remained for a century and a half.

The men who came to control New England's foreign trade became large figures in the affairs of the port towns; their influence extended into frontier villages and over wide stretches of uncleared land in the interior. Trade, in making material and real the value of men's labors in fields and on the sea, created dependences and networks of relationships which, though long-lasting and important to the whole community, had no preordained place in the Puritan scheme of things. They would have to be shaped to occupy a modest and respectable position. But the merchants who represented this new economic force had become, by virtue of the very services they performed for the public, parts of the separate, intractable world of Atlantic commerce. The Puritan magistrates found themselves dealing with men whose vitally necessary enterprises seemed at times to threaten the integrity of the established order but which could not be controlled without being made less useful. As time went on the problem of whether and how such control was to be exercised became overshadowed in importance by the increasing difficulty of containing the merchants at all within the structure of Puritan society.

The vision of New England as the center of a great fishing industry had been an attraction to Englishmen at least from the time of John Smith's American sojourn.[1] Occasional forays into New England waters had verified Smith's claims that this southern region had two fishing seasons instead of one as in Newfoundland and that the fishing grounds were not only fertile but also, being close inland, easily workable. Despite the failure of the Dorchester Company and the withdrawal of the New England Company's settlers from Cape Ann to Salem, the idea of a profitable New England fishery operated by English entrepreneurs persisted and was caught up by the undertakers of the Massachusetts Bay Company. . . .

A large part of the fish consumed by New Englanders before 1640, however, was obtained not from the local fishermen but from the west-country and foreign fishing vessels that occasionally came into New England waters. . . .

[1] EDITOR'S NOTE: John Smith (1580–1631) in 1614 proposed a plan for supporting a colony in New England on the profits of fishing. He is better known for his role in early Virginia.

This situation was entirely changed during the early years of the fifth decade. The normal commerce of England was interrupted by the upheavals of the Civil War. Sailors, fishermen, and ships were impressed for naval service. Ports were besieged and Bristol changed hands twice between 1642 and 1644. Though the royal forces held Devon and Cornwall, most of the west-country ports stood by Parliament and a number of them were the objects of damaging attention from the royalists. Even in ports untouched by war, business diminished rapidly as the effect of disrupted communications in the hinterlands was felt. The fighting extended to the sea, and vessels from the opposing sides pursued each other into distant ports where they attempted to seize or sequester the enemy. Under such conditions the English fishery in North America declined as the annual fleets to Newfoundland thinned out, and the relatively few vessels accustomed to visiting New England seemed to be disappearing altogether.

If the shock of civil war broke the thin ties of the west country to the New England fishery, its indirect effect on New England was, in part, to rouse the settlers to a greater effort in fishing. In response to the settlers' need for food and the merchants' desire for exchangeable commodities, experienced fishermen and farmers along the coast seeking winter employment went out in increasing numbers to test the wealth of the sea. Starting with the barest equipment, they began to work the local grounds diligently. Nantasket, Marblehead, the Isles of Shoals, Hog Island, and Monhegan Island soon became exclusively fishing communities populated by permanently settled New Englanders. As such, they were far from being model Puritan societies. Not a single inhabitant of Marblehead in 1644 could claim the freedom of the Commonwealth and by 1647 a court order ruled "that noe wimin shall live upon the Ille of Showles." But the industry flourished. Winthrop reported that in 1641 no less than 300,000 cod were caught and six years later £4,000 worth of fish was brought into Marblehead alone.

Ultimately, the success of the fishery depended as much on the ability of the merchants to organize and dispose of the yearly hauls as it did on the size of the catch, and during these same years the merchants entered the business in a large way. Besides buying the cargoes from the fisherman and equipping and supplying their voyages, they sent exploratory expeditions to such distant places as Sable Island off Nova Scotia and, in 1645, to Newfoundland. But as yet they were only serving a local market. They lacked the capital and business contacts to link the New England fishery to foreign markets.

Their needs dovetailed with the desires of certain London merchants who, in this decade of change and confusion, were furthering their ambition to share in the control of the North American fishery. There was no question of their competing with the west countrymen in the Newfoundland fishing industry itself, for the westerners had the advantage of a century's experience, a sufficient labor force, and complete equipment. What the Londoners sought was a share in the valuable carrying trade between the American fishing centers and the markets of Europe and the Wine Islands (Madeira, the Azores, and the Canaries)—a trade hitherto monopolized by west-country, Dutch, Flemish, and French shipmasters. Though they were able to write into the Navigation Act of 1651 clauses that extended to the fisheries the ban against foreign vessels trading in colonial products, they could not easily dislodge the established carriers from the profitable Newfoundland routes. The infant fishery of New England fitted into their plans smoothly. It offered the Londoners a rich and uncontested supply of American fish without involving them in the difficulties and risks of the fishing industry itself. Not only were there native fisherman at work in New England but the local merchants were becoming experienced in organizing the annual hauls and preparing them for wholesale disposal abroad. And the Londoners had precisely what the New England merchants lacked: capital, shipping, and established markets.

Men separated by three thousand miles of ocean, however, do not enter into business combinations automatically no matter how well their needs complement each other. Overseas commerce in the seventeenth century was capricious. Arrangements were interminably delayed by the accidents of sailing. Demand fluctuated incalculably as unforeseen crop failures created markets which the arrival of a few ships eliminated overnight. Reliable factors and correspondents were therefore of paramount importance, for frequently the success of large enterprises rested on their judgment. The London merchants might have understood the possibilities of the New England fisheries but they would not have ventured there without knowledge of the region's businessmen and its economic condition. There were in London, however, other merchants of established reputation who were already in touch with the New England businessmen. These men—City relatives and friends of the immigrant tradesmen—brought the two groups together. With their help certain New England importers were able to negotiate with groups of London merchants seeking shiploads of fish prepared for sale in southern markets. The result was a series of contracts between the two groups of men that accounts for one of the important early forms of the New England fish trade.

These agreements between the London and New England merchants varied greatly but had certain characteristics in common. The over-all enterprise was planned and launched in London; the Londoners kept the ownership of the goods throughout the voyage; the New Englanders acted as suppliers to the home country entrepreneurs. An example is the bond, dated February 20, 1646, by which Robert Houghton "of St. Olaves in Southwark merchant" pledged to George Gifford and Benjamin Whetcomb, London merchants, that Robert Sedgwick of Charlestown, Massachusetts, would load on their ship *Mary* 1,500 quintals of fish within twenty days of its arrival in Massachusetts. The merchants' plan was to make up an outwardbound cargo of manufactures to be sold in New England, pick up the fish as arranged in London, and dispose of them in Spain or the Wine Islands. The profits of the voyage would be returned to England either in bills of exchange[2] or in semi-tropical products to be sold in England.

The significance of this contract lies not only in its business arrangements but also in the importance of the individuals involved and in the relationships among them. Gifford and Whetcomb, together or in other *ad hoc* partnerships, became steady buyers of New England fish. Houghton, though himself a "brewer," was both son and brother of London fishmongers who may well have made the first contacts with the London buyers. Not only was Houghton a sympathetic friend of the New England settlers and probably a member of a Puritan church, but he was also Sedgwick's brother-in-law. He was thus in an excellent position to negotiate between the London fishmongers and the New England wholesalers and did so throughout the period. Sedgwick, whose organizing ability was to gain him an important role on the stage of European affairs, had previously been an importer of manufactures. Now, often in partnership with Valentine Hill, another Puritan tradesman new to the fishing business, he became one of the leading New England fish dealers.

Another, more complete, example of such an arrangement may be seen in this statement, signed in August 1650 at the Isles of Shoals:

Shipped by the grace of God in good order and well conditioned by mee Wm Davis of Boston in and uppon the good shipp called the George Bonaventure . . . now rideing at anchor at Marblehead and by Gods grace bound for Bilboa, to say, three hundd seventy six Kint of dry and merchantable New Engl. cod fish, and nine kint of refuse fish and is by the order and for the Acco of Mr Samuel Wilson of London mercht, being marked and numbred as in the Margent. and are to be d[elivere]d in the like good order and well conditioned at the aforesaid port of Bilboa (the danger of the seas only excepted) unto Mr Joseph Throckmorton or to his Assignes, he or they paying freight for the sd goods with primage and average accustomed.

[2] EDITOR'S NOTE: A bill of exchange was an order sent by one man, directing a second man to pay a specified sum of money to a third man. (The third man named in the bill might endorse it to a fourth.) The soundness of a bill depended on the second man (a) being able to pay, and (b) owing the money to the first or agreeing to extend him credit to the amount of the bill.

The *George Bonaventure* had arrived in July loaded with cloth which was sold for the accounts of the owners, John Leverett, Edward Shrimpton, and Thomas Bell and Company of London.

Documents such as these attest to the important role played by the London merchants in developing the New England fishery. The extent of the Londoners' involvement in this commerce cannot be estimated as no statistics remain, but the fact is indisputable that this type of trade served to introduce the New Englanders to the southern markets and supplied them with contacts and shipping during the first, critical years in the growth of New England's commerce.

This triangular trade of the Londoners, the most important form of business organization in the early New England fishery, was not inflexible. Variations were present from the start. Occasionally, the contracting partnership would include merchants in the Wine Islands or in Spain as well as in England. Frequently the master of the London ship would be a partner in the company and he would contract for the fish when his vessel arrived in New England. The arrangements could become quite complicated when each of the members of a large partnership was involved at the same time in other fishing contracts with the same suppliers and when most of the shipments went on the same vessel. In such cases bills of exchange circulated quickly among the Boston merchants as the agents and principals settled accounts. These bills were the credits the New Englanders sought; with them they could pay for the goods sent from England or invest in property.

Different as such combinations were, they had in common the confinement of the New Englanders to a relatively small part of the total flow of trade, and the profits that accrued to them as middlemen were less than they might expect if they could control the whole cycle. They sought continuously to enter larger and larger portions of the trade circuit and within certain bounds they were increasingly successful. Their expanded trade took two forms. First, by joining with other New England merchants they were able to finance independent voyages with fish to the southern ports, returning with wine and other semitropical products. And they became partners with the London merchants or with the agents in the southern ports for the total trip, entering their fish as capital and profiting proportionately to their investment.

Though such arrangements were increasingly common throughout the period, the merchants did not reach their ultimate goal of controlling the total circuit themselves. The critical line in the polygon of trade was the outward voyage from England in which the all-important manufactures were brought to the colonial ports. The cargoes carried on this leg of the voyage almost always remained the property of English merchants until sold in New England. It was only as minor shareholders that the colonials were able to claim some part of the profits from the outward passage. But they were able to gain full control of the secondary circuits between New England and the southern ports, relying on a further exchange of goods to secure the profits from this trade. By the Restoration the New Englanders not only were in complete command of their own fishery but also had a fleet of locally owned and operated vessels plying steadily between their home ports and the southeastern Atlantic markets. . . .

The fish trade and contact with the English trading centers served not only to supply the Puritans with an indirect form of returns but also to acquaint them with other needs of the islanders and Spaniards which they were capable of supplying. Fish was but one form of food; agricultural produce was equally desired. And on islands that lived by the wine trade, barrel staves, hoops, and all manner of timber products found excellent markets. All this, as well as fish, New England could supply, and as the fish trade progressed so too did the beginnings of the commerce in provisions and lumber.

The first known exchange of such goods for the wine of Spain and the eastern Atlantic islands was undertaken not by the Puritans but by one of their predecessors in the New World, that stubbornly independent Anglican of Noddles Island in Massachusetts Bay, Samuel Maverick. In 1641, when the Puritan fishing merchants were first being contacted by the Londoners, he was engaged in a triangular trade by which he paid for purchases in Bristol by sending whale oil to Anthony Swymmer, his agent in that west-country port, and clapboards to one William Lewis in Málaga on the Mediterranean coast of Spain, who remitted to Swymmer credits for Maverick's account in the form of Spanish money and fruit. In the following year the New Haven merchants launched one of their very few successful ventures by sending a vessel to the Canaries, and at about the same time an Englishman from Portuguese Madeira arrived in Massachusetts Bay, trading wine and sugar for pipestaves and provisions. In the next year two New England seamen contracted with an English business agent in Fayal, one of the Azores, to deliver fish, oil, pipestaves, and hoops.

This year, 1643, seems to mark the real birth of New England's independent commerce, for no less than five New England vessels cleared port for the ocean routes. Thomas Coytmore exchanged pipestaves and fish for wine and sugar at Fayal. The locally built *Trial* made a successful trip to the Spanish ports of Bilbao and Málaga while the *Increase* of Cambridge traded in Madeira. Within another twelve months four more New England vessels visited the Canary Islands where Edward Gibbons already was involved in complicated dealings with the local merchants.

And it was in that year that the first triangular slave voyage in New England history was made by one of the vessels trading in the Canaries, for she returned via Barbados where she bought tobacco "in exchange for Africoes, which she carried from the Isle of Maio." This voyage introduced New England to the trade in Negroes; but more important was the fact that its success stressed to the merchants the rich possibilities of commerce with the West Indies.

During the years when the permanent economy of New England was beginning to take shape, the islands of the Caribbean, settled just a few years earlier, sprang into the forefront of European commerce. By 1640, when the New England merchants began to look abroad, a string of European colonies in the Caribbean Sea had been added to the original Spanish settlements in Cuba, Hispaniola, and Puerto Rico. "After 1625," writes a leading historian of the West Indies, "swarms of English and French colonists poured like flies upon the rotting carcase of Spain's empire in the Caribbean, and within ten years the West Indian scene was changed forever." The Lesser Antilles became a battleground of the expanding European empires. The island of St. Christopher in the Leewards was jointly possessed by the French and English; Barbados, Nevis, Antigua, and Montserrat were indisputably English; Guadeloupe and Martinique were French; and Curaçao, St. Eustatius, and Tobago were in the hands of the Dutch. . . .

. . . The full picture of the Caribbean markets emerged only slowly, but it was quickly understood that the West Indians lacked the same commodities the New Englanders were already sending to the Wine Islands and Spain. And in return the New Englanders could obtain not only bills on English merchants but tobacco and the cotton they hoped to use in textile manufacture. Their high opinion of the slave trade gained from the earlier voyage was confirmed.

After 1644 the New England merchants turned their attention increasingly to the Caribbean. In 1645 some Bostonians sent a vessel to Africa which picked up wines at Madeira and sold its human cargo at Barbados. Several other direct contacts with that island were made in the same year, and a group of merchants sent a £400 letter of credit to an agent in Bermuda as the first step in opening trade relations with that island. Toward the end of the fifth decade it became known in New England that sugar was becoming a major product of Barbados. As early as 1647 Winthrop had it on good authority that men in Barbados "are so intent upon planting sugar that they had rather buy foode at very deare rates than produce it by labour, soe infinite is the profitt of sugar workes after once accomplished." The accuracy of such reports was soon tested, and before the decade was out this commodity had taken a preëminent place in the cargoes to New England. No sooner had the West Indians set up their first sugar mills than the need for horses to work them and to transport the crops from the plantations to the docks became felt, and New England added another item to its list of exports. In 1648 the *Welcome* of Boston was preparing to transport eighty horses, and in the following year William Withington of Rhode Island hired a Boston vessel of forty tons to take cattle on the first leg of a voyage "from Road Island . . . unto Barbados and Ginney; and backe to Barbados Anttego and Boston her port of discharge."

Meanwhile, contacts were multiplying in the east no less rapidly than in the west. Teneriffe in the Canaries was added as a permanent pivot of trade. The traffic in pipestaves to Spain, Portugal, and their dependencies was considered so valuable that the Massachusetts General Court ordered "all townes where pipe staves use to be shiped" to appoint two men to be "viewers" charged with seeing that no faulty staves were sent abroad.

In this first decade of effort by the merchants almost none of the goods which eventually figured in New England's trade were overlooked. Contracts were drawn up for shipping mast trees to England; shipbuilding rose to meet the growing need of the merchants for their own transportation and the steady demand for vessels by Englishmen and foreigners; and a growing fleet was dispatched to the tobacco plantations of Virginia and Maryland. By 1660 the outline of New England's permanent economy, formed in the forties and hardened in the fifties, was unmistakably clear. From that time until the American Revolution, though its magnitude and its place in the total life of the community increased, its main characteristics did not change.

The commercial system built by the first generation of New England merchants was part of a newly created economic world. In the first half of the seventeenth century, particularly from 1620–1650, the leading mercantile nations of Europe flung their commercial frontiers westward to the American continent and made of the whole Atlantic basin a single great trading area. The character of each country's involvement in the criss-crossing web of transoceanic traffic was determined by the resources it controlled and its place in European affairs. The shape of England's Atlantic commerce was a polygon formed by lines drawn between port towns in the British Isles, Newfoundland, the American mainland, the West Indies, the Wine Islands, and the continent of Europe. Outward from the larger ports in the British Isles flowed shipping, manufactures, and investments in colonial property, the enhanced value of which returned as colonial products to be sold at home or abroad.

The New England merchants became important agents in maintaining the efficiency of this mechanism. They entered the flow of England's

Atlantic commerce in an effort to pay for their purchases and to profit by advancing the exchange of European goods for colonial products. In no way was their commerce independent. Though the efficiency of the system permitted some of the New Englanders to limit their operations to a small area, a breakdown in any major part of the mechanism affected their trade immediately. Severance of the link to England would destroy the whole commercial system of New England.

Yet this intricate commercial mechanism with its many interrelated parts was not an impersonal machine existing above men's heads, outside their lives, to which they attached themselves for purposes of trade. The New England merchants of the mid-seventeenth century had witnessed the creation of this network of trade; they knew that human relationships were the bonds that kept its parts together.

The same principle was at work in the selection of agents, factors, and correspondents in the importing trade as operated in the fishery. Being both all important and extremely fragile and unreliable, commercial ties were best secured by the cement of kinship or long friendship. To a large extent the arrangements for the importation of goods that had existed in the thirties continued throughout the lifetime of the founding Puritan generation. Brothers, sons, and "in-laws" continued as agents of their English relatives. The old correspondences between the Shrimptons, the Footes and Joshua Hewes, the Hills, and the Cogans continued, but to them now were added new contacts among others entering the trade. Keayne's son Benjamin established himself as a merchant in Birchin Lane, London, and became his father's London agent. Thomas Fowle did business not only with his brother in London but with his brother-in-law Vincent Potter in Barnstable. Young John Hull built up his many-sided business with the help of his uncle, Thomas Parris, a haberdasher, and his "Coz Edw" Hull at the "Hatt-in-Hand" within Aldegate, London.

No longer was it necessary for the New England importers to face only east in their dealings; they also had to cultivate correspondences throughout the Atlantic world. To some extent they did so with the aid of relatives and old friends or the relatives of friends who had joined the movement to colonize the island dependencies; but they were also obliged to make fresh acquaintances among the merchants and planters in those areas. Two methods were most commonly used. Since most of the trade to the south was conducted in small vessels with small cargoes, a merchant would send his shipmaster to the markets he had selected with instructions to use his own discretion in selecting men to deal with. Over a period of time some of these transient contacts became firm commercial bonds which formed the framework of a lifetime of trade. But, for those who had capital to start with and some knowledge of the distant markets, the best method was to send a letter of credit to someone of good reputation and in this way to found an agency that could be relied on for advice on new opportunities or dangers to avoid.

The weaving of a network of correspondences was greatly facilitated by the migrations within the colonial area throughout the period. A number of New Englanders like William Vassal and Richard Vines transplanted themselves to the West Indies and became factors for their merchant friends in the Puritan colonies. Similarly, merchants were involved in the movement of people among and out of the West Indies and some of them became residents of the northern colonies. Thus John Parris, a relative of Hull, moved to Boston where he engaged in large operations in an attempt to stock his Barbados plantation with slaves; his ultimate success as a planter was no doubt partly the result of his transactions in Massachusetts. Men who moved south to the Caribbean like Vines or north to Boston like Parris carried with them friendships and a knowledge of affairs in their old home towns that were used in broadening the foreign connections of the New England merchants.

As a result, New Englanders contributed to the extension of a number of English family trading groups which in this period were spreading out over the Atlantic world. Younger sons seeking their fortunes were entering trade in the West Indies with the support of London relatives themselves anxious to profit from the importation of colonial goods. Often these families had kinsmen on the American mainland who joined in the growing enterprise. Thus the Winthrop family, starting with representatives in England and Massachusetts, ended with personal ties to Rhode Island, New London and Hartford, Connecticut; and, when young Samuel Winthrop moved from Teneriffe to Barbados and eventually to Antigua, to the West Indies as well. The most complete family commercial system of which we have knowledge is that of the Hutchinsons; it is an almost ideal type of this sort of arrangement.

The Hutchinson family trading unit, which may be reconstructed from Peleg Sanford's *Letter Book,* was based upon the continuous flow of manufactures exported from London by the affluent Richard Hutchinson to his brothers Samuel and Edward and his nephews Elisha and Eliakim. These four Bostonians, together with Thomas Savage who had married Richard's sister, retailed the goods in the Bay area and, through middlemen, sold also to the inland settlers. They conducted a large trade with the West Indies, sending provisions and cattle in exchange for cotton and sugar which they sold for credit on London. The West Indian trade of the Boston Hutchinsons was largely handled for them by Peleg Sanford of Portsmouth, Rhode Island, whose mother was another sister of Richard and who was, hence, cousin and nephew of the Boston merchants of the family.

Peleg, who had started his career as a commercial agent in Barbados, was in charge of the cattle farms in Rhode Island owned by the Bostonians; he exported their horses and provisions direct to Barbados where they were sold by his brothers, the Barbadian merchants William and Elisha Sanford. Peleg was entirely dependent on his Massachusetts relatives for his supply of manufactures, having to write to them not only for large cargoes of goods but also for halters for the horses and even for a frying pan. His own orbit of trade, reaching mainly to Boston and Barbados, also included Taunton and Bridgewater, Massachusetts, and Middletown and Hartford, Connecticut, for whose merchants he acted as middleman in the West Indies exchange.

Peleg and his Boston and Barbadian relatives operated in a constantly shifting series of combinations, as partners, as agents, or merely as customers to each other. What remained constant besides their locations and the direction of the trade flow was the ownership by the Bostonians of the imports, once they arrived in Massachusetts, and Peleg's agency for disposing of their cattle and sheep to the Caribbean markets. Peleg was an independent merchant in his dealings with the inland wholesalers and buyers and occasionally even in his West Indian trade, but not as an importer from England. . . .

. . . Their commerce illustrates not only the importance of kinship ties as a basis for commercial relations but also the consistency with which the New Englanders dealt with other Britishers whenever they could. For, though the New Englanders traded with the Dutch and French when their ships came to the New England ports or when they themselves went on peddling voyages to Canada or the West Indies, the overwhelming bulk of their commerce was conducted with other Englishmen. The reason for this was not that they paid the least attention to the navigation acts already in force or had moral objections to trading with foreigners, even with enemies of England, but that business relations with foreigners were much more difficult to establish and maintain than they were with other Britishers. In Spain, where Britons had been trading for a century, the merchants almost invariably dealt with Englishmen resident in the port towns. The same was true in the Spanish and Portuguese dependencies in the eastern Atlantic. And in the American trade, what reliance could be placed on the bonds of Frenchmen to the north who desired nothing more than the collapse of the British settlements in the New World?

The employment of Dutch carriers by New Englanders decreased less as a result of the effect of the Navigation Act of 1651 than as a consequence of the rise of shipbuilding in New England and the increasing interest of the merchants in freightage. The French West Indies were as yet not well enough developed nor the economic situation in the Caribbean tight enough to lead New Englanders to run the risks of attempting to start correspondences with unknown foreigners there. In long distance transactions they preferred to deal with their relatives and friends in the British Islands who, if necessary, could be brought to law in the British courts more easily than French merchants could. Their dealings in the French West Indies during this period were usually limited to face-to-face transactions carried on by shipmasters extemporizing cargoes.

The connection with England, in fact, continued to be the umbilical cord of their commerce. The failures of manufactures in New England meant that the colonists were utterly dependent on supplies from England, dependent, that is to say, upon the good will of a small group of London merchants. For the colonials could not compete with the English entrepreneurs in the home country markets and were obliged to purchase the goods they desired not from the producers in England but from the London exporters. Of the 204 "Cocquetts and Certificates of goods imported and exported" that were registered by William Aspinwall between 1645 and 1651, only eight were sent on the account of New Englanders.

The importance of this primary tie to England was felt by the merchants at every turn. Every transaction between the merchants had an indirect relationship to men in the home country. Bills of exchange were only as good as the drawee's reliability and the drawer's credit in England. Good connections with English merchants were of the highest value to a merchant's business, and John Hull's trips to the home country were significant in the solicitude they suggest for his reputation on the London Exchange.

Thus, despite their physical removal from the home country, and despite their advances into continental American trade routes, into the West Indies, and into Spanish markets, the New England merchants from the start conducted their trade mainly within the confines of the British commercial system. Nor was their involvement with England limited to economic matters. Politics and trade were as intimately connected in the New World as they were in the Old. The New England merchants could not escape entanglement in the tumultuous politics of Cromwellian Britain. . . .

. . . The confusions in England and the weakness of Parliament's power outside the British Isles permitted New England to enjoy full freedom to trade throughout most of the period, but when actual war among the imperial powers broke out Massachusetts was forced to ban trade with the Dutch and French. And in 1651, despite the protests of the influential merchants, the General Court was obliged to obey Parliament in outlawing traffic with the stubborn royalist colonies of Barbados, Antigua, Bermuda, and Virginia—though not without expressing horror at finding itself treated by Parliament as if "wrapped up in one bundle with all the other colonies," and vehemently rejecting Parliament's claim to the right of appointing colonial governors.

If England's colonial policies violated the interests of the New England merchants in this way it greatly favored them in others. In 1644 Parliament exempted all the trade of New England from the payment of the English import and export duties. Cromwell's expedition of 1655 which captured Jamaica was largely provisioned from New England; its naval purchasing agents became the largest single buyers of New England produce during the campaign. War threatened England's supply of naval stores from the Baltic and, fearful of being denied these essentials of sea warfare and transportation, the English government placed enormous orders for New England tar, timber, and turpentine. The merchants could not satisfy demands of such size, but they realized that the Navy Board in London was potentially their best customer and they did what they could to keep contacts alive for future transactions. This was simplified by the fact that a number of their group had returned to England and some of them had risen to positions of power in Cromwell's government. Not only did Robert Sedgwick, the Charlestown merchant, become a Major General in charge of part of the Jamaican expedition, but Edward Hopkins, the London "Turkey merchant" who had moved from Massachusetts to Connecticut, returned to England in 1651 where he became Member of Parliament, Commissioner of the Navy, Warden of the Fleet, and Keeper of the Palace of Westminster. Henry Vane, Hugh Peter, and a number of Winthrop connections occupied high positions in the English government, and Nehemiah Bourne, the New England shipwright and ship captain, after having been made "Rear Admiral of the Fleet of the Commonwealth of England and Captain of the St. Andrew" for his part in a sea battle with the Dutch, became one of the first Commissioners of Trade. The Charlestown shipwright Francis Willoughby, like Hopkins and Bourne, served the Commonwealth as Commissioner of the Navy. Most important of all, Richard Hutchinson, brother-in-law of the notorious Anne, and father, brother, and uncle of New England merchants, acquired great wealth as a London merchant and rose through the Navy Board to the treasurership of the Navy, one of the best posts in the entire British government for influencing the award of contracts for naval stores and provisions.

Enmeshed in the politics of Cromwellian England, New England's trade was already a formative influence on the development of colonial society. It determined the character of urbanization in New England, shaped the growth of the merchant group and its relations with other parts of the community, and led the merchants, for the most part Puritans themselves, to challenge the Puritan leaders on important points of policy.

As trade rose and the European shipmasters sought a familiar New England harbor where reliable merchants would be waiting to provide ship stores and cargoes, Boston, with its excellent harbor, access to the Massachusetts government, and flourishing agricultural markets, became the major terminus of traffic originating in Europe. To it were drawn the produce not only of the surrounding towns but also of New Hampshire, Rhode Island, and Connecticut as well. With the exception of Salem and Charlestown, the other promising mercantile centers slipped back toward ruralism. Plymouth, which had been the first trading center east of Manhattan, was described in 1660 as "a poor small Towne now, The People being removed into Farmes in the Country." The commercial promise of Newport faded within a decade of its settlement by the exiled Bostonians, not to be revived until the end of the century. And New Haven, whose optimistic merchant leaders had laid out "stately and costly houses," was "not so glorious as once it was" with its "Merchants either dead or come away, the rest gotten to their Farmes." Nothing had come of the grand schemes of Ferdinando Gorges;[3] Maine continued to be a sparsely settled district of fishermen and trappers. The inhabitants in the string of settlements along the Piscataqua lived by farming and the lumbering made lucrative by the enterprises of the merchants. The whole hinterland from the Merrimac River to New London had become the producing area for the marts around Boston Bay. Food, worked timber, and cattle were carried from the inland towns to the port city where they could be exchanged for manufactured goods. The islands of Narragansett Bay had proved to be excellent grazing lands for cattle. The towns along Long Island Sound and the Connecticut River, though not within the immediate sphere of Boston, contributed to the stocks of produce and cattle sought by the merchants.

This is not to say that these essentially rural districts had no trade except to Boston and Manhattan. On the contrary, there were men in the Connecticut River towns and along the Sound and Narragansett Bay who managed a considerable exchange of goods; but their dealings were different from those of the Bostonians. They dealt in a secondary orbit of

[3] EDITOR'S NOTE: Sir Ferdinando Gorges (1568?–1647) was the most persistent non-Puritan promoter of New England colonization. From time to time he backed several plans to establish a feudal principality, regulate fishing, and establish a commercial enterprise in New Hampshire and Maine.

trade, sending a small but steady flow of local produce to the southern colonies or occasionally to the West Indies. They had fallen completely out of contact with the European sources of manufactures. The Connecticut River grandees were, like the younger Pynchon, primarily landed squires and only secondarily merchants. The few men in the coastal towns of Connecticut or Rhode Island who, like Edmund Leach and Walter Newbury, did devote themselves primarily to trade operated within a commercial sphere subordinate to that of the Bostonians and the Dutchmen.

The towns differed in appearance and size according to their position in the orbits of trade. First, there were the secondary market centers, usually but not always inland. These communities, among which were now included Hartford, New Haven, and Plymouth, were the collection points for the agricultural surplus of the neighboring farming hamlets. There were among their leading inhabitants men who trafficked in these commodities, furnishing "the Sea Townes with Provisions as Corne and Flesh, and also they Furnish the Merchants with such goods to be exported." But these men were not full-time merchants; they derived their status in the community from the traditional values of rural Englishmen.

The "Sea Townes" which were supplied by the inland market centers, were distinguished by some sort of external commerce, varying from that of Strawberry Bank (Portsmouth, New Hampshire) which supplied the neighboring ports with timber and provisions, to Milford, Connecticut, which had "gotten into some way of Tradeing to Newfoundland, Barbados, Virginia." In these towns there were men who devoted themselves entirely to trade, but their interests did not dominate the affairs of their towns.

In three towns, however—the three towns in continuous commercial contact with Europe—the merchants imposed themselves on the lives of their fellow-townsmen with unique force. In Charlestown, Salem, and especially Boston, they exercised a decisive influence in public affairs. The satisfaction of the physical needs of their commerce transformed the appearance of the towns. Their expanding businesses required wharves and storehouses, shops and market places; the preparation and disposition of their cargoes called for laborers, handicraftsmen, and highways into the interior; the equitable conduct of trade called for official regulation of markets, weights and measures, the care and protection of the harbors, and easily accessible courts of law. Offering to the settlers not only the manufactures of Europe but also wealth and contact with the greater world left behind, they were not refused. Their mark was left most clearly on that commercial hub, the "Metrapolis" of New England, Boston. . . .

As obvious to contemporaries as was the impact of the Boston merchants on the physical development of the towns was the extent of their power over the lives of their neighbors. To the farmers and fishermen, forced to supply their constant needs with the fruit of irregular production, the merchants dictated prices and the terms of credit. The limited money supply of New England flowed into their hands. By 1650 good bills of exchange on England could be found only in the Boston Bay towns and in Salem.

Complaints of the greed and injustice of the Boston merchants came from the fishermen of the north as from the farmers and cattle raisers of the south. The heir of Ferdinando Gorges asked the royal commission visiting New England in 1664 to consider ways of founding a port city in Maine as a "Means to relieve the Inhabitants from the great Inconveniency they are at by being forced to carry their Goods to the Bay of Boston and there also to buy at Second or Third Hand all such Goods of [those] Parts as are necessary for them. . . ." One observer of the New England scene described the lack of shopkeepers in Maine as the result of the practices of the "damnable rich" Massachusetts merchants who supplied all things needed,

. . . keeping here and there fair Magazines stored with *English* goods, but they set excessive prices on them, if they do not gain *Cent per Cent,* they cry out that they are losers, hence *English* shooes are sold for Eight and Nine shillings a pair, worsted stockins of Three shillings six pence a pair, for Seven and Eight shillings a pair, Douglass that is sold in *England* for one or two and twenty pence an ell, for four shillings a yard, Serges of two shillings or three shillings a yard, for Six and Seven shillings a yard, and so all sorts of Commodities both for planters and fishermen, as Cables, Cordage, Anchors, Lines, Hooks, Nets, Canvas for sails, etc. . . .

Similarly, in 1658 the General Court of Rhode Island wrote to its London agent complaining of the treatment the Rhode Islanders were receiving from the Puritans. Since "ourselves are not in a capacity to send out shippinge of ourselves, which is in a great measure occasioned by their oppressinge of us," they wrote,

wee cannot have any thinge from them for the suply of our necessities, but in efect they make the prices, both of our comodities, and their own also, because wee have not English coyne, but only that which passeth amonge these barbarians, and such comodities as are raised by the labour of our hands, as corne, cattell, tobbacco, and the like, to make payment in, which they will have at their own rate, or else not deale with us. Whereby (though they gaine extraordinarily by us), yett for the safeguard of their own religion may seem to neglect themselves in that respect; for what will men doe for their God.

The extent of the economic power of the merchants cannot be explained merely as a result of their control of goods and money. It was also the consequence of three peculiar conditions of their business enterprises: specialization was impossible; expansion required an increasing control over certain natural resources; and real property was the most secure, if not the only secure, form of investment.

Specialization in trade is possible only when a freely flowing medium of exchange or a banking system makes it possible for a merchant to realize the profit of his sales without entering into a further exchange of goods. In New England during this period, as, in fact, throughout most of the following century, the balance of trade and the supply of coin or paper was such that currency flowed out as fast as it entered, and no amount of legislation by mercantilist-minded colonials could reverse the process. Despite the establishment of the Massachusetts mint and the passage of laws against the exportation of coin, New England suffered from so chronic a deficiency of currency that as early as 1663 Winthrop, Jr. was led to propose to the Royal Society a scheme for a "banke without mony." Payments to merchants for their goods were, for the most part, made in kind, and thus the larger a merchant's sales the greater the variety of goods he accumulated. The merchants sold manufactures, for example, not for coin or good paper but for crops, animals, fish, and percentages of ships or of current voyages. A man had only to enter trade in one commodity to become immediately involved in the exchange of several more.

The necessary variety of commodities dealt in by a merchant helps to explain the fact that shopkeeping did not become a separate occupation as the Boston merchants rose in wealth and power. All the leading merchants in the town, no matter what their economic or social position, maintained shops—general stores—where they sold imported goods and the produce of the New England farms in small quantities. The shops were valuable to the merchants not only because retail sales to the growing Boston population were lucrative but also because these retail stores provided a necessary outlet for the odd lots of goods left over from wholesale exchanges.

To be a merchant in Boston in 1660 meant to be engaged, wholesale and retail, in the exchange of a great variety of goods, to be ready to accept payment in all sorts of unexpected commodities and currencies, always to be seeking new markets in which to sell new kinds of goods and new kinds of goods to satisfy new markets. Versatility was one of the keys to success; to specialize was to decline. The merchants reached deeper and deeper into the inland regions of New England seeking control of the resources they needed for the expansion of their trade, especially timber, rough for masts and spars, or worked into planks, pipestaves, and barrels. If horses and sheep were valuable, why not raise them oneself instead of relying on a number of small farmers for a supply? With freight charges a considerable burden to a merchant, would it not be better for him to build his own vessels and add carriage and the vessel itself as salable commodities?

The merchants felt the necessity of expansion, and in the twenty years after the crisis of 1640 they spread their influence more and more widely. Two Hutchinsons bought control of the nineteen sawmills on the Great Works River in New Hampshire in order to assure themselves a continuous flow of lumber products. John Hull, the merchant mint-master of Boston, bought timber land and sawmills in New Hampshire, together with the Broughtons who had started out as fish wholesalers; he also raised cattle on his land in Rhode Island. A glance at the first fifty pages of the *Aspinwall Notarial Records* shows that during the single year 1645–1646 Valentine Hill dealt in fish, wheat, peas, pork, corn, cattle, ships, pipestaves, clapboards, tobacco, indigo, and sugar. Joshua Hewes, the ironmonger's nephew, started as a retailer of manufactures and ended his career as a dealer also in lumber products, tobacco, and sugar. And Edward Gibbons' multifarious enterprises included exchanges in every conceivable type of colonial commodity, from Nova Scotia furs, Spanish wines, and New England provisions, to lumber, ships, and cattle. The merchants in the port town developed the New Hampshire lumber industry, opened the Narragansett area of Rhode Island to cattle grazing, established and maintained the shipbuilding industry, and provided the markets for provisions that led to the quick cultivation of large and increasing numbers of firms.

There were, of course, stresses placed on certain commodities by individual merchants, but these resulted not from a desire to specialize but from the accidents of demands placed on them by their correspondents and the resources they happened to command. But one commodity absorbed the intense interest of every merchant without exception—land. In an economy lacking both coin and a reliable and unfluctuating system of paper property, real estate was the best form of investment. The surviving records tend to exaggerate the importance of dealings in land because every land transaction was legally registered to assure clear title while every commodity exchange was not. Nevertheless, it is an unmistakable fact that the merchants were extraordinarily involved in the buying and selling of land. The balance of land transactions in the total recorded business life of Valentine Hill and the Boston Hutchinsons is so high as to suggest that they were primarily real estate agents, not merchants at all. What explains their endless trafficking in land is the satisfaction it gave to certain powerful desires which they could fulfill in no other way.

The first generation of New England overseas merchants were London tradesmen in origin, and they conceived of the rewards of a life of trade in terms characteristic of their class. For centuries the goal of the London businessmen had been to prosper in trade, marry into a family of higher social standing, provide themselves with landed estates, and begin the process of transferring their family from the status of tradesmen or merchants to that of gentlemen. The great social magnet was a secure place among the landed county families where alone might be enjoyed "the unbought grace of life." The New England merchants sought the same goal. Some of them remained in New England only long enough to make their fortunes and then returned to the home country where they bought into the land. Those who remained in the New World sought to recreate the process under different circumstances. Most of the merchants were engaged throughout their active lives in accumulating contiguous pieces of land which they eventually consolidated into large estates. They were aided in this by the grants of land made to them by the government in recognition of their services either as investors in the original Massachusetts Bay Company or as public benefactors. They bought from the natives, foreclosed on unfortunate debtors, and accepted land willingly as payment for debts. When enough property had been bought or granted to them they staked out their estates, built a house and out-buildings, and, like Robert Keayne at Rumney Marsh, Francis Champernowne at Greenland, New Hampshire, and Kittery, Maine, and Anthony Stoddard in Roxbury started the process of transforming themselves into New England country gentlemen.

Landed property was a particularly valuable form of wealth for the merchants also because commerce was not transferable as such from father to son. The heart of a merchant's business lay in his reputation and the number and quality of his correspondents. The only business property he could claim besides a wharf, a shop, and parts of ships, was the stock of goods on hand and shares in current voyages. The merchants sought solid investments for their profits, investments that could be transferred to their children. This they found in real property—land and buildings.

Such land as could conveniently satisfy a merchant's social ambitions or prove of use to his children was, of course, within the periphery of settlement. But increasingly through the period the merchants invested in land that could not serve these purposes—blocks of unsurveyed wilderness land in New Hampshire, Maine, and western Massachusetts. Such places they did not expect to visit, let alone inhabit. These purchases were the beginnings in New England of a consuming interest in land speculation. . . .

Seeing in real property a means of social fulfillment, a form of transferable property, and a promising object of speculation, the New England merchants bought and sold, bequeathed and inherited, mortgaged and released land in a bewildering maze of transactions. By 1660 they were so involved in the ownership of land that the least disturbance of values or titles would bring them instantly forward in defense of their rights.

The effectiveness of such a defense would depend largely upon their access to political power, the institutional forms of which were solidifying during the same years that saw the growth of the commercial structure. Most influential in town affairs in the ports of Boston, Charlestown, and Salem, the merchants joined to form a separate political interest only in the Massachusetts legislature. Even here, however, they were not dominant. Though the representatives of the three largest ports were consistently merchants and though certain other delegates were inclined to support them on many issues, the preponderance in the House of Deputies was held by men from rural, inland towns whose sympathies were frequently antagonistic to the merchants. And throughout the period the upper chamber, the Council of magistrates, despite the fact that occasional members like Gibbons were merchants of dubious enthusiasm for Puritanism, remained faithful to the aims of the Founders who knew the value of trade but who believed it served the community best when subordinated to the goals of religion. As a result the Massachusetts merchants were able to swing the General Court to policies that favored them as a separate faction only when these policies harmonized with the desires of the bulk of the legislators or when they bore no relation to them at all.

Thus in 1643 the General Court lifted the 8 per cent ceiling on interest rates in the case of bills of exchange, which, relating mainly to transfers of commercial credits, satisfied the merchants without directly affecting other groups. It was only when economic conditions improved that the laws passed in the early forties to protect consumers against creditors and sellers were repealed. By 1646 it was no longer considered necessary to permit contracts in money to be paid in kind, and in 1650 the law permitting debtors to avoid payment and evade the usual consequences of attachments and confiscation of their property was repealed. But, when in 1651 it was decided by the majority of the deputies that the tax burden was unequally distributed owing to the easier assessment of visible property, "the estates of marchants, in the hands of neibours, straungers, or theire factors [being] not so obvious to view," the best efforts of the merchants and their sympathizers could not block the passage of a law assessing "all marchants, shopkeepers, and factors . . . by the rule of our common estemation . . . havinge regard to theire stocke and estate, be it presented to view or not . . ."

Such laws were not efforts to penalize the merchants but merely to right what appeared to be a bad balance of interests. The importance of commerce to the Commonwealth was, in fact, well recognized by the members of the Court, and in the fifties they moved to support the merchants, though always in ways that promised little if any conflict with other groups. In 1650 a committee of six was appointed to "peruse and duly consider of the booke intituled Lex Mercatoria [Gerard Malynes' *Lex Mercatoria*], and make retourne of what they conceave therein may be necessarily, usefully, and beneficially improoved, for the dividing of maritine affaires in this jurisdiccion." Two years later the Court, following the precedent of the English Parliament, set up a board of trade to which all men might "come to discover theire greivances, and to advise of meanes for remedie, as also to propose their severall ingenuous waies for the promoting of trade." Apparently the committee did little if anything, and in 1655 the General Court, determined "to use our utmost endeavors for the procuring of suitable supplies," appointed separate committees for each of the four counties "to consider of some such way as whereby both merchandizing may be encouraged and the hands also of the husbandman may not wax weary in his imployment . . ."

Economically all-powerful, politically influential but circumscribed, the merchants—willingly or not—were prime movers in a gradual, subtle, but fundamental transformation of New England society. Their involvement in the world of Atlantic commerce committed them to interests and attitudes incompatible with life in the Bible Commonwealths. Most of them did not seek the destruction of the Puritan society; but they could not evade the fact that in many ways commercial success grew in inverse proportion to the social strength of Puritanism.

The continued spiritual health of the Puritan community required both isolation from the contamination of Old World sin and the unquestioned authority of the Puritan magistracy. Evil was cancerous, spreading uncontrollably once it took root in sensitive flesh. If good men ruled the Bible Commonwealths the disease could only originate abroad. By performing their indispensable economic function the merchants robbed the Commonwealths of their cherished isolation. If the health of Puritanism required isolation and the most rigorous selection of newcomers, the well-being of trade demanded the free movement of people and goods and a rising population. Should strangers come freely to New England shores? Should the sailors and merchants of all nations traffic in the Massachusetts ports? On these points Puritanism and commerce flatly disagreed. "But now behold the admirable Acts of Christ," fluted Edward Johnson in surveying the success of the Puritan settlement:

the hideous Thickets in this place were such, that Wolfes and Beares nurst up their young . . . in those very places where the streets are full of Girles and Boys sporting up and downe, with a continued concourse of people. Good store of Shipping is here yearly built . . . also store of Victuall both for their owne and Forreiners-ships, who resort hither for that end: this Town is the very Mart of the Land, French, Portugalls and Dutch come hither for Traffique.

But in a different mood, contemplating the dangers that would confront the settlers, the same rhapsodist wrote,

. . . and whereas he [God] hath purposely pickt out this People for a patterne of purity and soundnesse of Doctrine, as well as Discipline, that all such may finde a refuge among you, and let not any Merchants, Inkeepers, Taverners and men of Trade in hope of gaine, fling open the gates so wide, as that by letting in all sorts you mar the worke of Christ intended.

The same attitude appeared in the legislation of the Bay Colony. Trade was welcomed by the Massachusetts leaders, but the General Court stood firm against the thronging strangers who followed in its wake. In 1645 Emmanuel Downing, Nehemiah Bourne, Robert Sedgwick, and Thomas Fowle led a group that protested against a law limiting the residence of unaccredited strangers in Massachusetts to three weeks and also against the banishment of Anabaptists. Many of the Court, wrote Winthrop, agreed with the merchants in their desire to revise these laws, but the church elders lectured them so powerfully on the dangers of leniency that the Court ruled "that the laws mentioned should not be altered at all, nor explained."

The laws stood but the problem persisted and in fact grew with the increase of trade. In 1650 the Court felt obliged to require that every stranger over sixteen years of age present himself upon arrival to two magistrates who would pass immediately on his fitness to remain, and in the following year this regulation was given the force of law. In 1652 the Court demanded a written oath of fidelity to the Massachusetts government of all whose loyalty was suspected and particularly "of all straungers who, after two moneths, have theire aboade here." How many individuals like David Selleck, a well-known shipmaster and merchant who was fined for allowing some Irishmen to come ashore in Massachusetts, felt the effect of these laws cannot be estimated, but the spate of legislation reflected the magnitude of the problem which tended to separate the interests of commerce and of Puritanism.

The question of strangers was part of the more general and fundamental problem of the toleration of dissent in a Bible Commonwealth. The orthodox view, which had triumphed in the Antinomian controversy of 1637, was that toleration was an unmitigated evil, a sinful welcome to Satan's clamorous hordes. But it had become clear that this precept, made effective in law, was as harmful to trade as it was beneficial to the perpetuation of orthodoxy. Persecution, a growing number of merchants discovered, was simply bad for trade; it "makes us stinke every wheare," as the business-minded George Downing wrote to Winthrop, Jr. Not only did it lessen the appeal of New England to immigrants, but it also blackened the reputation of New Englanders in English trading circles. At each point of controversy merchants appeared in defense of a softer, more latitudinarian policy.

The Remonstrance and Petition to the General Court of 1646 attacked the very basis of Puritan society by demanding the broadening of church membership and of the civil franchise. The seriousness of its consideration by the magistrates reflected both the importance of its originators and the widespread sympathy it found among the settlers, particularly those of the younger generation. It was largely the work of the enterprising Dr. Robert Child who, though a medical man by profession, was a metallurgist by avocation and one of the leading spirits in exploiting the resources of New England. . . . Yet he, like all but one of the signers, was outside the membership of the New England churches. Of the other six signers, three—Thomas Fowle, Samuel Maverick, and David Yale—were Boston merchants and a fourth, John Dand, though apparently not engaged in trade in New England, had been a grocer in London. Their petition, expressing the increasing dissatisfaction with the civil and ecclesiastical limitations of Puritan orthodoxy, was rejected by the General Court after it had justified its position in a powerful counterblast. The remonstrants were lectured on their sins and fined severely, Child receiving the stiff penalty of £200. After enduring a number of indignities, Fowle who had been one of the most active merchants in Boston, the imaginative and energetic Child, and the affluent David Yale returned permanently to England. Orthodoxy had triumphed again, but its victory had been costly.

In a series of less sensational disputes the merchants also found themselves in conflict with New England Puritanism. William Vassal, a merchant from Stepney, Middlesex, who had been one of the first magistrates of the Bay Colony, received similar treatment by the Commonwealth when he petitioned for greater tolerance in civil and ecclesiastic affairs and he too eventually returned to England to restore his fortunes as a West Indian merchant and planter. Conformity proved to be too confining even to that typical first generation Puritan merchant, William Pynchon, whose return to the home country in 1652 was stimulated by the public burning of his treatise *The Meritorious Price of Man's Redemption,* which was written in the form of a dialogue between a tradesman seeking enlightenment and a minister. The Salem merchants William Hathorne and Henry Bartholomew were among those who came to Pynchon's defense in the

Court. Anthony Stoddard, the Boston merchant, was jailed for insolence to the governor. Stoddard and Edward Hutchinson objected to the way the church treated the thorny problem of the admission of members' children, the latter requesting dismissal from the church over the issue. In 1651, when the General Court endorsed the Confession of Faith and Discipline written by the Synod of 1646 as the official statement of orthodoxy, among the fourteen deputies who dissented were the merchants William Hathorne, Henry Bartholomew, Thomas Clarke, John Leverett, Jeremiah Houtchin, and William Tyng. The same men objected to the General Court's fining of the Malden church for its toleration of the "errors and unsaffe expressions" of its pastor Mr. Mathews.

If certain of the merchants stood in opposition to the institutions of Puritan orthodoxy, none of them did so as anarchists. Their dissent turned on points of dogma and of civil and ecclesiastical policy, but as men of property they joined ranks with the most enthusiastic Puritans against the fanatical Quakers during the first phase of their persecution. Like the church elders, the merchants saw in the Quakers' "superadded presumptuous and incorrigible contempt of aucthoritie" the destructive "Spirit of Muncer [Münster], or John of Leyden revived . . ." Though the treatment accorded Quakers by the Salem merchant Edmund Batter was extraordinary in its brutality, a large number of merchants joined in a petition to the General Court for more severe laws against them.

In general, however, the merchants for a wide variety of personal reasons, all reflecting their discomfort in the constrictions of orthodoxy, sided with the dissenters in the attacks, small and large, directed at the reigning magistracy. To be sure, there were men like John Hull who managed to maintain the delicate balance between the total acceptance of social Puritanism and an active participation in commerce, but they were a small minority of the whole merchant group. By the 1650's the merchants had become so clearly identified with the principle of toleration that the devout Edward Johnson attributed a series of ship disasters to the "hand of the Lord" being against them. The merchants, he wrote,

> . . . being so taken up with the income of a large profit, that they would willingly have had the Commonwealth tolerate divers kinds of sinful opinions to intice men to come and sit down with us, that their purses might be filled with coyn, the civil Government with contention, and the Churches of our Lord Christ with errors. . . .

Nor did the future promise a greater harmony between the merchants and the orthodox magistracy. By the mid-1650's the character of the rising generation was discernible and to the entrenched oligarchy it seemed pitifully weak. The children of the Founders, however well-intentioned they might have been, knew nothing of the fire that had steeled the hearts of their fathers. They seemed to their elders frivolous, given to excess in dress and manners, lacking in the necessary fierceness of belief. The General Court voiced a common thought of the older colonists when in 1659 it included among the reasons for proclaiming a day of humiliation "the great security and sensuallity under our present injoyments" and "the sad face on the rising generation." Among the merchants the spiritual distance between the two generations stretched widest. Young Winthrop evinced a spirit far different from the one that in 1633 had enjoined him to "feare nothinge more than securitie, and carnall confidence" when, twenty-two years later, he wrote to his brother Fitz-John,

> I perceive by your letter that you were much possessed with the feare of Death, you must be [care]full that Sathan doth not delude you, it is good to be alwaies mindfull and prepared for death, but take heede of distrusting, perplexed thoughts about it, for that will encrease the sicknesse.

The writer, merchant and scientist as well as public leader, was a far different man than his father had been, and the difference between them typifies the gap between the first two generations of Puritan merchants.

> John Winthrop the elder is severe, dignified, stern, introspective, medieval; John Winthrop the younger is eager, outgoing, genial, responsive, modern. The younger man was broad-minded, but never sounded the depth of religious experience as his father had done; the elder had seen much of life, but only from the angle of a puritan magistrate.

It is Winthrop, not John Hull, who typifies the second generation of native merchants.

The character of the merchant group was changing not only as a result of the differences between the first and second generations but also because by mid-century the group was being recruited in part from a different portion of English society. The growing economic promise of New England was beginning to attract men intent on careers in trade who were not only strangers to New England orthodoxy, but to Puritanism itself. They were adventurous Englishmen seeking their fortunes and they brought with them the spirit of a new age.

Within the single decade during which the first generation mercantile leaders were dying off—Keayne died in 1656, Cogan in 1658, Hill in 1661, Shrimpton in 1666, Allerton in 1659, Gibbons in 1654, William Tyng in 1652, Webb in 1660—the new men began to appear. The first to make his presence felt was Thomas Breedon, who, in 1648, entered the records of New England as a supercargo on the *Thomas Bonaventure* of London, bound from Málaga to Boston. By 1652 he had settled in the New England port, bought property there, and started his tempestuous career as a New England merchant. From the start it was clear that he was alien corn. His interests were entirely commercial, and he had little sympathy with Puritanism. His personality reflected a strange light from every facet. Even his dress was foreign:

He appeared in Boston [a contemporary wrote] in a strange habit with a 4 Cornerd Cap instead of a hat, and his Breeches hung with Ribbons from the Wast downw[ard] a gr[ea]t depth, one row over another like shingles on a house: The Boyes when he came made an outcry, from one end of the streete to the other calling him a Devill, which was so greate, that people woundering came out of there houses to see whatt the matter was.

Leagued with a group of English merchants, Breedon was after big game in the commercial hunt and lost little time in joining with other New Englanders of similar interests and abilities. In 1658 he became the Boston agent, banker, and supplier of Colonel Thomas Temple ("Honest Tom Temple," as he claimed Charles I on the scaffold had referred to him) who by careful manipulation had managed to gain control of Nova Scotia with all its trade. Temple, another newcomer, an aristocrat and royalist, was extremely well connected with certain individuals in the ruling circles of England. As a relative of Lord Say and Sele he had access to the inner clique of merchants and government officials whose influence grew so rapidly under the Commonwealth and Protectorate.

Temple and Breedon shared a broader view of British commerce and affairs in general than had been possible for the first Puritan merchants or even for their sons. Their eyes were constantly focused on England to which they hoped to return and whose interests they considered second only to their own. Breedon, like another important new arrival of the fifties, Richard Wharton, was an economic imperialist, "interested in business as a source of private wealth, of public prosperity, and of natural expansion." Breedon and especially Wharton, who became one of the biggest operators in New England commerce and real estate, were the complete antitheses of that troubled Puritan, Robert Keayne. The devout shopkeeper of Birchin Lane was a gnarled and petty figure next to the ebullient Wharton whose interest in trade and land speculation, we are told by his biographer,

. . . was dependent on more than the material success he hoped they would bring. He enjoyed 'playing the game,' as his bouyant and enthusiastic letters testify. His imagination, power of organization, courage in taking risks, ability to inspire confidence in prospective investors, driving force, tireless energy, optimism, are all characteristic of the successful captain of industry.

Wharton and Breedon were Restoration Englishmen—royalists, Anglicans, and commercial imperialists—who went to New England as John Parris had gone to Barbados, as fortune seekers in the almost untouched area of colonial commerce. To them the attitudes and institutions of Puritanism were annoying archaisms. In the years after 1660 such men proved to be effective catalysts of changes that favored their interests.

Declension in a Bible Commonwealth

PERRY MILLER

Bailyn, Maclear, Rutman, and others have seen fundamental changes in New England Puritan culture within its first decade or two. Bailyn saw change mainly as a departure from the original purposes; Maclear and Rutman, as the creation of an orthodoxy out of inchoate aspirations. Perry Miller, though he saw changes of both these sorts between 1630 and 1662, still believed that the covenant theology dominated Massachusetts and Connecticut for much longer. Briefly in "Declension in a Bible Commonwealth," at length in *The New England Mind; from Colony to Province,* he explored the long losing battle of this system of thought with the realities of life in New England. The abridged version of "Declension in a Bible Commonwealth" reprinted here is intended to present the essential features of Miller's thought and to serve as an introduction to his later book. While he found the merchants playing a role similar to that which Bailyn gave them, Miller believed that the outcome was reached less quickly. This difference in interpretation arose in part from a difference of subject matter under examination, but more significantly from a difference of opinion about what evidence reveals the tone of a society. Bailyn examined the way in which merchants conducted their affairs; Miller examined the words of the recognized public spokesmen of the community, believing that the ideas of that segment expressed—perhaps more fully than the average man could have done—the ideas that the bulk of the population used to make sense of their lives.

I

EVEN A PURITAN SOCIETY, EVEN A PEOPLE CHOSEN OF GOD, IF THEY undertake to settle a wilderness, will meet with hardship and sometimes with disaster. Leaders will die, since men cannot live forever; winds and earthquakes strike equally the chosen and the unchosen; caterpillars will consume the grain of the righteous unless God contrive a very

Perry Miller, "Declension in a Bible Commonwealth," *Proceedings of the American Antiquarian Society,* Vol. LI (1941), pp. 37–94; also in P. Miller, *Nature's Nation,* 1967, pp. 14–49. The article is reprinted here without footnotes and with deletions where indicated.

exceptional providence to divert them, while saints no less than other men must run the hazard of pestilence, drought, the measles, or shipwreck. When such afflictions overtake a community of the unregenerate, they know not what to do. They put the blame upon second causes or upon blind chance; they have no way to overcome the evil and must either endure or perish. But a holy commonwealth of Puritan saints is fully equipped with a method for meeting emergency. At the first flick of the lash, the whole body politic assembles for a ceremony of public humiliation and communal repentance, wherein the people take the responsibility for the disaster upon themselves, asserting that the fault is entirely theirs and that God has punished them justly and necessarily for their sins. Thereupon the way for accomplishing their relief becomes obvious: they must resolve to mend their ways and beseech the Lord to look with favor upon their reformation. Whole days should be officially set apart for these observances, called in New England "days of humiliation" or "fast days," to be observed not with complete fasting—that extremity was Popish superstition—but with abstinence from all but the essentials of life, even, according to one instruction, from the pleasures of marriage. The principal action of the day should be the delivery of a public sermon before all the society, in which the minister, the spokesman for the community, would set forth the issues of the occasion, review the affliction, and make articulate the determination of the group henceforth to banish whatever sins had brought the distress upon it.

From the beginning Puritan settlements employed this method, and at first with spectacular success. At Plymouth in July, 1622, the colony was suffering from a drought which, continued a few days more, would have reduced it to starvation; the authorities appointed a day of humiliation and the next day rain fell, whereupon a second day was set apart for universal thanksgiving. The advance guard of the Massachusetts Bay Company, even before it reached American shores, was saved from storms and seasickness whenever the Reverend Mr. Higginson bade them observe a fast aboard ship. . . .

The meticulous promptness with which God answered these early fasts left an indelible impression upon the New England mind and furnished the models for later imitation. For a time there seems to have been some indecision as to who should issue the summons. Ideally the call ought to come from the churches, since it was in the churches that men would confess their sins and pray for relief. At the Bay they did originally determine the event, and when the General Court first took the initiative, on September 3, 1634, it contented itself with expressing merely a "generall desire" that a day of humiliation be observed throughout the several plantations. For years many congregations went through the form of voting to concur in fasts proclaimed by the state, and the politicians were always assumed to be acting at the desire of the churches, many fasts being ordained explicitly "upon the motion of the elders." Yet gradually, because public distresses affected all alike, the legislatures assumed the function of calling the people to repentance, and soon entrusted to governors and councils the right to proclaim fasts during the recess. The General Court in Massachusetts first openly commanded a fast in 1637 when it designated a day on which all inhabitants should bewail the Antinomian dissensions—the occasion on which Wheelwright delivered his "incendiary" sermon and almost frustrated the purpose of the Lord. Antinomianism so obviously endangered the whole body politic that it behoved the central government both to take over the one method that would insure the public safety and to make certain that all the public took part. The Plymouth codification of 1636 officially required the Governor and Assistants to command days of fasting and thanksgiving "as occasion shall be offered." In Connecticut, as in Massachusetts, the churches first determined the days, but gradually the General Court assumed the power of choosing those observed by the whole colony, and in 1655 delegated it to the magistrates during the intervals between sessions. However, particular churches were everywhere free to observe fasts in order to deal with local difficulties, and during the English Civil Wars, when colonial governments were obliged to tread softly lest their sympathy with Parliament cause them to offend the King, they ordered few public observances and left the churches to keep their own as they saw fit.

Thus the colonies settled upon a ritual, and the custom throve through the seventeenth century. Whatever afflicted them or grieved them became the occasion for a day of communal humiliation, when worldly pursuits were laid aside and the people gathered in the churches to acknowledge their sins, to promise reformation, and to pray for relief. Fasts were proclaimed because of dissensions and evil plots, "to prepare the way of friends which wee hope may bee upon comeing to us," for lack of rain or too much rain, for excessive snow, cold or heat, for hail-storms, fires, winds, plagues, pests, the smallpox or witchcraft, for the deaths of leaders or ominous prodigies like eclipses or comets. Some of the later days were not quite so clearly and decisively rewarded as were the first. . . . Innumerable colonial and local fasts were observed during the dark months of King Philip's War,[1] and theological perplexities sprouted anew as day after day was followed by military disaster, but the clergy had a ready explanation: the people had not sufficiently abased themselves or truly

[1] EDITOR'S NOTE: King Philip's War (1675–1676) took place in southeastern New England; related Indian conflicts continued in northern New England even longer.

repented. Therefore they should keep not fewer but still more days of public humiliation.

Behind the practice of these fasts lay a conscious theory, which in the first place was an inevitable corollary of Calvinism, and in the second was for these colonists immeasurably reinforced by the peculiar theology of New England. In Calvinist eyes the physical universe is under the continuous and unceasing direction of God's providence. Whatever comes to pass, a rainstorm, an attack of the smallpox, an earthquake, does not result from mere natural law; it is an event specifically ordained by an intelligent being for intelligible reasons. Afflictions do not just happen, but are sent from on high; public calamities are moral judgments upon a sinful people, literally "acts of God." The moral status of a people is therefore written out in events: if they are sinful, they suffer; if they are virtuous, they prosper. . . . When they come under the rod of His wrath, and then foregather for repentance, He may listen to their prayers and grant them deliverance. When He is pleased to bless them, if they promptly show their gratitude in a day of thanksgiving, He is the more likely to continue their felicity. In the forefront of the Calvinist mind was the conception of an absolute sovereign whose will decreed the smallest event, and therefore Calvinists devised the ceremonial of a public humiliation as the best and surest method of relieving public misfortunes.

In the colonies this general Calvinist conception of providence was further particularized, and thereby further implicated in the career of the societies, by certain additions which New England theologians made to the original idea. Long before they came to America, they had become members of a school of doctrine now known as the "federal" or "covenant" theology. They revised or amplified pure Calvinism by defining the relationship between the predestined elect and his God not merely as the passive reception of grace, as did Calvin, but as an active covenant, after the model of that between Abraham and Jehovah in the Book of Genesis. According to this doctrine, the saint was redeemed not simply by an infusion of grace, but by being taken into a league with God, an explicit compact drawn up between two partners, wherein the saint promised to obey God's will and God promised infallibly to grant him salvation. Starting with this notion of a personal and inward covenant, the theologians extended it to the church and the state. They argued that a nation of saints, all of whom were personally in covenant with God, would also be in covenant with Him as a body politic, that as each individual had inwardly subscribed the bond, so a society formed by their regenerate action would swear to the covenant in outward unison. Hence, not alone in the privacy of their devotions, but in the forum of the commonwealth they would draw up a concrete treaty, they and God setting down the terms they would observe each toward the other, they promising to obey His law and He to reward their obedience. Under these happy conditions the New Englanders believed that their governments, alone among the nations of the earth, had been founded, and the circumstances of settlement lent plausibility to their belief. . . . Here the people entered into a holy society upon their own volition, inspired by their devotion to the word of God and their desire for pure ordinances; they joined in the migration deliberately in order to found sanctified commonwealths, and by that very act swore a covenant with God not merely as individuals but as a people. Thus John Winthrop expounded the idea in his magnificent sermon aboard the flagship of the Great Migration, before the society had set foot in Massachusetts. We are, he said, entered into a covenant with God to undertake this work together; the people have drawn up and subscribed the articles, "wee have professed to enterprise these Accions upon these and these ends." The first and the unquestioned premise of the New England mind was the conviction that unlike other states these had not come into being through accident, by natural growth or geographical proximity, but were founded in the conscious determination and the free will of saints, who had migrated for the specific ends of holy living. Voluntarism was reconciled with authoritarianism, in politics as in private life, by the hypothesis that none should have the benefit of the law but those who had subjected themselves to it. Just as the liberated will of the saint is at once submitted to the rule of the Bible, so the sovereign power of the holy commonwealth is committed through a national covenant to performing only those actions which God commands, while God will be the patron only of such nations as freely put themselves under His sway.

The covenant of God and the nation was necessarily different from the covenant of God and the individual in one important respect: a society cannot receive the rewards of obedience in another world, for only particular individuals can be translated to heaven. Consequently, the compensations of social rectitude must be given here and now, in the tangible form of material success and victory over enemies. Of course a Calvinist God was originally free to dispense misery and happiness according to no rule but His tyrannical pleasure. He still deals with heathen nations just as He wishes, though He is apt to observe a few principles of common equity and will generally give more prosperity to the sober and industrious than to the violent and rapacious. With a Christian people who are not yet in covenant with Him, He is equally free to behave as He likes, and may afflict them when they are virtuous and prosper them when they are sinning, though with Christians He is more apt to accord His dispensations to their behavior, and we may be fairly certain that a sinning nation will sooner or later come to grief. But the situation is altered when a nation is formally in covenant with God. Then the master of the universe, the absolute monarch of creation, has limited His awful power to the terms of the covenant; He is bound by His own consent, but nevertheless He is bound. Thereafter He can inflict punishment only when the society has deserved rebuke. A nation so fortunate as to be in His covenant is no longer exposed to inexplicable and irrational distress; its public welfare will wax or wane with its morality, and it will receive nothing either of good or evil but what it merits. The saints had been reluctantly forced to admit that God's dispensations with England seemed to come under the head of His dealing with a heathen people rather than with a Christian society, let alone with a covenanted tribe. Hence nothing could be accomplished there, for God was not bound to treat England by any rule of justice, but in New England, as Winthrop told the settlers, men would always know where they stood: after God ratifies this covenant, which He will do by bringing us safely to Massachusetts Bay, if then we strictly perform the articles of our bond, all will go well with us, but if we neglect the ends we ourselves have propounded, if we "shall fall to embrace this present world and prosecute our carnall intencions," the Lord will break out in wrath against us as a perjured people. . . . Consequently, when they had violated the agreement, and were reminded of their lapse by the sudden descent of a whirlwind or a plague, there was but one way in which a covenant people could find deliverance, by admitting their fault, undertaking to reform their errors, and begging God to remember His covenant. The ceremony necessarily had to be a public one, with the entire society participating, because God had covenanted with the whole people. When He will not look at us any more and exposes us to evil, said Cotton, if now "we returne and bewaile our breach of Covenant with God, how little good we have done, and how little serviceable we are, then is he wont to let us see, that his Covenant was never so far broken, but he can tell how to be good to us, for the Lord Jesus Christs sake." Unless men push their violations so far that God is obliged to annul the covenant entirely, they can always come back into the benefits of the promise by renewing the letter of their bond. Hence the necessity for setting aside a day of public humiliation and for enacting a renewal of the covenant by the whole society, for only thus could God be induced to become once more the ally of the society, as He had been at the founding, and be persuaded to withdraw whatever terrors the sins of the people had caused Him to send amongst them.

For two decades after 1630 both the theory and practice of the fast day remained exactly as the founders first worked them out, and the effectiveness of the rite was amply attested. . . . The ceremonial of the humiliation day, being proved the right method for securing such blessings, was quickly standardized. The formula can be seen, for example, in the call issued by the General Court of Massachusetts in 1648. First the afflictions were recited, in this case the distractions in England, an unknown disease which the Lord had visited upon New England, a drought that was endangering the corn, and the morality of our countrymen in the West Indies; this was followed by the resolution that these matters be "intimated" to the churches; then came the appointment of a day to be kept as a day of humiliation, and finally the peremptory order, "all p[er]sons are here[by] required to abstaine from bodily labor that day, & to resort to the publike meetings, to seeke the Lord, as becomes Christians in a day of humiliation." In 1648, as in previous years, the rite worked the desired result, at least as far as New England health and corn were concerned.

In this proclamation, as in all the earlier ones, a meticulous distinction was observed between the physical afflictions, the disease and the drought, and the sins of the people which were assumed to have produced the afflictions. The theory held that travails were sent upon mankind to remind them of their obligation, whereupon they were to bethink themselves of their sins and take to repentance. However, in the Massachusetts proclamation for October, 1652, a subtle modification of the formula was introduced: a fast was ordered for a number of reasons, most of them conventional—storms and rains, wars in England, the growth of heresy—but at the same time, among the provoking occasions for this fast were listed "the worldly mindednes, oppression, & hardhartednes feard to be amongst us." For the first time, the sins themselves were enumerated as evils from which the society was suffering along with such external afflictions as hitherto had furnished the causes for a ceremony. The original theory held that sensible deprivations were a just retribution for the people's sins; it looked upon them as reminders through which God made the people aware of what they had been doing. The Puritans, in other words, had first conceived the relationship between God and the society in objective terms, and looked outward to read their inward condition by the course of events. At this point they began to turn their eyes from external happenings to internal misgivings, and to transfer the sins of the people into the column of causes in a way that had not been contemplated in the original theory. The modification in the formula, the shift from regarding a sin as something to be reformed *after* the physical affliction to considering it as in itself a sufficient reason for ceremonial mortification, is so slight that it would hardly deserve our notice did not this instance mark the beginning of an alteration that grew perceptibly with the years. Within a decade the formula was completely transformed, and the implications of the new version were subtly but profoundly different from the old. The proclamations steadily and increasingly listed sins rather than manifest troubles; though such calamities as King Philip's War still furnished occasions for fasts, the announcements of the '60's and '70's became progressively recitals of spiritual shortcomings rather than catalogues of misfortunes. Hard-heartedness, security, sloth, sensuality, lack of zeal among the rising generation, declension from "primitive affections," formality, hypocrisy were intruded among what had originally been the sole kind of provocations, such as mildew, droughts, caterpillars, shipwrecks and other such visible "tokens of God displeasure." Very shortly the visible tokens were offered as distinctly secondary to the sins. There was, in short, a steady drift toward emphasizing the subjective factors before the objective; the focus of attention was turned inward, and the authorities were more apprehensive over the hearts of the people than over their sufferings in the flesh. The significance of this transformation is not lessened by the fact that in all probability it was wrought unconsciously; it was in effect a silent revolution within the New England mind, or at least within the New England sensibility, with the result that between 1660 and 1690 the relationship of the society to God came to be felt in terms that practically reversed the primitive conception.

The altered emphasis of the proclamations was encouraged, if not actually instigated, by the clergy. In the first decades they had naturally devised a special kind of sermon to be delivered upon fast days. Inevitably it arraigned the sins of the society and exhorted the people to repentance. It was bound to present the state of affairs in a grave light and to persuade audiences that without reform still more serious consequences would follow. For the first ministers the delivery of fast sermons had been but a small part of their intellectual activity; they were engrossed in the larger issues of theology and of international Protestantism, and their energies were principally devoted to the complicated question of church polity. They had not fled into a provincial solitude but had moved to America in order to carry on the great struggle of the Reformation, to produce the model of a perfect church which all Europe was to imitate. After 1660 such matters were of less concern to the New England clergy, but the spiritual health of their own societies was all-important. Protestantism did not heed the New England model, and after the Restoration the colonies had perforce to rest content with their modest provincial status. Meantime their theology, having been vindicated against all possible heretics, Arminians or Antinomians, was codified in the Westminster Confession which the Synod of 1648 adopted as its own, so that there was no longer urgent need for constructive thinking in affairs of doctrine. But with the isolation of New England, everything now depended on the maintenance of zeal and devotion among the people, for these societies had been founded upon the assumption that they were in covenant with God and would forever be active in His service. Hence the later ministers concentrated upon the fast-day sermon, the call to humiliation and repentance, not only in the towns but above all in the General Court either on days of humiliation or on the annual days of election. . . . Where the characteristic writings of the first generation were learned treatises upon polity or such profound musing upon the labyrinth of sin and regeneration as the great studies of Hooker, Shepard, and Cotton, the preëminent productions of the second generation—and also after 1660 of those of the first who, like Richard Mather or John Davenport, outlived their contemporaries—fall mainly into the category of the jeremiad. The most polished, thoughtful, and impressive creations of these decades, with few exceptions, are lamentations over the "declension" of New England and tirades against its lengthening list of sins. The pattern of the jeremiad took shape as a public review of the shortcomings of the society, designed to be spoken on formal occasions, when the people or their representatives were met together, and the form soon became as fixed and stereotyped as the funeral sermon or Latin oration. The people gathered year after year, doubtless knowing in advance exactly what they would hear, and every General Court, as soon as it had assembled in the spring, would listen once more to an arraignment of public evils before settling down to business. . . .

. . . The published remains of the period 1660 to 1690 give a very one-sided picture of what was actually preached on ordinary Sabbaths, and manuscript notes taken by faithful listeners show that normally the general doctrines of theology and morality were exhaustively discussed. Yet the fact remains that on the great occasions of communal life, when the body politic met in solemn conclave to consider the state of society, the one kind of sermon it attended was not an exposition of doctrine, not a description of holiness or of grace, not a discourse on what had once been the preoccupation of New England, the reformation of polity, but instead was a jeremiad in which the sins of New England were tabulated over and over again, wherein the outward judgments which God already had inflicted were held to presage what He would increase in violence unless New England hastened to restore the model of holiness.

Michael Wigglesworth sketched out the pattern of the jeremiad in his best verse, "God's Controversy with New England," in 1662. Higginson's election sermon of 1663, *The Cause of God and His People in New England,* approaches the form which achieved definitive shape with Jonathan Mitchell's *Nehemiah on the Wall* in 1667 and William Stoughton's *New Englands True Interest* in 1668. Thereafter the type lay ready to hand for every preacher, and was assiduously imitated in every pulpit. Later practitioners improved upon Mitchell and Stoughton only by extending the list of sins, by going into greater detail. Year by year the stock enumeration grew, and once a new sin was added to the series it kept its place in subsequent renditions. The great jeremiads of the 1670's were the literary triumphs of the decade and deserve to rank among the achievements of the New England mind; some of them made so deep an impression that they were cited and quoted down to the eve of the Revolution. Fifty years after the Great Migration, the literary form in which the New England mind found its most appropriate expression was a jeremiad. By 1680 forensic indictments of an apostatizing New England in the name of an idealized picture of its primitive sanctity had already become traditional and conventional.

Year after year the sins of New England were catalogued, the expanding list testifying to a steady deterioration. Though the preachers still dwelt upon calamities, and continued to point out that these were inflicted for breach of contract, their first concern was to press home the vast array of the sins themselves, and days of humiliation were celebrated not half so much because of losses to life and property as because of an acute self-consciousness among the children that they could not measure up to their fathers. . . . In 1679, after even an Indian war had not caused New Englanders to reverse their descent, the leaders assembled in Synod at Boston for a supreme effort to remedy what for years they had been condemning. By now they were wholly concentrated upon the offenses and very little occupied with the punishments, which were assumed to be obvious. They issued a report that epitomized and systematized the contents of the jeremiads. More faithfully than could any traveller or royal commission, the clergy here composed a study of social trends in New England, except that, being federal theologians, they cast their findings into the form of an enumeration of the accumulated misdeeds, which they offered in part as an explanation for financial and military reverses, but more importantly as an inducement to public sorrow. That the compilers disapproved of everything they saw, and vainly called upon the populace to forsake its ways in an effort to reachieve the spirit of 1630 does not interfere with the accuracy or the historical validity of their description. Nor was their statement the superficial work of a moment, for they drew upon the jeremiads in which the story had been minutely and continuously documented.

The authors of the Synod's *Result,* of whom Increase Mather was the chief penman, were trained in the logic of Ramus[2] and knew that when

[2] EDITOR'S NOTE: Petrus Ramus (1515–1572), a French philosopher, invented a system of logic and rhetoric based on a set of categories designed to sweep away Aristotelian complexity. Controversial when originated, the system was revered in the seventeenth century by New England Puritans, but has subsequently been discarded everywhere as nearly useless.

they subjected the themes of the jeremiads to the rules of "method" they should place the most important first; first on their list, therefore, was "a great and visible decay of the power of Godliness amongst many Professors in these Churches." In a Puritan state, as Urian Oakes made clear in 1673, a spiritual apathy among the saving remnant of the righteous, even though it produced no overt crimes, was more dangerous than the most flagrant of immoralities. . . . It was not that all the citizens were actively evil: "Many have gone a great way by civill honesty and morality," but that those who went thus far were generally "accounted to be in a state of salvation." There is risen up a generation, said Increase Mather in 1674, "who give out, as if *saving Grace and Morality* were the same." No doubt, he countered, morality is necessary, but by itself it is not enough; a godly education is a great help, but if it alone is rested in, "without experience of a regenerating work of the Spirit, then a man's case is sad," and in New England of the 1670's he found too many born of Christian parents, baptised and educated in religion, who grew up to profess what they had been taught and who thought they needed no other conversion. . . . Could the founders have imagined a more ghastly mockery than that their descendants should be carried to religious duties "from external considerations only, by a kind of outward force without any spiritual life or vigour or delight in them." . . .

From this basic defect flowed at once the most serious of all sins, according to the Puritan ethic: pride, manifesting itself variously as a rebellion of subordinates against superiors, as contention in the churches, and, most shockingly, as extravagance in apparel. Concepts of sin are subject to the vagaries of circumstance, and in ages of scarcity or in pioneer societies, frippery in dress is an especially heinous offense; in the Puritan colonies it was still more serious because by indulging in this vice the lower orders pressed upon the upper and endangered the stratified structure of the state. . . . The same spirit of sinful pride manifested itself in the congregations during the hot disputes over the Half-Way Covenant[3] that embroiled the churches in the 1660's and almost produced open conflict in 1670, when the Old South seceded from the First Church of Boston. The original assumption of the New England order had been, said Stoughton,

[3] EDITOR'S NOTE: The "Half-Way Covenant" was a practice recommended to the New England churches by a synod of ministers in 1662. Before that time, children of church members who had been baptised but grew up without an inward spiritual experience of divine grace could not become members of a church in good standing, and so could not present their children for baptism or become voters. In churches that adopted the Half-Way Covenant, a baptised person who felt no conversion experience could profess belief in the doctrines and put himself and his family under the discipline of the church, and then could have his children baptised, but could not vote in church or colony affairs.

that in all disagreements "strict and impartial Examination would yield large matter of uncontrollable Conviction," but when saints degenerate and are content with a formal piety, they no longer can be persuaded by even the most infallible syllogisms. The third evil, according to the Synod, was a direct consequence: the appearance of heresies and errors, not merely those imported by Quakers and Anabaptists but those emanating from formal professors who "hearken & adhere to their own fancyes & Satans delusions."

From this point on, the Synod came down to specific practices. The increase of swearing, which in 1676 Increase Mather said had gone so far that even children in the streets were guilty, was naturally associated with the vice of cards or dice and with the vicious habit of sleeping at sermons. The fifth evil was Sabbath-breaking. "Since there are multitudes that do profanely absent themselves or theirs from the publick worship of God, on his Holy day, especially in the most populous places [of] the land," and there was a steady lament that on the "night after the Sabbath . . . there is more wickedness committed usually . . . than in all the week besides." The Puritan Sabbath began at sundown on Saturday and ended the next evening, and the pent up energies of a rebellious generation seemed particularly explosive on Sunday nights. In the sixth place there was the sad decay of family government; heads of families were accused of no longer praying or reading the scripture, of becoming "cockering" parents, indulging their children in licentious freedoms, "letting them have their swinge, to go and come where and when they please, and especially in the night." Seventhly, there was the rank flowering of inordinate passions into innumerable lawsuits, with a frequent resort to lawyers, in spite of the Puritan belief that attorneys ought to be suppressed because they "will for their own ends espouse any Case right or wrong." The eighth head of the Synod's *Result* incorporated material which always bulked large in the jeremiads, the sins of alcohol and of sex. Increase Mather heard some say by 1673 that more wine was drunk in Boston than in most towns of its size in the Christian world, and certainly, if the ministers are to be believed, militia training days had become such occasions as are not traditionally associated with the word "Puritanical": "every Farmers Son, when he goes to the Market-Town, must have money in his purse; and when he meets with his Companions, they goe to the Tavern or Ale-house, and seldome away before Drunk, or well tipled." Taverns, of course, had long been looked upon askance, but the Synod was forced to the admission that they were frequented not alone by "town-dwellers" but even by "church-members" who misspent their time there to the dishonor of the gospel and the setting of bad examples. About the beginning of King Philip's War the preachers first discovered that the demon rum was becoming responsible for a new offense, that traders in the back country were using it to debauch the Indians and take advantage of them, which was a particularly crying sin, the Synod declared, because the planters came to this colony with a design to convert the heathen. As for sexual morality, the proclamations and sermons would give the impression of a rapidly thriving promiscuity. Fornication in 1665 was "much increasing among us," and in 1668 the General Court was obliged to take some means "for the easing of tounes where bastards are borne"; in 1672 "the sinn of whoredom & uncleanes growes amongst us, notwithstanding all the wholesome lawes made for the punishing & suppressing such land defiling evills," and in this year Alice Thomas made the first recorded attempt to supply Boston with a brothel, "giving frequent secret and unseasonable Entertainmen[t] in her house to Lewd Lascivious & notorious persons of both Sexes, giving them opportunity to commit carnall wickedness." She was taken and whipped through the streets, but that was small comfort to the ministers who were forced to suspect that if so much fornication had been publicly discovered, "how much is there of secret wantonness & wicked dalliances?" The Puritans were wise enough to know that in any society "that which is seen is nothing in comparison of that which is not."

The ninth and tenth of the Synod's findings testify, in the fashion of the jeremiads, to a growing worldiness that was the moral consequence of an increase in wealth. The ninth told of frauds and deceits invented by a shrewd people in their business affairs, and commenced an indictment of the Yankee trader which many other critics were soon to take up. Still more significant for the student of the social history was the tenth topic: "inordinate affection to the world." The first comprehensive meditation on this theme had appeared in Higginson's election sermon of 1663: the Lord stirred up the founders to come to this land not for worldly wealth or a better livelihood for the outward man; there were no "rationall grounds to expect such a thing in such a wilderness as this," but God has blessed us with many earthly comforts and many "have encreased here from small beginnings to great estates." But it followed, said Higginson, that our prosperity is not the result of our efforts or our resources, but of our piety, and if our piety fails so then will our comforts. New England, he declared in words that were to be quoted for a century, was "originally a plantation of Religion, not a plantation of Trades. Let Merchants and such as are increasing Cent per Cent remember this." . . . John Cotton had detected as early as 1642 a popular disposition to figure "if we could have large elbow-roome enough, and meddow enough, though wee had no Ordinances, we can then goe and live like lambs in a large place." If this, he promised, should become your frame of mind, "you may have part in

Reformation of Churches, but no part in the resurrection of Christ Jesus." But New England elbows grew sharper and longer with the years, and the Synod professed for all the world to read, "There hath been in many professors an insatiable desire after Land." "Land! Land! hath been the Idol of many in New-England," cried Increase Mather; whereas the first planters were satisfied with an acre a person and twenty for a family, "how have Men since coveted after the earth, that many hundreds, nay thousands of Acres, have been engrossed by one man, and they that profess themselves Christians, have forsaken Churches, and Ordinances, and all for land and elbow-room enough in the World." Charles Chauncy[4] became aware in 1655 that there were men in New England who would prefer to settle far into the wilderness without any ministry or schools or means of civilization if they might have their liberty; untroubled by strict sabbaths they could then follow their worldly interest any time, "and their children may drudge for them at plough, or hough, or such like servill imployments, that themselves may be eased." The lament over frontier plantations, where no ministry was settled, swelled to a constant cry in the next decades.

Meanwhile, as the frontier was extended, trade increased. Even in 1639 certain of the magistrates had protested against the fining of Robert Keayne for having dared to buy as cheaply as he could and to sell for the highest price he could get; they objected that in spite of all learned cogitation on the question, "a certain rule could not be found out for an equal rate between buyer and seller." It had taken all the authority of John Cotton and the Word of God to silence them, to make the community accept the rule of the "just price." The later ministers repeated Cotton's dicta, but they were no longer able to force them upon the citizens. And still more horrifying was the fact that the lower orders, comprehending what treatment they were receiving from their employers, had begun to reply in kind. Oakes could tell in 1673 of much "Griping, and Squeezing, and Grinding the Faces of the poor"; what wonder that by 1679 "Day-Labourers and Mechanicks are unreasonable in their demands"? . . . How far New England in fact had departed from the theory in which it had been conceived can be seen by comparing the censure of Keayne in 1640 with Mather's lament in 1674, "A poor man cometh amongst you and he must have a Commodity whatever it cost him, and you will make him give whatever you please, and put what price you please upon what he hath to give too, without respecting the just value of the thing." The medieval and scholastic concept of the just price, like the medieval attitude toward

[4] EDITOR'S NOTE: Charles Chauncy (1592–1672) arrived in New England in 1638 and served as minister at Plymouth before being chosen President of Harvard College in 1654.

usury, was simply dropping out of the economic code of New England, though the ministers were still, in the name of the original ideal, fulminating against a process that they could not hinder.

The last of the Synod's paragraphs described the fatal unwillingness of the people to reform, even after the Lord had called upon them in a series of severe judgments, and the corresponding decay of what in the seventeenth century was called "public spirit," which meant a disinclination to pay the public charges, a neglect of education, and a reluctance to support the ministry. At this point the ministers were clearly fighting for the Puritan intellectual ideal, for the existence of a religious leadership that would be learned as well as pious, scholarly as well as fervent, against a spreading disposition among the people to prize education less than profits, and an academic discourse less than emotional rant. "Young men prefer cheap knowledge, easily come by, to wholesome wisdom." The jeremiads ceaselessly bewailed the state of "inferiour schools" and of "the Colledge," that "School of the prophets," without which religion would fail and the light of the sanctuary flicker out. Furthermore, Puritan scholars had to be maintained not only at school but in their libraries, for the pursuit of learning in the Puritan code was a lifetime occupation. The people no doubt are "generally poor and low enough" Oakes admitted, but if the "Common Wealth of Learning" is once allowed to languish, there will be an end also of our civil and ecclesiastical state; unless there is a supply of learned men, and unless learned men are paid in the proper style, "who sees not what Ignorance, and Rudeness, and Barbarism will come in like a Floud upon us?" "Should Academical Learning fall in this land," Increase Mather joined in the chorus, "darkness shall then cover the earth, and gross darkness the people." Not that the Holy Spirit was "locked up in the narrow limits of Colledge learning," but assuredly ministerial gifts were not to be acquired "in a Shoemakers Shop." To the last ditch the Puritan ministers would defend the ideal of learning and scholarship, even after they were induced to surrender the doctrine of the just price and to countenance the taking of interest, but there were forces at work in their society as early as the 1670's which were challenging the ideal and creating a demand for religion more adapted to the appetites of an unlearned, land-grabbing, hard-drinking, and excitable people.

The Synod did not pretend that its digest of offenses was an original document. "The things here insisted on," it declared, "have . . . been oftentimes mentioned and inculcated by those whom the Lord hath set as Watchmen to the house of Israel, though alas! not with that success which their Souls have desired." Even its systematic and devastating presentation appears to have wrought little of the success desired by the watchmen, and after the *Result* was published in 1680 they resumed the preaching of jeremiads. But now a new theme appeared along with the enumeration of particular breaches of conduct: a frank recognition that the jeremiad had become a kind of literary stereotype. . . . The pattern had become conventional, and the preachers were compelled to admit that the people were getting bored. There were some, apparently, who grumbled that the jeremiads were "nothing else but the mistakes of an irregular (though well minded) zeal, or the dumps and night visions of some melancholick spirits." Yet, though such sermons were "condemned by some, contemned by many more, scarcely believed by any," and though the ministers had to confess as much, they resolutely persisted through a further succession of fast days and days of election. The best works of the 1680's were, monotonously, jeremiads: Willard's *The Only Sure Way to Prevent Threatened Calamity* in 1682, Samuel Torrey's *A Plea for the Life of Dying Religion* in 1683, and William Adams' *God's Eye on the Contrite* in 1685. The line was interrupted by the revocation of the charter and the establishment of the Dominion of New England, during which the ministers had to restrain their denunciations. But no sooner was Andros deposed than the provisional government of the saints met once more to hear a jeremiad, delivered by the young Cotton Mather and complete with all the old array of sins. Under the new charter the form was cultivated with new vigor, and persisted well into the eighteenth century, although from time to time an election preacher might lay it aside and devote himself to discussing the principles of political science. . . .

II

We must, of course, make allowance for ministerial exaggeration when we go to the jeremiads for a picture of life in the seventeenth century. Also we must remember that a group of worried preachers calling upon the people to repent were not chronicling the history of their times in a scientific and objective spirit. Yet the sequence of their denunciations does provide a neat chronological summary of a chapter in the economic growth of New England. What they called sins are recognizable as manifestations of social change, and the phenomena they singled out are equally important to the modern historian. The jeremiads tell the story of a society that had been founded by men who believed, rightly or wrongly, that it was motivated solely by religion and was dedicated to realizing on earth the explicit revelation of God, a society organized on theological principles and ruled by an economic code that was a survival from the Middle Ages. They further testify that, in the course of the century, by the very necessities of its predicament, the society became increasingly involved in the work of settlement, of fishing and of trade, that it emerged by slow and insensible degrees into the now familiar outlines of a commercial and capitalist economy. The jeremiads are evidences of the grief and bewilderment that this uncomprehended evolution caused the leaders, who were conscious only of their inability to resist it. But the modern observer cannot help being struck with one remarkable fact about the whole series of denunciations: while the ministers were excoriating habits and tempers that were the direct result of the process, while they were lamenting the worldly spirit of merchants and frontiersmen and demanding that they come to humiliation, they at no time condemned the pursuit of wealth or the expansion of the frontier. They berated the consequence of progress but never progress itself. They deplored the effects of trade upon men's religion, but they did not ask men to cease from trading. They arraigned men of great estates, but not the estates. . . . New England merchants, farmers and shipbuilders increased "cent per cent," and the results were a decay of godliness, lust for possessions, class antagonisms, expensive apparel, and a lessened respect for learning. In these respects New Englanders seemed to be deserting the great tradition of their fathers. But they would have deserted it still more had they not labored in their callings with a diligence that was bound to increase their estates and widen the gulf between the industrious and the shiftless, the rich and the poor, between those who made money and those who borrowed it—and paid the interest!

That every man should have a calling in this world and should work in it faithfully was a first premise of Calvinism and Puritanism. William Ames, whose textbook of ethics was standard in seventeenth-century New England, laid down the dictum that even he who has an income must nevertheless work in a calling; each man has a talent for something, whether for government or banking or ditchdigging, which is given him of God. It is no disgrace according to Ames's teachings for a man to suffer poverty if the circumstances are beyond his control, for then the bad fortune is sent from God as a correction or a trial, but it is a loathsome crime for a man to accept poverty which he could avoid or remedy. As the Puritan conceived the order of things, God had cunningly contrived that men, if they would live at all, must seek the physical necessities of life in the earth or the sea, but in His benevolence He also provided that the objects of their search are there to be found, if men will only bestir themselves to hunt. . . . Ames's doctrine was recapitulated at the end of the century by Samuel Willard in his immense *summa* of all Puritan knowledge, *A Compleat Body of Divinity,* wherein Puritans were informed that they were bound by their allegiance to God to engage themselves in an outward calling, for "Man is made for Labour, and not for Idleness."

John Cotton composed the finest exposition in the authentic language of New England Puritanism of what, since Max Weber, has come to be generally called the "Protestant ethic." He made abundantly clear that Puritan philosophy did not expect men to desist from profit making—on the contrary, it positively encouraged them—but it did expect them to get the profits without succumbing to the seductions. Civil life in the world, no less than the life of contemplation, is lived by faith, Cotton declared, and just as soon as a man finds faith in his heart he is drawn to live in "some warrantable calling," "though it be but of a day-labourer." The true Christian does the work that providence sets before him sincerely and faithfully, not shirking the most homely or difficult or dangerous tasks. "If thou beest a man that lives without a calling, though thou hast two thousands to spend, yet if thou hast no calling, tending to publique good, thou art an uncleane beast." But the distinctive cast of the Puritan theory—in which it contrasts radically with the prevalent assumptions of the nineteenth century—appears first in Cotton's emphasis upon "the publique good" and second in his insistence that though a man have great gifts for his calling, he depend not upon his own powers but upon God for rewards and profits. The Puritan conception was far from "rugged individualism"; a man might not make all the money he could or spend it as he chose, for he was bound to serve the good of the whole, else he was an unclean beast. Furthermore, he was obliged to keep constantly in mind that his gifts were from God and that the providence of God governed his success or failure, not the state of the market or the rate of exchange. If the saint worked at his business in such a spirit, he could not be corrupted by success. He would take all good fortune, according to Cotton, "with moderation," he would be an ascetic in the midst of prosperity, and no matter how much he outstripped the fathers of New England in wealth he would not fall below them in piety.

The Puritan ideal can be perceived in dramatic form in a little allegory that enjoyed great popularity among Puritans of both Englands during the seventeenth and even into the eighteenth century. *A Rich Treasure At an easy Rate; or, The ready Way to true Content,* purportedly by one "N.D.," was first published in London in 1657 and reissued in Boston at least in 1683 and again in 1763. According to this simple narrative, at one end of town lives Poverty with his wife Sloth, "in a sorry ruinous Cottage; which shortly after fell to the ground, and he was never able to repair it," while at the other end dwells Riches with his servants Pride, Oppression, Covetousness, Luxury, and Prodigality. He once had two sons, Honour who died young and Ambition who came to an untimely end; his daughter Delicacy has a bastard child Infamy, and daughter Avarice produced Misery, while his chaplain, Sir John Reader, stumbles through the prayers in a book and then gives himself to drinking and swearing. Into town comes Godliness, with his servants, Humility, Sincerity, Repentance, Experience, Faith, Hope, Charity, Temperance, and Sobriety. He tries living first beside Riches and then beside Poverty; Riches insults him, and Poverty raises such a hullabaloo by coming home every night from the alehouse drunk as a beggar that Godliness is in despair. For a time he is tempted to go into a cloister, but he remembers—and here we have the essence of the Protestant ethic—"that Man was made for Society" and that he is bound "to honour God, as much as was possible, by doing good to humane Society." At this juncture he meets with Gravity, who advises him to live in the middle of the town, half-way between Riches and Poverty, beside old Labour, the best housekeeper in the parish, and his good wife Prudence. Godliness and Labour get on famously, with the help of Labour's servants, Forecast, Diligence, Expedition, Cheerfulness, and Perseverence, "early Risers and at their work." As soon as Labour becomes the friend of Godliness, he prospers marvellously. Godliness teaches him to pray, and Labour's estate increases still more, until at last Content comes to live with him, bringing in his train Justification, Adoption, Assurance and Sanctification. Labour's happiness knows no bounds: "he had never prayed before, but now *Godliness* had throughly instructed him, and taught him a better Art, and the way of thriving."

This all too transparent allegory might be taken for a symbolic rendering of the lives of a thousand New Englanders in the age of the jeremiads, most notably, perhaps, for the career of the mintmaster, John Hull. He was no child of "Riches," for his father was a blacksmith, and he had but little "keeping" at school; he hoed corn for seven years, until "by God's good hand" he was apprenticed to the trade of a goldsmith. At the age of twenty-three he joined hands with "Godliness," for the Lord had brought him under very choice means, the ministry of John Cotton, and had made the means "effectual"; so he found "room in the hearts of his people" and was received into the fellowship of the First Church of Boston. The economic virtues that waited upon both Labour and Godliness were all his; he was an early riser and at his work, "and, through God's help, obtained that ability in it, as I was able to get my living by it." He kept his shop so well that shortly it not only kept him but supplied him a surplus to invest in ships and land, and John Hull became one of the first merchant princes of Massachusetts. But always, whether tradesman or merchant or banker, he went in the fear of God, looking to Him for all rewards and submitting everything to His will. When the Dutch got his ships, he knew where to seek for consolation: "The loss of my estate will be nothing, if the Lord please to join my soul nearer to himself, and loose it more from creature comforts." However, when his foreman at Point Judith Neck stole his horses, the Puritan saint knew what to say to him: "I would have you know that they are, by God's good providence, mine." Business and piety mingled in his instructions to his captains; the Lord should be worshipped in his vessels, sabbaths sanctified, and all sin and prophaneness suppressed. "That the lords presence may bee with you & his blessing bee upon you . . . is & shall be the prayer of yor friends & owners," but also, he wrote with the same pen, "Leave noe debts behind you whereever you goe." . . . Religion to a man of his temperament meant precisely seizing the main chance and getting ahead in the world, and sin was synonymous with wasted opportunities. He took into his shop two apprentices, Jeremiah Dummer and Samuel Paddy; by Puritan standards Dummer was a good boy, but Paddy was a wastrel, and after Master Hull was compelled to turn him out he went, as was to be expected, from bad to worse. There was no mercy for the prodigal in the heart of John Hull; years afterward he told Paddy off in a severe letter embodying the grim contempt of the successful Puritan for those who do not unite godliness and labor in their callings: "Had you abode here and followed your calling you might have been worth many hundred pounds of clear estate and you might have enjoyed many more helpes for your sole. Mr. Dummer lives in good fashion hath a wife and three children and a good estate is a member of the church and like to be very useful in his generation." John Hull died worth some six thousand pounds, and would have been worth twice that had he not supported the colonial treasury out of his own pocket. . . .

Thanks to this spirit among its citizens, to the fact that there were many Hulls and Dummers as well as Paddys, providence blessed New England with a flourishing portion of this world's goods, much more, as Higginson remarked in 1663, than could have been expected from its slim resources and stony soil. The amazing truth is simply that the society denounced continuously in the jeremiads was not economically declining but advancing. . . . For the first ten years New England lived happily and comfortably off its immigrants, the newcomers bringing in foreign goods and at the same time providing the market for New England produce. It can hardly be too much stressed that the orthodoxy of New England, the "New England Way" both in church and state, was formed during the halcyon decade of 1630–1640 when the economic problem took care of itself, in what Hubbard called "the first and golden age in this new world," and the New England mind bore the impress of its origins in its inability thereafter to comprehend how any economic question could ever rise into such prominence. But this happy era was brought abruptly to an end when the calling of the Long Parliament shut off immigration and threatened New England with starvation. Then, for the first time, the colonies perceived the situation into which the providence of God had led them: they were in desperate need of English wares which they could not manufacture for themselves and without which they would not survive, but at the same time they possessed a limited and inadequate number of articles that could be sold in England; therefore in order to live, they had to find some way of converting their fish, lumber, wheat, flour and livestock into a means of paying for English cloth and tools. For reasons best known to himself, God had not laid before His saints the easy problem He set the Godless Virginians, who found at their doorsteps a crop that could be marketed in London and needed only to harvest it. The New Englanders had to learn commerce or perish. They did not perish, though once again they professed that they were not indebted solely to their own ingenuity or their capacity for hard work: . . . "Our Maritan Towns began to encrease roundly" wrote the pious historian in 1650, but he had seen only the beginning; the Restoration was a grievous set-back for the Puritan orthodoxy and John Hull was among the most depressed, for he found "the face of things looking sadly toward the letting-in of Popery"; yet he and his commercial colleagues had little cause to complain of the government of Charles II. The Navigation acts and the exclusion of the Dutch created a golden opportunity for the merchants of New England, and in this ironic fashion, at the hand of the most flagrant immoralist of the age, the providence of God compensated Puritan colonies for the ravages of King Philip. In 1691, when the spokesmen for Massachusetts were defending their society against criticism from the outside, they could conveniently forget the burden of the jeremiads and announce to the world that the people of New England had shown "that Necessity and Freedome could do wonders," that they in a few years had grown to a height and greatness that had brought more riches, industry and glory to the English nation than ever any colony had done. Thus wealth did in fact accumulate, and if a man had the right spirit, if he rose early and worked in his calling, if he trusted to God for the return, he was almost certain not to be disappointed. Men who started as millers, being paid in grain, were compelled to find buyers and so grew to be traders, perceiving therein the guiding hand of providence; men who started as artisans settled down in workshops, took apprentices, and shortly were capitalists. Merchants imported the indispensable stocks and advanced them to farmers and frontiersmen on credit and so became bankers, and could crack the whip of discipline over their inefficient debtors, as did John Hull: "I am afraid lest by keepeing a drinkeing House you learn to tipple yor selfe and thereby stifle the voice of yor Conscience that else would call upon you to bee Righteouse me thinks some fruits might have come to mee last winter." They bought up the fishing fleet as soon as God had made clear that the cod was to be the mainstay of Massachusetts, and by the beginning of the eighteenth century a few capitalists dominated the industry. By that time also the merchants had taken hold of their providential opportunities with such forecast, diligence, expedition, and perseverance that not only had they succeeded the Dutch as the principal competitors of the English merchants but also they were steadily draining the interior of whatever had a market value, syphoning off money from Newfoundland, bringing in cargoes from southern Europe, diverting the coinage of the Caribbean into their pockets, and finally, to cap the climax of their brilliance, earning the freight-charges on everything they handled and then selling their very ships at a handsome profit! . . . By 1670 there were said to be thirty merchants in Boston worth from ten to thirty thousand pounds; they modestly denied they had yet reached such figures, yet by the end of the century the families of Lillie, Faneuil, Belcher, Foster, Phillips, Wharton, Clarke, Gallup, Sewall, were a long way from penury, and Ned Ward reported that "In the Chief, or high Street there are stately Edifices, some of which cost the owners two or three Thousand Pounds." . . . The holy commonwealth was turning into a commercial society, so much so that the very language of piety was affected, and even those ministers who denounced worldliness expounded their theology in the imagery of trade. Joshua Moody, for example, would deliver a Thursday lecture in which he declared that salvation yielded a hundred per cent clear gain, and "It is rational that Men should lay out their Money where they may have the most suitable Commodities and best Pennyworths"! Samuel Willard's *Heavenly Merchandize* in 1686 was exactly what the title indicates, and Boston merchants could easily grasp every sentence. The Puritan tenet that men must know the conditions of redemption in addition to believing the Gospel came out as: "A prudent buyer will see his wares, & try them before he will buy them"; that one effect of sin is to make men try to haggle with God over the terms of salvation was thus expounded: "He that really intends to buy, will first cheapen; every one hath such a principle, that he could buy at the best rates; to have a thing good, and have it cheap, is most men's ambition." Willard concluded that Christ was a good buy and could be had not too dearly.

The question thus is forced upon us, why did New England of the late seventeenth century express itself most frequently and most earnestly in elaborate self-denunciation? Why did the spokesmen for a society that had triumphed over the frontier and the sea, that was piling up money and building more stately mansions on the high street, incessantly call upon that society to abase itself before the Lord, as though it were a loathsome and contagious leper? And why did the people listen, why did they read such jeremiads, why did they fill up their own diaries with similar meditations and include themselves in the general condemnation, even when, like John Hull or Samuel Sewall, they were fast progressing along the road to wealth? We must remember that the jeremiad sermons were delivered always on the most formal occasions, when the whole people assembled with the conscious purpose of taking stock of their condition. And always, either in their churches or in the General Court, they heard what already they had been told a thousand times, the only variation being that year after year the number of their sins increased. These ceremonies were obviously formal purgations of some sort, periodic gatherings for the solemn purpose of self-condemnation; the rite was kept up with gusto for a generation and was still being practiced, though with lessening conviction, a century later.

Explanation would be easy if the jeremiads had been directed solely at non-church members. Occasionally the ministers did bewail the presence of Philistines among the children of Israel. . . . But had the sins of New England, enumerated in the jeremiads, proclaimed in the fast day bulletins, and tabulated by the Synod, been merely the sins of the reprobate, all would have been well. Instead, however, there was a universal confession that the saints themselves were guilty, that they especially furnished examples of declining zeal, security, hard-heartedness, and the like, for only the regenerated could exhibit these particular declensions. The sins of pride and contention were more evident inside the churches than without. The decay of New England was definitely not a matter merely of the multitude; it was a backsliding of the children of the covenant.

Whereupon a second hypothesis suggests itself: did anybody really believe in the declension? Were the jeremiads merely rhetorical gestures? Was this one more instance, in the long history of sanctimonious pretense, of a confession of sinfulness on Sunday to be followed on Monday by raising the interest rate or foreclosing a mortgage? Did the people listen on the day of humiliation to an attack on their fine apparel when they had come to church in order to exhibit it? To some extent this may have been true; but Puritan diaries and other evidences do not as a whole bear out such an impression. On the contrary, they show a people who were sincerely and genuinely overwhelmed with a sense of their own shortcomings. The mixture of business and piety in Hull's instructions to his captains was not hypocrisy, it was the natural expression of a man to whom religion and business were equally real, and he humbled himself most ardently on the days of fasting. The jeremiads bespoke something deeper than a pious fraud; they were the voice of the community, and they patently proceeded from some more profound anxiety, some apprehension of the spirit and trouble of the heart that needed constant and repeated assuaging.

The problem becomes more complex if we ask whether there really was in fact so terrible a degeneration as the jeremiads portrayed. If we took them at face value, we should conclude that New England was swept with what in modern parlance would be called a crime wave that lasted over forty years, and would expect that by 1700 it had become complete chaos. When Hutchinson reviewed the literature and studied the Synod of 1679, judging by the worldly and secularized standards of an eighteenth-century gentleman, he was compelled to interpolate, "we have no evidence of any extraordinary degeneracy." No doubt one could collect enough instances from the court records to create the impression of extensive depravity, but the point would have to be made that these crimes were the exception rather than the rule and that even in the supposedly decayed state of public morality they still were punished. As for the mass of the people, whether full members or Half-Way members or merely inhabitants, they were hard at work, raising their families, clearing the land, attending church, searching their souls, praying for the grace of God and humbling themselves for their unworthiness. Above all, in accordance with the dominant ethic of the society, they were at work; they were obeying the Biblical injunction to increase and multiply, and they were, with some interruptions, receiving the rewards of pious industry in the form of material prosperity.

But as the rewards came in, and New England adjusted itself to different circumstances, it was perforce compelled to take cognizance of other matters than sanctity and polity. The truth of the matter seems to be not that New England was declining but that it was changing; it had become something other than it had started out to be, in spite of the fact that many who were responsible for the change still desired with all their hearts that it remain unchanged. The orthodox colonies were, as they themselves proudly admitted, "theocracies," which meant that they were medieval states, based upon the fixed will of God, dedicated to the explicit purposes of Revelation, that they were societies of status and subordination, with the ranks of man arranged in a hierarchical series, the lower obedient to the higher, with gentlemen and scholars at the top to rule and direct. They were to be governed with a view to the religious end of mankind, not to the profit motive. Things were right or wrong intrinsically, not relatively, and a just price for all merchandise could be determined absolutely by theologians. The ideal was not mere theory; it was implemented by such prosecutions as that of Robert Keayne and by repeated legislation fixing the prices of commodities and the wages of workers. Three generations of experience in a changing world that would not remain obedient to the prescriptions of the founders could not shake the faith of the clergy in their code of social regulation, which Samuel Willard reproduced in the last decade of the century as part and parcel of the "body of divinity." From the textbook of Ames to the folio of Willard all agreed that rights to property were invalid if founded only upon "civil law" and not at the same time upon natural and divine law, which meant upon the moral law as well. All the relations of life, natural, economic, ecclesiastical, were held to be fully covered by the rules of the Bible, and especially the social, which by divine appointment were always to take the form of an orderly progression of ranks, classes and degrees. . . . The jeremiads constantly endeavored to hold up in the face of a changing society the ancient ideal of a due subordination of Superiors and Inferiors, the static hierarchy of gentlemen, priests, scholars, burghers, and peasants. The most eloquent on this subject was William Hubbard's remarkable *The Happiness of a People* in 1676 which, though betraying on every page an awareness of altering conditions, of internal divisions and conflicts, pled fervently for the primitive conception of "order." The infinite and omnipotent creator had made the world of differing parts, "which necessarily supposes that there must be differing places, for those differing things to be disposed into, which is Order." Especially must this subordination be observed in the political world, and "whoever is for a parity in any Society, will in the issue reduce things into an heap of confusion." . . . "In fine," Hubbard concluded, "a body would not be more monstrous and deformed without an Head, nor a ship more dangerous at Sea without a Pilot, nor a flock of sheep more ready to be devoured without a Shepheard, then would humane Society be without an Head, and Leader in time of danger." And though he disagreed with other preachers on many points, Hubbard was at one with them in contending that religion alone held such a society together, bound rank to rank, kept each in its place, and made all work toward the same inclusive end. "The Interest of Righteousness in the Common wealth, and Holiness in the Churches are inseparable," said Urian Oakes, "The prosperity of Church and Common wealth are twisted together. Break one Cord, you weaken and break the other also."

By this ideal the jeremiads judged the society, and by this standard they found it failing. They testify, therefore, to the fact that the reality was corresponding less and less to theory and that men were conscious of the discrepancy even while they were unable to cope with it. The change came on apace, irresistible and terrifying, for no one could see where it was leading, though all could see it coming. Instead of zeal there was simple piety and industry; scholars became less influential as the pioneer and the business man became more important. Class lines drawn upon the basis of inherited status had to be redrawn on the basis of wealth. The social leadership of New England was later to become very adept at receiving into its ranks new men of wealth or ability, but it could do so with ease only after New England put aside its original social theory and gave itself entirely to the ethic of a commercial age. In the seventeenth century the shock was great when some fine names were dimmed and upstart families, Symonds, Brattles, and Whartons, forged ahead. In vain Samuel Willard preached that a civil deference ought to be paid to the gentlemanly class, "tho' the Providence of God may bring them into Poverty"; by 1689 Cotton Mather could only shake his head in amazement over the changes New England had seen: "If some that are now rich were once low in the world, 'tis possible, more that were once rich are now brought very low." Nor did a family have to work its way to the very top of the social scale in order to upset the religious hierarchy. It was enough if a Robert Turner, for instance, admitted as an indentured servant to the church of Boston in 1632, should become the master of the tavern, "The Sign of the Anchor," and die in 1664 with an estate of sixteen hundred pounds, or if a John Kitchin should start as the servant of Zachery Bicknell, and his grandson Edward be a merchant prince the equal of the Endicotts. Samuel Shrimpton began as a brazier, but he ended by owning a large part of Beacon Hill, while Thomas Savage, the son of an English blacksmith, began as a tailor, then erected wharves on Fleet Street, and finally made £2500. The social structure refused to stay fixed and classifications made by God Himself were transgressed with impunity. Thanks to the pious industry of the saints, or the near-saints, New England ceased to be a holy city set upon a hill, where men remained forever in the station to which they were born, where all ranks meekly submitted to the dictation of gentlemen and scholars.

Of course, had the fluctuation meant merely that a few social leaders were recruited from the abler among the lower ranks it would not in itself have endangered the Puritan social ideal. But the process by which the successful business man rose in the world played havoc with the primitive constitution of the society. John Josselyn sagely observed that in New England the diligent hand made rich, but that those of a "droanish disposition" became wretchedly poor. . . . In the first decades New England had thought it might be an exception to the prophecy that the poor would always be with us, but by the end of the century it knew better. Still worse, however, the process which built up the fortunes of the few worked hardship not only upon the droanish poor, but upon the yeomen farmers, men of virtue and industry, who were permitted by the providence of God to accumulate estates worth no more than two or three hundred pounds. The workings of the economic system forced them to pay a reluctant tribute to the merchants, millers and ship-builders. They went into debt for the imported goods; they paid the merchants with their produce, but they received only the first cost and their little store of cash flowed into Boston coffers. The rural districts were reduced to trading on a commodity basis, in what was called "country pay," which figured prices at a higher rate than the goods would fetch in sterling, yet the merchants collected their debts at the rate of sterling and not at the higher level, and the back country began to agitate for cheap money. The class antagonism and the regional hostility which the jeremiads deplored were not figments of an overheated imagination, they were bitter realities, becoming more bitter with the years, and they were tearing the holy and united commonwealth apart. As the lines were more sharply drawn, even the upper class of inherited position, the sons and daughters of Winthrops, Nortons, Dudleys, Saltonstalls, Bradstreets became less dedicated leaders of a religious crusade and more a closed corporation of monopolists. They married among themselves, Winthrops with Bradstreets, Dudleys with Saltonstalls, while ministerial families also intermarried extensively and each group took on the character of a caste. Though the church always offered an avenue of escape to the abler youth of the lower orders, to such men as John Wise, the son of an indentured servant, or Thomas Barnard, the son of a malster of Hartford, yet the ministers of New England no less than the magistrates and the merchants were formed into a vested interest by the end of the seventeenth century—which was not exactly what the founders had envisaged.

The new men, especially the new men of wealth, came up by a different ladder from that which Winthrops and Cottons had ascended, and they showed the effects of their training almost at once. Edward Johnson was horrified as early as 1650 to discover that merchants and vinters "would willingly have had the Commonwealth tolerate divers kinds of sinful opinions" because they were more interested in increasing the population, "that their purses might be filled with coyne," than in upholding an orthodox régime. Thirty years later the merchants of Boston and Salem were generally eager to come to terms with the English government even to the extent of surrendering the sacred charter. A Samuel Shrimpton would as soon serve as a councillor for Andros as an assistant for the commonwealth, and Thomas Maule, who started as a cloth worker in Salem and grew to be a large importer and exporter, was actually a Quaker. But even if the new men were loyal to the theocracy, they would not abide by its regulations in matters of business. The long succession of laws in which the Puritan authorities attempted to fix wages and prices, to decree proper fashions in dress for the different classes, and to hold the merchants in check as John Cotton had restrained Robert Keayne, fell to the ground. "Those good orders," Hubbard sighed, "were not of long continuance, but did expire with the first and golden age in this new world." In 1639, he noted, to seek a profit "above 33 per cent" had been to invite exemplary punishment, but "since that time the common practice of the country hath made double that advance no sin." . . . It was a complete defeat for the original plan of New England that frontier towns should be settled without a ministry, but, as Cotton Mather declared in 1690, the insoluble problem was how "at once we may Advance our Husbandry, and yet Forbear our Dispersion; and moreover at the same time fill the Countrey with a Liberal Education."

And all this time, when the advance of husbandry and the increase of trade was dispersing the society and dividing the classes, husbandmen and traders were constantly encouraged by the code of Puritanism itself to do exactly those things that were spoiling the Puritan commonwealth. They worked in their callings, and they created multiplicity instead of unity; they waited upon God for the reward and they became social climbers instead of subordinates; they took advantage of their opportunities and they brought about laissez-faire instead of sumptuary regulation. But in so doing they were blessed, for the injunction they obeyed was as much derived from the primitive creed as was the ethic of regulation and subjection. The more the people worked in the right spirit, the more they transformed the society into something they never intended; the more diligently they labored on the frontier, in the field, in the counting-house or on the Banks of Newfoundland, the more surely they produced what according to the standards of the founders was a decay of religion and a corruption of morals.

The jeremiads, therefore, were more than a complaint of the saints against worldlings in their midst, more than a hypocritical show, more than a rhetorical exercise. They were necessary releases, they played a vital part in the social evolution because they ministered to a psychological grief and a sickness of the soul that otherwise could find no relief. They were the profession of a society that knew it was doing wrong, but could not help itself, for the wrong thing was also the right thing. They were social purgations, enabling men to make a public expiation for sins they could not avoid committing, freeing their energies to continue working with the forces of change. A predicament that was produced by the providence of God, a declension that was aggravated at every point by a precise obedience to the edicts of God, could be faced by a bewildered people only with a humbling of themselves before the inexplicable being who brought them into it. From such ceremonies men arose with new strength and courage; they had done the best they could, they had acknowledged what was amiss, they could now go back to their fields and benches and ships, trusting that the covenanted Lord would remember His bond, but when again they grew apprehensive they could look into their own hearts, read what was amiss there and hasten once more to cleanse their bosoms of poison by public confession. The jeremiads called over and over for reformation, not merely for humiliation and repentance, but for an actual change in the social habits; they produced nothing of the sort, but only more days of humiliation. They did not really signify a resolution to reform, because the people were powerless to resist the march of events. Hence, knowing their impotence, the people needed some method for paying the necessary tribute to their sense of guilt and yet for moving with the times. They knew inwardly that they had betrayed their fathers, or were betraying them; they paid homage to them in the ceremony of humiliation and thus regained something of their self-respect, though paradoxically they had to acquire it by confessing their iniquities.

A literary form does not come into flower unless it answers some necessity in the emotional and social environment. The drama was a true expression of Elizabethan society and the jeremiad sermon was a perfect articulation for the little societies in New England, once the first rush of settlement was over and they were caught in the web of colonial economy. The form perfectly suited the needs of the moment, for on the one hand it satisfied the passionate desire to remain loyal to the Puritan tradition and on the other it sanctioned the pious ethic of godly labor which was destroying the tradition. Devotion to business, the accumulation of riches, the acquisition of houses and lands, these were the duties of all Christians, and what they earned in the way of elegance or luxury was the just reward of their holy diligence. But business and riches meant devotion to the world, and luxury was also a symbol of pride. The sins lamented in the jeremiads were not those of the notoriously scandalous, but such sins as were bound to increase among good men who worked in their callings according to the right Puritan ethic, even though the results of their labor had to be condemned by the ideal which engendered it. Hence these sins had to be professed and denounced, the more so because they were incurable. After the proper obeisance had been offered to an ideal that it was abandoning, the society then had deferred to the past, and so was the more prepared to march into the future.

The Puritan Tradition

ALAN SIMPSON

The hardest question to answer about New England Puritanism remains, How has it affected modern America? Effects have been sensed by many people, though often Victorian prudery has been included by mistake. Ruling out such obvious blunders still leaves a swamp of disagreement. So far, the most thoughtful approaches to the problem have come from the Harvard school—Ralph Barton Perry's *Puritanism and Democracy* (1944) provides an extended commentary on aspects of the question; Clifford K. Shipton's "Puritanism and Modern Democracy," in the *New England Historical and Genealogical Register,* vol. CI (1947), 181–198, is also important; and Kenneth B. Murdock has made a useful contribution in *Literature and Theology in Colonial New England* (1949). In some ways, though, Alan Simpson has treated the question best, if only by pointing out candidly how difficult it is to solve and cautioning against casual answers. Simpson, who is now president of Vassar College, taught history at the University of Chicago when he wrote *Puritanism in Old and New England.* By considering both places where Puritanism is commonly conceded to have left effects, he had an especially good perspective on the problem, though he had to define Puritanism in rather broad terms. His thoughts on the long-range results of Puritanism should be read in the light of his formulation. "The essence of Puritanism," he wrote, "is an experience of conversion which separates the Puritan from the mass of mankind and endows him with the privileges and duties of the elect. The root of the matter is always a new birth, which brings with it a conviction of salvation and a dedication to warfare against sin."

HOW DOES ONE ASSESS THE INFLUENCE OF SOME PROFOUND experience on the subsequent history of a people? The effort of these Puritan saints to seize and dominate the life of English-speaking people in the seventeenth century was obviously such an experience, and everyone who inspects the national consciousness of Englishmen and Americans today finds Puritanism a part of its makeup, whether the inspection is made by ourselves or by strangers who look at us with the

Reprinted from *Puritanism in Old and New England* by Alan Simpson by permission of The University of Chicago Press. The passages reprinted are pp. 99–100, 103–114, without footnotes and with deletions where indicated.

incredulity—sometimes kindly, sometimes irritated—of visitors from another world. But what is this Puritanism which has a continuing history? Obviously, it is not the Puritanism which I have been discussing in this book. That is a historical movement with a beginning and an end. It does not repeat itself. Nor is the Puritanism with a continuing history the sum total of the connections which can be traced to Puritanism. Unitarianism can be traced to Puritanism and Transcendentalism to Unitarianism, but is Emerson to be regarded as part of the Puritan tradition? I should say "Yes" only if it could be shown that Emerson was attempting to solve his problems as he believed that Puritans tried to solve theirs or if his solutions bore some direct resemblance to Puritan solutions. Let me foreshorten this type of question and make it more extreme. There were Puritans in the seventeenth century who telescoped into their own lives a history which might take fifty years to work itself out in a dissenting congregation; that is to say, they began as dogmatic Puritans with an intense conviction of their election and ended as lukewarm deists with a few Puritan inhibitions. Is such a man to be considered a Puritan after he has worked his passage from the ages of faith into the ages of reason? I should say not, if the term is to have any meaning at all. Similarly, I should say that the continuing history of Puritanism, if it is to have any useful meaning, must be the continuing history of attempts to solve problems in a Puritan spirit.

To limit it to this is still to leave it sufficiently ambiguous, for it is in the nature of such attempts that they represent selections and adaptations of the original experience. . . .

If one is looking for the broadest definition of the original Puritanism, it obviously falls into the category of religious revivals. This has been a recurring rhythm in the history of Christian culture, and a more general view than I am taking . . . would relate Puritanism to earlier revivals. However, if one is to ignore this previous history, and to start with Puritanism, one finds that it has certain drive and that it goes through the typical history of self-discovery, enthusiasm, organization, and decay. It derives its drive from its view of the human predicament. When the Puritan surveys the world within the terms laid down by Christian tradition, he is struck by the profundity of human sin, by the necessity for a work of grace in his own soul to redeem him from the lot of fallen humanity, and by the demand for a disciplined warfare against sin which God makes on those he has saved. His pilgrimage is therefore a search for regeneration, which is usually achieved through an experience of conversion, and for the development of the type of character which is appropriate to the regenerate—a character marked by an intense sense of personal responsibility to God and his moral law, which expresses itself in a strenuous life of self-examination and self-denial. So much for the drive. As for the typical history, it takes rather more than a century to work itself out. The origins of English Puritanism are to be found among the Protestant Reformers of the mid-sixteenth century; it takes shape in the reign of Elizabeth; produces thrust after thrust of energy in the seventeenth century, until the final thrust throws up the Quakers; and then ebbs away.

This revival is clearly followed by another, [the Wesleyan movement in England and the Great Awakening in America] working within the same tradition, having a similar drive, and much the same scope in time. . . . On both sides of the Atlantic the same symptoms have appeared; they quickly reinforce each other, and they form the beginning of an evangelical movement which continues to pulse through the English-speaking people until it reaches a climax of influence in the second half of the nineteenth century, and then once again ebbs away. In America it is the chief means through which the Protestant churches undertake the enormous task of Christianizing a continent. In Britain there is the same problem of impressing religion and morality on an expanding population both at home and overseas.

I have already touched on some of the contrasts between this second revival and the first. Let me make some of them more explicit.

One contrast lies in the relationship between the Puritan and the intellect of his age. Though I have said in a previous chapter that I think the picture of the Puritan as an intellectual has been overdrawn, to the extent that Puritanism was always more an affair of the heart than of the head, the fact remains that the earlier Puritan did not have to maintain his faith in spite of or against the evidences of philosophy or science. Many Puritans, in my definition, which includes the anti-intellectuals as well as the intellectuals, were neither interested in these evidences nor capable of judging them, but those who were could feel that the truths of Scripture were in harmony with all learning and experience. There was much in the philosophic tradition to support the Puritan. There was little in historical science to shake his faith in Scripture or his conception of human history as the field in which God gathers his elect. There was nothing in the older physical science to cause him great concern: no mechanistic theory of the universe, no displacement of this planet from its central place, no doctrine of evolution. His use of the prophetic books of the Bible to interpret human history, his doctrine of special providences in which God was constantly setting aside the ordinary operations of nature to achieve his purposes, seemed eminently reasonable to him. The result was that among the Puritan scholastics—the last representatives of the medieval ambition to synthesize all experience—it was possible to achieve a fusion of intellect and emotion that was less and less possible for their descendants. Increasingly, it becomes necessary to bury difficult questions in a wise silence or to compromise with them in a way which robs the Puritan impulse of some of its otherworldliness or to shunt them aside. On the whole, evangelism has chosen either to bury or to shunt. Although it has been able to impart its ethical impulse to almost all classes of society, so that even the high aristocrat in Victorian England cultivates a sense of duty and the agnostic himself is a very earnest moralist, it has been less and less able to sound intellectually respectable. And in its extremer forms it becomes a religion of feeling without any intellectual structure at all.

The second contrast lies in the relationship between the Puritan and the religious organization of his society. When the first revival began, his society had a dogmatic religious commitment, and no such thing as toleration existed, apart from the concessions which politicians have always made to expediency. Working within this tradition, the first impulse of the Puritan was to turn his community into a rigorous theocracy. Government of the people, by and for the saints, might be described as his idea of good government. However, partly as a result of divisions among the saints, and of the genuine theory of religious liberty which some saints developed, and partly as the result of developments for which the saints can claim no credit, what emerged from that enterprise was not a theocracy but a regime of toleration. The second revival begins under that regime. In America it is turned into a regime of religious liberty, with the state separated from the church. The diversity of religions left no alternative so far as the federal government was concerned, and the rationalists combined with the evangelicals to get the state churches disestablished. In Britain, religious toleration is turned into a system where no religion is discriminated against, but an established church remains. All this means that the second revival is working within either a liberal or a democratic community. But its theocratic impulse dies hard. The converted soul is likely to cling to its conviction that it has a superior insight into God's design for the social order—a conviction which irritates the unconverted and which is not based on any experience. The belief of Roger Williams that the state should be left to the natural reason which God has bestowed on all his creatures, with the Christian only playing his part as one witness, would seem to be more appropriate. However, if political leaders, like Lincoln, are sometimes afflicted by preachers who insist that God demands the immediate abolition of slavery, these reformers are no longer in a position to use any force but argument.

So much for the obvious contrasts. As for the comparisons, there is the conversion experience, which I have chosen as the central feature of the original Puritanism. There is the fission process, the endless splintering, the Babel of heresies, or the flowering of the sects, whichever you prefer to call it—a process which demonstrates once again how fundamental the individualism of the Protestant Reformation has proved to be compared with its superficial collectivism. There is, furthermore, the same bewildering variety of consequences which the search for regeneration can have; the same variety as it had during the Puritan Revolution. Some activities no doubt tend to be shared: an educational mission, a philanthropic mission, a mission to preserve Sabbatarianism or to promote the adoption of Puritan morals, an evangelical impulse which prompts the converted to adopt causes of one description or another. But in this last category it is noticeable that the southern churches feel little disposition to adopt the antislavery cause and that the conversion experience is compatible with every kind of social outlook. John Wesley is a Tory, but the movement he starts will produce liberals, chartists, and socialists. English nonconformity, smarting under the legal privileges and social snobberies of parsons and squires, is either middle or lower class; but English evangelicalism will make as many converts within the privileged classes as outside. Jacksonian democrats like Orestes Brownson are in the tradition of seventeenth-century Levellers, and they are resisted by Puritans in the tradition of seventeenth-century Brahmins. Evangelicalism can mean an individualistic search for salvation or a social gospel. It can reinforce capitalism or produce experiments in communism. It can sustain the privileged or rally the underprivileged. The insights of the converted, as they survey the social scene, are simply not to be marshaled under any single formula.

The final similarity is, of course, in the character. I have said enough . . . about the heroic virtues. The defects have often been made the subject of jibes, and I shall try to restrain myself.

The Puritan has a very limited sense of humor, as one can see from a glance at his portrait. I am thinking not of Grant Wood's "American Gothic" but of seventeenth-century portraits. The corners of the mouths in the divines, at least, are almost invariably pulled down. Emerson has a good phrase for his ancestors. He calls them "the great grim earnest men who solemnized the heyday of their strength by planting New England." I will only add that life seldom struck them as funny. I know that the historian of New England can produce one humorist in Nathaniel Ward; but I have not been so fortunate with the English Puritans. The nearest I came to it was in a Puritan diary, where the author admits he cannot repress his desire to tell a good story, but he tries to keep the account straight by capping every joke with what he calls "a savoury morsel" of divinity. Cromwell's characteristic humor is a sort of horseplay; this is the Cromwell who throws cushions at his officers, who is said to have spattered an officer's face with ink while they were signing the king's death warrant, or who gets a good laugh watching a soldier tip a pail of milk over another soldier's head. Perhaps it is a relief from tension with a touch of hysteria about it; or perhaps it is just the bucolic antics of a plain russet-coated captain. Later in the history of Puritanism a certain humor develops, but it is naturally rather wry—or it has to be indulged when the great Taskmaster is not looking. Of course I do not want to imply that the Puritan, while he is being a Puritan, cannot make a good remark. I have always liked the reply of the revivalist preacher who had not much grammar and was one day ridiculed for it. "That's all right, brother; what little I have I use for the Lord. What do you do with yours?" But you see he is keeping his eye on the main business. Of all the gifts of humor, the only one which blends naturally with the Puritan's purpose is satire: the sort of satire which Carlyle used to such effect in producing conversions.

The other defects of the Puritan character all spring from the fact that he has stripped himself of nonessentials for the struggle and finds it grim. He makes very little contribution to literature outside the didactic sphere. He is likely to regard the arts as the trimmings of life. And he can degenerate into a kill-joy. Macaulay's jibe about the reason why the Puritans suppressed bear-baiting has a grain of symbolic truth in it. They suppressed it, not because it gave pain to the bear, but because it gave pleasure to the spectators.

In conclusion, let us return to the Puritan's impact on politics. Among his virtues I would list:

1. *His contribution to our system of limited government.*—The original Puritans had a genuine basis for their distrust of arbitrary power in addition to their experience of arbitrary government. They thought that man was too sinful to be trusted with too much power. They were likely to make an exception of the saint, but, once saints were prevented from ruling, they have kept their conviction that nobody else should be trusted. The Puritan tradition, with its everlasting insistence that only God is worthy of worship, is one insurance among Anglo-Saxon people that the state has no claim to worship. Fortunately, there are many other securities, but no one will undervalue the stubbornness of this one. They have defended, in season and out of season, the right to preach, to criticize, and to judge. A shrewd observer of the English scene after the Puritan Revolution was struck by the difference it had made to the power of authority to procure respect for its pronouncements: "He [the author] thinketh that the Liberty of the late times gave men so much Light, and diffused it so universally amongst the people, that they are not now to be dealt with, as they might have been in Ages of less enquiry; and therefore tho in some well chosen and dearly beloved Auditories, good resolute Nonsense

back'd with Authority may prevail, yet generally Men are become so good Judges of what they hear, that the Clergy ought to be very wary how they go about to impose upon their Understandings, which are grown less humble than they were in former times, when the Men in black had made Learning such a sin in the Laity, that for fear of offending, they made a Conscience of being able to read; but now the World is grown sawcy, and expecteth Reasons, and good ones too, before they give up their own Opinions to other Mens Dictates, tho never so Magisterially deliver'd to them."

2. *His contribution to self-government—to the development of initiative and self-reliance in the body of the community.*—The Puritan pilgrimage has been a perpetual pilgrimage in self-help. The significance of the dissenting chapel as a training ground for working-class leadership in English history has often been emphasized, and much the same services have been performed by the free church tradition in America. Nor should we forget, in the nineteenth century as in the seventeenth, the direct transfer from church affairs to political affairs of certain techniques of action. The political meeting of the nineteenth century owes an obvious, if not wholly healthy, debt to the camp meeting of the revivalist preacher.

3. *His contribution to education.*—The most anti-intellectual Puritan has been obliged to master at least one book—and that a great one. The most intellectual Puritans, in their desire to promote saving knowledge, have thrown up academy after academy, college after college, until their influence has been writ large over the history of education in England and America.

4. *His contribution to morality.*—The Puritan code has its repellent features, but it is no bad thing to have habits of honesty, sobriety, responsibility, and hard work impressed on a community. It seems probable that the acquisitive energy of the nineteenth century would have created far more havoc than it did without the restraining influence of this evangelical spirit.

Finally, there is the contribution which Puritanism, within the religious tradition of Anglo-Saxon peoples, has made to "the class peace." Almost the worst thing that can happen to the politics of a modern society is to have them polarized around social classes. Any force which works across these divisions, and either conceals or cements them, has a permanent claim on our gratitude.

As the limitations of Puritanism have been sufficiently stressed . . . I shall quote only one passage which seems to sum them up. I might have chosen for censure the *cri de cœur* of the nonconformist conscience in nineteenth-century English politics as it appears in the protest of the famous preacher Hugh Price Hughes: "What is morally wrong can never be politically right." Instead, I shall take a passage from an American sermon called "Puritan Principles and the Modern World," which was delivered in 1897:

"Puritanism stands for reality; for character; for clean living as a condition of public service; for recognition of responsibility to God; for the supremacy of the spirit. When Oliver Cromwell entered Parliament in 1653, and said, pointing to one member, 'There sits a taker of bribes'; to another, 'There sits a man whose religion is a farce'; to another, using the hardest name possible, which I soften, 'There sits a man whose personal conduct is impure and foul'; and then in the name of Almighty God broke up the Parliament, he was the impersonation of Puritanism; and for one, I wish he would rise from his grave and in the same spirit enter some of our halls of legislation, both state and national."

That passage, with its conviction that righteousness ought to prevail, with its tendency to make the Puritan's own moral character a test of political fitness, and with its pressure to turn politics, which ought to be the art of reconciliation, into a moral crusade, reminds us of the darkest blot on his political record.

SELECTIVE BIBLIOGRAPHY

Only a few of the many valuable studies of Puritanism and early New England can be listed here. Fortunately, a splendid bibliography by George McCandlish is available in the "Harper Torchbooks" edition of Perry Miller and Thomas H. Johnson, eds., *The Puritans,* 2 vols. (paperback*). A good shorter bibliography is in Daniel J. Boorstin, *The Americans; the Colonial Experience* (1958; paperback).

The most enjoyable way into New England Puritanism is by Samuel Eliot Morison's *Builders of the Bay Colony* (1930; paperback)—the paperback edition has an extra biography; or Edmund S. Morgan, *The Puritan Dilemma, the Story of John Winthrop* (1958; paperback); or Alan Simpson, *Puritanism in Old and New England* (1956; paperback). Almost as good are S. E. Morison, *The Puritan Pronaos* (1936), republished as *The Intellectual Life of Colonial New England* (1956; paperback); Kenneth B. Murdock, *Literature and Theology in Colonial New England* (1949; paperback); and a fine combination of primary and

* Dates in parentheses are original publication dates. The word "paperback" indicates that the work is now available in paperback. If only the word "paperback" appears after the work cited, its original publication was in a paperback edition.

secondary sources, E. S. Morgan, ed., *The Founding of Massachusetts* (paperback).

Original sources are especially appealing for early New England. Miller and Johnson, eds., *The Puritans* (1938; paperback) has an excellent introduction and selections. William Bradford's *Of Plimmoth Plantation* is a masterpiece—it should be read in either the Worthington C. Ford edition (1912) or the S. E. Morison edition (1952; cheap reprint). Next best among Puritan histories are John Winthrop's *Journal* (1825–1826 or 1908 edition) and Edward Johnson, *A History of New England . . . the Wonderworking Providence of Sions Saviour in New England* (1654 and later editions). E. S. Morgan's anthology, *Puritan Political Ideas* (paperback), is good in its field. Charles F. Adams, ed., *Antinomianism in the Colony of Massachusetts Bay, 1636–1638* (1894) makes fascinating reading. Cotton Mather's style is an acquired taste, but *Magnalia Christi Americana* (1702 and later editions) has absorbing passages.

For interpretations other than the Puritan and the current ones, see Thomas Hutchinson, *The History of the Colony of Massachusetts-Bay* (1764–1828 or 1936) for the first good native secular work; Joseph B. Felt, *Ecclesiastical History of New England* (1855–1862) or Henry M. Dexter, *The Congregationalism of the Last Three Hundred Years* (1880) for denominational points of view; John G. Palfrey for filiopietism; Charles F. Adams or Brooks Adams for antifiliopietism; James T. Adams, *The Founding of New England* (1921; paperback) and *Revolutionary New England, 1691–1776* (1923) for an economic interpretation; Charles M. Andrews, *Our Earliest Colonial Settlements* (1933; paperback) or his *The Colonial Period of American History* (1934–1938; paperback), or Viola F. Barnes, *The Dominion of New England* (1923) for an analysis of early New England in the framework of a developing British empire; or Vernon L. Parrington, *Main Currents in American Thought* (1927–1930; paperback) for a blend of economic determinism and ideological conflict.

The Harvard school's monuments of erudition—all, fortunately, well written—include Perry Miller, *Orthodoxy in Massachusetts, 1630–1650* (1933; paperback), the two volumes of *The New England Mind* (1939, 1953; paperback), *Roger Williams* (1953; paperback), and *Errand into the Wilderness* (1956; paperback); Samuel E. Morison, *The Founding of Harvard College* (1935) and *Harvard College in the Seventeenth Century* (1936); E. S. Morgan, *The Puritan Family* (1944; paperback); Clifford K. Shipton's volumes in *Sibley's Harvard Graduates*—IV to XIII, so far; and in a sense, Ralph Barton Perry, *Puritanism and Democracy* (1944; paperback).

Dissatisfaction with Miller's treatment of the importance of the requirement of conversion experience for church membership and the related puzzle of the Antinomian furor have occasioned several important studies: E. S. Morgan, *Visible Saints* (1963; paperback); Larzer Ziff, *The Career of John Cotton* (1962); Emery Battis, *Saints and Sectaries* (1962); and Norman Pettit, *The Heart Prepared* (1966).

The study of law in early Massachusetts has been advanced by George L. Haskins, *Law and Authority in Early Massachusetts* (1960); Richard B. Morris, *Studies in Early American Law* (1930); Mark DeWolfe Howe and Louis F. Eaton Jr., "The Supreme Judicial Power in the Colony of Massachusetts Bay," *New England Quarterly,* vol. XX (1947), 291–316; Jules Zanger, "Crime and Punishment in Early Massachusetts," *William and Mary Quarterly,* vol. XXII (1965), 471–477; and several essays in George A. Billias, ed., *Law and Authority in Colonial America* (1965). The subject of ecclesiastical justice has been treated in Emil Oberholzer Jr., *Delinquent Saints* (1956).

Notable economic studies include Bernard Bailyn, *The New England Merchants in the Seventeenth Century* (1955; paperback) and *The Apologia of Robert Keayne* (paperback); E. N. Hartley, *Ironworks on the Saugus* (1957); and Edgar A. J. Johnson, *American Economic Thought in the Seventeenth Century* (1932).

Important recent studies of New England towns are to be found in Darrett B. Rutman, *Winthrop's Boston* (1965); Sumner C. Powell, *Puritan Village* (1963; paperback); John Demos, "Notes on Life in Plymouth Colony," *William and Mary Quarterly,* vol. XXII (1965), 264–286; Philip J. Greven Jr., "Family Structure in Seventeenth-Century Andover, Massachusetts," *William and Mary Quarterly,* vol. XXIII (1966), 234–256; and Kenneth A. Lockridge and Alan Kreider, "The Evolution of Massachusetts Town Government, 1640–1740," *William and Mary Quarterly,* vol. XXIII (1966), 549–574.

Topics of great intrinsic interest are well handled in: E. S. Morgan, "The Puritans and Sex," *New England Quarterly,* vol. XV (1942), 591–607; Lawrence W. Towner, "'A Fondness for Freedom': Servant Protest in Puritan Society," *William and Mary Quarterly,* vol. XIX (1962), 201–219; Alden T. Vaughan, *New England Frontier: Puritans and Indians, 1620–1675* (1965); Douglas E. Leach, *Flintlock and Tomahawk: New England in King Philip's War* (1958; paperback); Richard S. Dunn, *Puritans and Yankees: The Winthrop Dynasty of New England* (1962); and Ola E. Winslow, *Master Roger Williams* (1957).

Miscellaneous items noteworthy for interpretive skill include: Alan Heimert, "Puritanism, the Wilderness, and the Frontier," *New England Quarterly,* vol. XXVI (1953), 361–382; Kai T. Erikson, *Wayward Puritans: A Study in the Sociology of Deviance* (1966); Peter Gay, *A Loss of Mastery; Puritan Historians in Colonial America* (1966); and Anthony Garvan, *Architecture and Town Planning in Colonial Connecticut* (1951).

555

68 69 70 71 7 6 5 4 3 2 1